The Academic Portfolio

The Academic Portfolio

A Practical Guide to Documenting Teaching, Research, and Service

Peter Seldin

J. Elizabeth Miller

JOSSEY-BASS
A Wiley Imprint
www.josseybass.com

Published by Jossey-Bass
A Wiley Imprint
989 Market Street, San Francisco, CA 94103-1741—www.josseybass.com

Library of Congress Cataloging-in-Publication Data

Seldin, Peter.
   The academic portfolio : a practical guide to documenting teaching, research, and service /
Peter Seldin, J. Elizabeth Miller.—1st ed.
      p. cm.
   Includes bibliographical references and index.
   ISBN 978-0-470-25699-2 (pbk.)
1. Portfolios in education.   I. Miller, J. Elizabeth, 1958-   II. Title.
   LB1029.P67S44 2008
   378.1'224—dc22   2008027383

Printed in the United States of America
FIRST EDITION
PB Printing   10 9 8 7 6 5 4 3 2

The Jossey-Bass
Higher and Adult Education Series

Contents

Preface

An important change is taking place in higher education: faculty are being held accountable—as never before—for how well they do their jobs. Current interest in appraising faculty performance grows out of the demand by government, the general public, and accrediting agencies for more accountability.

Reflective and deep information on teaching, research and scholarship, and service—and how those three legs of academic work fit together—has been skimpy at best. The result has been that the general and routine approach to evaluating faculty performance has often relied on student ratings, a testimonial letter or two, and lists of publications, presentations, and college or university committees on which the faculty member served.

The focus has been on the "what," not the "why" or the "how." Thoughtful reflection and context were not built into the evaluation system. And neither was an explanation of the significance of the professor's work, an especially important omission when promotion and tenure committee members are not in the same discipline as the professor and have difficulty understanding the nature of the professor's research and scholarship and its value.

Unless the faculty member developed a teaching portfolio, little or no attention was paid to this person's teaching philosophy and methodology. But even if he or she did develop a teaching portfolio, it focused on only one leg of the three-legged stool of faculty work. Nothing was said about the nature of the professor's research and scholarship, the significance of selected publications, the context of his or her work, his or her most noteworthy accomplishments, and role on institutional committees. And nothing was said about the integration of the three legs of faculty work or about how one leg informs the others.

The best way the writers know to get at the individuality and complexity of faculty work is the academic portfolio, a careful gathering of documents and material highlighting the professor's performance and suggesting its scope and quality. Importantly, it is based on depthful reflection and provides the "why" and the "how," not just the "what." It can be used to present the hard evidence on teaching, research and scholarship, and service effectiveness. It is flexible enough to be used for personnel decisions and provide the stimulus and structure for self-reflection about areas of faculty performance in need of improvement.

The academic portfolio concept has gone well beyond the point of theoretical possibility. Today it is being adopted or pilot-tested in various forms by an increasing number of institutions. Among the current users or experimenters with portfolios are Jackson State (Mississippi), Texas A&M University, Texas Christian University, University of Alabama at Birmingham, Drexel University (Pennsylvania), the New School (New York), and Loyola College in Maryland. Significantly, among the users or experimenters with portfolios today are institutions of every size, shape, and mission.

This book focuses squarely on academic portfolios, which may prove to be the most innovative and promising faculty evaluation and development technique in years. It identifies key issues, red-flag warnings, and benchmarks for success. It describes the what, why, and how to develop academic portfolios and includes an extensively tested, step-by-step approach to create a portfolio. It lists twenty-one possible portfolio items covering teaching, research and scholarship, and service from which faculty choose the ones personally most relevant.

The portfolio template included in this book is the result of extensive research. More than two hundred faculty members and department chairs from across disciplines and institutions (large and small, public and private) provided suggestions and recommendations as to its content. The result is a comprehensive portfolio template that can easily be adapted to individual faculty and department needs. The motto, "Adapt, rather than adopt," applies here.

The thrust of this book is unique:

- It provides time-tested strategies and proven advice for getting started with portfolios.
- It outlines key issues, red-flag dangers, and benchmarks for success.
- It discusses the portfolio as a way of documenting faculty performance.

- It includes specific guiding questions to consider as prompts when preparing every section of the portfolio.
- It spells out important points to consider in evaluating portfolios.
- It offers eighteen model academic portfolios from across disciplines and institutions, ranging from small liberal arts colleges to research universities. For balance, the portfolio contributors are at different points in their career trajectories.

In short, *The Academic Portfolio* offers colleges and university administrators and faculty the kind of research-based, ready-to-use information required to foster the most effective use of portfolios.

It is written for faculty members, department chairs, deans, and members of promotion and tenure committees. They are the essential partners in developing successful academic portfolio programs. Graduate students, especially those planning careers as faculty members, will find the book useful. The language used is straightforward and nontechnical.

Chapter One discusses the academic portfolio concept; how it includes the scope, quality, context, and significance of a professor's achievements; why the content depends on the purpose for which it is to be used; how it is based on structured reflection, thoughtfully selected information on teaching, research and scholarship, and service activities that portray an appropriate balance of professional activities; and that it provides solid evidence of their effectiveness.

Chapter Two describes the many possibilities from which the faculty member can select portfolio items relevant to his or her academic situation, discusses the factors to consider in choosing items, outlines the five main categories of the narrative (the preface, independent sections on teaching, research and scholarship, and service, and a section on integrating professional work and goals), provides suggestions as to the length of each category, presents a detailed table of contents, and includes nearly one hundred prompt questions to guide the preparation of each part of the portfolio.

Chapter Three examines in important detail the four cornerstones of successful academic portfolio programs: the value of self-reflection, the importance of collaboration, the vital need to discuss expectations, and how to gain acceptance of the concept.

It offers practical advice and takes a hard look at what works and what does not.

Chapter Four presents a list of specific helpful suggestions to faculty members who prepare their portfolios. Among others, the detailed recommendations include housing the portfolio in a binder with tabs; including specific information, not generalities; explaining the evidence; enhancing the narrative section; limiting the number of student and faculty colleague comments; and revising the portfolio every year.

Chapter Five spells out how to evaluate academic portfolios for personnel decisions, what should be evaluated, and how it should be done; discusses the key requirements of acceptability, practicality, and relevance; and outlines the crucial differences between strong and weak portfolios. It also provides practical advice: a nineteen-point suggested checklist of items for evaluating academic portfolios that emerged from discussions with more than 150 members of personnel committees at different colleges and universities.

Chapter Six offers pragmatic answers to many questions commonly raised about developing and using academic portfolios. Here are guidelines for getting started and a discussion on how portfolios differ from the usual faculty report to administrators. It also addresses how much time it takes to develop a portfolio, why portfolio models and mentors are so important, and why an elegant portfolio cannot disguise weak performance in teaching, research and scholarship, or service.

Chapter Seven contains the actual academic portfolios of eighteen professors from different disciplines and institutions.

———————

PETER SELDIN
Pleasantville, New York
October 2008

J. ELIZABETH MILLER
DeKalb, Illinois
October 2008

Acknowledgments

We applaud the professors who contributed their portfolios to this book for their professionalism and good-humored acceptance of deadlines and rewrites. Working with them has truly been our pleasure.

About the Authors

Peter Seldin is Distinguished Professor of Management Emeritus at Pace University in Pleasantville, New York. Formerly an academic dean, department chair, and professor of management, he is a specialist in the evaluation and development of faculty and administrative performance and has been a consultant on higher education issues to more than 350 colleges and universities throughout the United States and in forty-five countries around the world.

A well-known speaker at national and international conferences, Seldin has presented programs at more than thirty American Council on Education national workshops for division and department chairs and deans specifically designed to enhance departmental leadership.

His well-received books include:

Evaluating Faculty Performance, with associates (Anker, 2006)

The Teaching Portfolio, third edition (Anker, 2004)

The Administrative Portfolio, with Mary Lou Higgerson (Anker, 2002)

Changing Practices in Evaluating Teaching, with associates (Anker, 1999)

The Teaching Portfolio, second edition (Anker, 1997)

Improving College Teaching, with associates (Anker, 1995)

Successful Use of Teaching Portfolios, with associates (Anker, 1993)

The Teaching Portfolio (Anker, 1991)

How Administrators Can Improve Teaching, with associates (Jossey-Bass, 1990)

Evaluating and Developing Administrative Performance (Jossey-Bass, 1988)

Coping with Faculty Stress, with associates (Jossey-Bass, 1987)

Changing Practices in Faculty Evaluation (Jossey-Bass, 1984)

Successful Faculty Evaluation Programs (Coventry Press, 1980)

Teaching Professors to Teach (Blythe-Pennington, 1977)

How Colleges Evaluate Professors (Blythe-Pennington, 1975)

He has contributed numerous articles on the teaching profession, student ratings, educational practice, and academic culture to such publications as the *New York Times,* the *Chronicle of Higher Education,* and *Change* magazine. Among recent honors, he was named by the World Bank as a visiting scholar to Indonesia. In addition, he was elected a fellow of the College of Preceptors in London, England. This special honor is given to a small number of faculty and administrators who are judged to have made an "outstanding contribution to higher education on the international level." For his contributions to the scholarship of teaching, he has received honorary degrees from Keystone College (Pennsylvania) and Columbia College (South Carolina).

J. Elizabeth Miller is associate professor of family and child studies at Northern Illinois University in DeKalb, Illinois. She has taught graduate courses in research methods, family and child studies, and adolescent development and undergraduate courses in family theories, marriage and family, and life span human development. Three times she has been honored with excellence in teaching awards.

Previously she was the founding director of the Teaching Assistant and Training Development Office, which provided extensive training to more than eight hundred teaching assistants. Many of those who received such training are now faculty members at colleges and universities throughout the United States and in numerous other countries around the world. Miller is the outgoing chair of the Women's Caucus of the American Association for Higher Education and has served on the board of the National Council of Family Relations. A presenter at numerous national and international conferences, her research interests focus on the interplay between feminist teaching and learner-centered instruction, as well as the improvement of college teaching. She has extensive experience mentoring faculty members and graduate students at her institution and others as they prepare their teaching portfolios.

She is the author of the well-received *Exploring Family Theories* (2003, with associates) and has published journal articles in family theory, work and family in higher education, religion and family, and mentoring graduate students.

About the Contributors

Shivanthi Anandan is associate professor of bioscience and biotechnology at Drexel University. She serves as chair of the undergraduate program committee in that department and is an in-house mentor to other Drexel University faculty in the preparation of their teaching portfolios. Her teaching and research interests are in biotechnology, microbiology, and genetics.

Carrie Liu Currier is assistant professor of political science and director of Asian studies at Texas Christian University. Her research focuses primarily on the effects of economic reform on women in China. In addition, she has conducted research on population policy in China, women and the sex industry in Southeast Asia, and China's strategic relationship with Iran.

Pamela A. Geller is associate professor of psychology, Ob/Gyn, and public health and director of the student counseling center at Drexel University. She teaches courses in counseling at both the undergraduate and graduate levels. Her research focuses largely on women's health issues, including the mental health consequences of pregnancy loss.

Charles N. Haas is the L. D. Betz Professor of Environmental Engineering and head of the Department of Civil, Architectural, and Environmental Engineering at Drexel University. He is a fellow of the American Academy for the Advancement of Science, the Society for Risk Analysis, and the American Academy of Microbiology. His research focuses on the assessment and control of human exposure to pathogenic microorganisms, and in particular the treatment of water and wastewater to minimize microbial risk to human health.

Gina Jarman Hill is an assistant professor in the Department of Nutritional Sciences at Texas Christian University and a registered and licensed dietitian who has been actively involved in local, state, and national professional organizations. Her current research interests include lactation, medical nutrition therapy, dietary supplementation, and the relationship between nutrition and behavior.

Robert Kirkbride is associate professor of product design at Parsons The New School for Design, New York, and director of the architectural design firm studio 'patafisico. His work has been exhibited and published widely. He has been a visiting scholar at the Canadian Centre for Architecture and architect-in-residence at the Bogliasco Foundation in Genoa, Italy. His research on architecture and memory received the Gutenberg-e Prize from the American Historical Association and will be soon published by Columbia University Press.

Sheri Spaine Long is associate professor of Spanish and chair of the Department of Foreign Languages and Literatures at the University of Alabama at Birmingham. Her teaching and research interests are Spanish language and culture and literature, with a special focus on Madrid in literature. She serves as editor of *Foreign Language Annals* and is the coauthor of *Nexos: Introductory Spanish* (2005) and *Pueblos Intermediate Spanish in Cultural Contexts* (2007).

Robert M. Maninger is assistant professor of education at Texas Christian University. He teaches a technology applications course for preservice teachers and a variety of other courses for preservice teachers and administrators. His research focuses on the use of technology in higher education, specifically its effectiveness in teacher preparation.

Kelly Murray is assistant professor of pastoral counseling and director of Ph.D. clinical education at Loyola College in Maryland. Her research interests focus on women and personality styles in relation to success, and health and psychological states during war. Her clinical work focuses on women's health, trauma, particularly posttraumatic stress disorder, and personality disorders.

Ranjan S. Muttiah is an assistant professor in the Department of Geology at Texas Christian University, where he runs the Center for Geographic Information Systems and Remote Sensing. He teaches courses in environmental science and geographic information systems. His research focuses on the use of computer models to solve water resource problems, and he has received grants and published several papers in this area.

Lisa A. Oberbroeckling is an assistant professor in the Department of Mathematical Sciences at Loyola College in Maryland. She teaches classes primarily in calculus and analysis. Her research is in theoretical mathematics, specifically operator theory, which is a subfield of functional analysis.

Clement A. Seldin is a professor in the Department of Teacher Education and Curriculum Studies at the University of Massachusetts, Amherst. He has received many teaching awards including the university's highest faculty honor, the Distinguished Teaching Award. He has contributed numerous articles to such publications as *Educational Research Quarterly, Phi Delta Kappan,* and *Urban Education,* and served on research teams for The Schools of Education Project, a study of the nation's twelve hundred schools of education.

Marlene K. Sokolon is an assistant professor in the Department of Political Science at Concordia University in Montreal, Canada. Her research specialization includes ancient political philosophy, the philosophy of emotions, and the role of poetry and literature as pedagogy. She is the author of *Political Emotions: Aristotle and the Symphony of Reason and Emotion* (2006).

Annalise Sorrentino, MD, is assistant professor of pediatric medicine in the Division of Pediatric Emergency Medicine at the University of Alabama at Birmingham. Her research focus has been on medical education and faculty development in medical schools. She is the national faculty representative for the American Heart Association's Pediatric Advanced Life Support program, as well as the medical director for the classes held at UAB Medical School. She serves as editor of *The Polhill Report: Dedicated to Lifelong Learning,* a quarterly pediatric newsletter that reviews medical research.

Lynda Henley Walters is a professor in the Department of Child and Family Development at the University of Georgia. Her teaching and research interests include families and law, cross-cultural comparisons of families, and issues in adolescent development. She is the past president of the National Council on Family Relations and has been an active member of seven other professional organizations. She has authored numerous articles and chapters and served as a reviewer for thirteen journals.

Timothy M. Wick is professor and chair of the Department of Biomedical Engineering at the University of Alabama at Birmingham. He is also codirector of UAB's BioMatrix Engineering and Regenerative Medicine Center. His research focuses on tissue engineering and cell adhesion, and he has published prolifically in this area. He is a fellow of the American Institute for Medical and Biological Engineering and is an active member of several other professional societies.

Reginald Workman is an associate professor at The New School (Jazz and Contemporary Music Department). A bassist/composer, he is recognized as one of the most technically gifted bassists in modern music. A member of the John Coltrane Quartet, his fifty-year career includes performances and recordings with almost every notable figure in the jazz world, including Thelonious

Monk, Art Blakey, and Miles Davis. He has received numerous awards for both jazz and jazz education. Current projects include *Trio 3,* the African-American Legacy Project, and the Sculptured Sounds Music Festival.

John Zubizarreta is professor of English and director of honors and faculty development and former dean of undergraduate studies at Columbia College. A C.A.S.E. Professor for South Carolina, he has published and consulted widely on teaching, learning, academic leadership, and honors education. His most recent book is *The Learning Portfolio: Reflective Practice for Improving Student Learning* (2004), and he is vice president and president elect of the National Collegiate Honors Council.

The Academic Portfolio

Chapter One

The Academic Portfolio Concept

An important and welcome change is taking place on college and university campuses: evaluating faculty performance is being taken more seriously. Countless institutions are examining their evaluation methods and exploring ways to improve them. As for faculty, they are being held accountable, as never before, to provide solid evidence of the quality of their teaching, research, and service. The new focus is not just what they have accomplished but the skills, abilities, attitudes, and philosophies that enabled them to achieve professional excellence.

What is behind the movement to seek new and more effective ways to evaluate faculty performance? The growing number of parents and students facing swiftly rising annual costs of higher education led to demanding questions about the quality of faculty performance. And strident demands for faculty accountability from newly aroused legislatures and institutional governing boards added to the pressure on campuses.

But perhaps the most compelling force was the growing chorus of complaints from administrators and professors themselves that the current evaluation system was not geared to assisting review committees to understand the rich quality of their work and its significance. True, they probably have student ratings and a curriculum vitae that lists publications, honors, presentations, and research grants. But student rating numbers and lists of scholarly achievements do not describe one's professional priorities and strengths. They do not present a rationale for choices made, expectations realized, circumstances that promoted or inhibited success. And, importantly, they do not describe the significance of one's work.

Yet in the absence of such information, how can performance be evaluated? How can it be rewarded? How can it be improved? And how can institutions give teaching, research, and service their proper role and value?

Is there a way for colleges and universities to respond to the pressures to improve systems of faculty accountability? The answer is yes. A solution can be found looking outside higher education.

Architects, photographers, and artists all have portfolios in which they display and highlight their best work. An academic portfolio would do the same thing. It would enable faculty members to display their accomplishments in teaching, research, and service and discuss the significance of those accomplishments for the record. At the same time, it would contribute to sounder promotion and tenure decisions, as well as the professional development and growth of the individual faculty member.

What Is an Academic Portfolio?

An academic portfolio is a reflective, evidence-based collection of materials that documents teaching, research, and service performance. It brings together, in one place, information about a professor's most significant professional accomplishments. It includes documents and materials that collectively suggest the scope, quality, and significance of a professor's achievements. As such, it allows faculty members to display their accomplishments for examination by others. And in the process, it contributes to sounder personnel decisions as well as the professional development of individual faculty members. Zubizarreta (2006, p. 202) describes the academic portfolio as a ". . . judicious, critical, purposeful analysis of performance, evidence, and goals—the kind of reflection and keen scrutiny of achievement and future directions that leads to authentic professional development, meaningful assessment, and sound evaluation."

In order to be useful, a portfolio must be manageable and cost- and time-efficient. A challenge in portfolio construction is to decide "how much information is enough," especially when the portfolio is to be used for promotion and tenure decisions. Too many data can be unwieldy and, worse, misleading by creating the impression that the candidate is unable to discriminate or is attempting to overwhelm the committee with paper. Yet too sparse a portfolio may convey a lack of richness, substance, and experience.

The academic portfolio is not an exhaustive compilation of all of the documents and materials that bear on an individual's performance as a faculty member. Instead, it culls selected information on teaching, research, and service activities that portray an appropriate balance of professional activities and provide solid evidence of their effectiveness. The focus is on the quality and significance of the work, such as an especially innovative teaching technique, an article from a highly competitive journal, or a particularly time-consuming campus committee. Being selective does not mean creating a biased picture of one's teaching, research and scholarship, and service performance. Rather, it means providing a fair and accurate representation of it.

The logic behind portfolios is straightforward. Earlier assessment methods, such as student ratings, lists of publications, and campus committees, were like flashlights: they illuminated only the activities and abilities that fell within their beams and therefore shed light on only a small part of a professor's performance. But with portfolios, the flashlight is replaced by a searchlight. Its beam discloses the broad range of professorial skills, attitudes, and philosophies, as well as the significance of one's achievements to students, colleagues, the academic discipline, and the institution. It has the capacity to convey a true, rich picture of an academic professional life.

Millis (1991) offers reasons for the viability of teaching portfolio development, a view that is readily adaptable to the academic portfolio:

1. Portfolios are cost-effective since they can be integrated into current evaluation processes without major disruption by rethinking and reallocating faculty time and commitment.
2. They are an effective tool for instructional improvement since portfolios are grounded squarely in discipline-related pedagogy.

3. Since portfolios involve both documentation and reflection, and faculty "own" the portfolio process, they are more likely to act positively as a result of their own reflections.
4. Good portfolios are collegial efforts. Valuable assistance can come from a department chair or a faculty colleague in structuring the portfolio and deciding what goes into it.

Using the Portfolio

Faculty members are busy, even harried, individuals. Why would they want to take the time and trouble to prepare an academic portfolio? Seldin (2008) says that the two most frequently cited reasons for preparing one are to provide evidence for use in personnel decisions and to improve performance.

Personnel Decisions

Providing a rational and equitable basis for promotion and tenure decisions is a central reason for preparing an academic portfolio. In today's climate of increasing accountability, colleges and universities are looking toward portfolios as a rich way, and with greater depth, to get at the complexity and individuality of faculty performance. These institutions have concluded that personnel decisions (evaluation) should rest on a holistic examination of faculty teaching, research, and service performance. The portfolio provides evaluators with hard-to-ignore information on what they do, why they do it, how they do it, and the significance and outcome of what they do.

At some institutions, faculty members who elect to dedicate most of their waking time to a major research program are excused by the department chair or dean from some faculty responsibilities. At other institutions, research and publication are mildly encouraged, and professors are expected to focus on their teaching duties. But at most colleges and universities, professors must learn to divide themselves, like Gaul, into three parts: teaching, research (and publication), and institutional or community service. They are accountable in all three areas.

Some argue that professors should be given unrestricted freedom to select the items that best reflect their performance. That approach works well if the portfolio is developed for improvement, but not if the portfolio is developed for personnel purposes (evaluation). Why? Because the contents are based on a combination of availability of supporting materials, the nature of the portfolio, the faculty position, the discipline, and the mission and objectives of the institution. The resulting lack of standardization makes comparability across portfolios very difficult.

One answer is to require portfolios being used for personnel decisions to include certain mandated items along with the elective ones. Such mandated items might include summaries of student evaluations, innovative course materials, representative course syllabi, description of faculty research, selected samples of publications or creative works, external funding obtained, selected samples of department or institution committees, and a description of three major professional accomplishments and an explanation of why they are noteworthy. All additional items in the portfolio would be selected by individual faculty.

Professors stand to benefit by providing their portfolios to evaluators of their performance. Portfolios provide evaluators with rich evidence on which to make judgments about their effectiveness. If certain items in the portfolio are standardized, comparison of faculty performance (for example, three professors from one large department seeking promotion to full professor) becomes possible.

Does the portfolio approach really make any difference? Consider the comments from professors whose portfolios were used for personnel decisions:

> *A political science professor in North Carolina:* "The portfolio was particularly helpful as I prepared my material for tenure. It helped me articulate who I am academically to people outside my discipline. That was invaluable."

> *A history professor in Kansas:* "The portfolio made a big difference when I submitted my material for post-tenure review. I sailed through!"

> *An economics professor in Pennsylvania:* "By completing the academic portfolio, I've been able to easily gather the important documents that I need to support my application for promotion."

From a clinical science professor in Washington: "My portfolio helped me to get ready for the promotion process! I felt much more prepared. Internal feedback on my portfolio was very positive, and several colleagues have now asked me to mentor them as they prepare their own portfolios."

How do members of promotion and tenure committees feel about academic portfolios? Consider the following comments from members of committees:

A committee member at a large research university in Florida: "It took time to learn how to evaluate the portfolios. But once we did, the richness of the data and the integration of material made our job much easier."

A committee member at a small liberal arts college in Vermont: "Without doubt, we make better tenure and promotion decisions with academic portfolios. The reflection component is essential."

A committee member at a comprehensive university in New York: "I wish the portfolio idea had come along twenty years ago. Why? Because (a) the integration of material; (b) incorporation of a reflective component; and (c) limited length (sixteen pages here) would have saved the committee considerable time and helped us make much better decisions."

It is important to keep in mind that use of the portfolio for personnel decisions is only occasional. Its primary purpose is to improve teaching, research, and service performance.

Improve Performance

There is no better reason to prepare a portfolio than to improve performance. The process of thoughtful reflection augmented by the gathering of documents and materials on performance provides data with which to assist the faltering, motivate the tired, and encourage the indecisive.

Faculty are hired by institutions in expectation of first-class performance. To help them hone their performance is nothing more than an extension of this expectation. Improvement becomes possible when the professor is confronted with portfolio data showing strengths and weaknesses—data that the professor accepts as fair and accurate. Preparation of a portfolio can thus serve as a springboard for performance improvement. It is in the very process of reflecting on their work and creating the collection of documents and materials that the professor is stimulated to reconsider policies and activities, rethink strategies and methodologies, revise priorities, and plan for the future.

The academic portfolio is an especially effective tool for improvement because it is grounded in the tripartite role of a professor working in a specific discipline at a particular college or university at the present time. It focuses on reflective analysis, action planning, and self-assessment.

The bottom-line question, of course, remains: Do portfolios actually improve faculty performance? For most faculty, the answer is yes. Experience suggests that if the professor is motivated to improve, knows how to improve, or knows where to go for help, improvement is quite likely.

Consider these comments:

An English professor in California: "The process of taking a fresh look at my teaching, scholarship, and service was motivating and even eye-opening. I especially valued the opportunity to reflect on how my efforts in the proverbial trinity of the professoriate are not as integrated as I originally thought. I'll work to improve that situation."

An engineering professor in Indiana: "Developing the portfolio enabled me to take a more systematic look at everything that I've been doing in the classroom, as department chair, and in professional activities and then tying the threads together. Areas for improvement are more clear now."

A foreign language professor in Illinois: "The portfolio helped me reassess the many movements that I make in a day and think about how to keep my 'eye on the ball.' Working in academe is so full of distractions. Looking at myself through the academic portfolio helped me refocus on the core of what I do."

A clinical psychology professor in New Jersey: "Taking the time to step back from the daily work demands and gain a broader perspective allowed me to create some specific career goals. This was both inspiring and effective in helping me lay out a plan for how to direct my efforts in the next few years."

A *music professor in Illinois:* "Preparing the portfolio helped me recognize and articulate the connections among my teaching, research, and service; prior to writing it, I hadn't realized how tightly these professional activities were woven."

When used for improvement purposes, the portfolio contains no mandated items. Instead it contains only items chosen by the faculty member. For example, a professor might decide to include teaching philosophy and methodology; documentation of teaching improvement activities; comments from peer reviewers on submitted articles and proposed conference presentations; feedback on student advising; description of how his or her teaching, research, and service contribute to professional growth and development; and description of professional goals still to accomplish.

There are three important reasons that the portfolio is such a valuable aid in professional development: (1) it is grounded in discipline-based performance; (2) the level of personal investment in time, energy, and commitment is high—since faculty develop their own portfolios—and that is a necessary condition for change; and (3) it stirs many professors to reflect on their performance in the areas of teaching, research, and service in an insightful, refocused way.

Ideally, academic portfolio development is not a "one-shot" activity but rather a cumulative, reflective process that extends throughout a professor's professional career. Froh, Gray, and Lambert (1993) view the portfolio as integral to advancement to the next stage of one's academic career. Why? Because portfolio development can help professors reflect on their accomplishments and activities, chart future goals, and provide documentation to hiring and promotion and tenure committees.

Ongoing examination of professional accomplishments may lead to new directions in academic lives. For example, a faculty member who brings in a major research grant might decide to take up the challenge of incorporating more extensive use of technology in the classroom. A faculty member who completes a new book might agree to chair an institution-wide self-study committee.

Other Purposes

Although it is true that most portfolios are prepared for purposes of personnel decision or improvement of performance, some are prepared for other reasons—for example:

- Graduate students are preparing portfolios to bolster their credentials as they enter the job market.
- Professors are preparing portfolios to take on the road as they seek a different position. Generally the portfolio is submitted in advance of an interview.
- Some institutions are requiring academic portfolios from finalists for academic positions.
- Portfolios are used to help colleges and universities determine winners of awards for outstanding faculty performance or for merit pay consideration.
- Professors nearing retirement are preparing portfolios in order to leave a written legacy so that faculty members who will be taking over their position will have the benefit of their experience.
- Portfolios are used to provide evidence in applications for grants or released time.
- Colleges and universities are asking faculty to prepare portfolios so they can provide data on their performance to persons and organizations operating off campus, such as government agencies, boards of trustees, alumni, the general public, and advocacy groups.

Chapter Two

Choosing Items for the Academic Portfolio

There are many possibilities from which items can be selected that are especially relevant to an individual professor's particular academic situation. The items chosen for the portfolio depend on (1) the purpose for which the portfolio is being prepared, (2) the institutional context, (3) the discipline, (4) the importance assigned by the faculty member to different items, (5) any content requirements of the faculty member's institution, and (6) personal predilection and style of the professor. Differences in portfolio content and organization should be encouraged to the extent that they are allowed by the department and the college or university.

Since the academic portfolio is a highly personalized product, like a fingerprint, no two are exactly alike. The information revealed in the narrative and documented in the appendix bears a unique stamp that personalizes the portfolio.

Nevertheless, given the nearly universal need in faculty evaluation today that professors document the three-legged stool of teaching, research, and service, the following list should be helpful. It does *not* comprise items a professor *must* include. Rather, it includes many possibilities from which the faculty member can select items relevant to his or her particular academic situation. Also, there may be some other items, not on this list, that are particularly relevant to an individual professor and can be selected for their portfolio.

The portfolio takes a broader view of teaching, research, and service than the traditional curriculum vitae compiled by faculty to document their achievements because it integrates the values of the faculty member with those of the discipline, the department,

11

and the institution. This is accomplished by work samples and reflective commentary that speak to such an integration of values. Thus, the portfolio transforms the traditional dossier to reflect the work of each individual faculty member and the unique contribution that he or she has made in relevant areas of teaching, research, and service.

A word of caution: All college and university faculty have seen poor student work dressed in fancy covers. The point of the academic portfolio is not a fancy cover. Instead, it is the thoughtful, integrated compilation of documents and materials that make the best case for the professor's effectiveness.

The portfolio narrative has a hierarchical structure. Typically it contains five main categories: the preface, independent sections on teaching, research, and service, and a section on integrating professional work and goals. An appendix provides evidence that supports the narrative section.

Within the main categories, professors create subcategories that provide rich details on their professional activities, initiatives, goals, and accomplishments and thoughtful reflection on their performance.

An important word about the academic portfolio template that follows: this is its ninth iteration. More than two hundred deans, department chairs, and faculty members contributed to its development. They work at large universities and small colleges, public and private institutions, unionized and nonunionized campuses. Settings vary, of course, but the questions that need to be considered and the materials that need to be collected are similar across all contexts.

What differs from institution to institution are the policies and procedures followed, the criteria used to assess the evidence of teaching, research and scholarship performance, and the relative weighting of various activities. For that reason, readers are urged to develop their individual portfolios bearing in mind the context of their own campus culture.

Preface

This section, which is usually about a half-page in length, spells out the purpose (tenure? promotion? improvement?) for which the portfolio is being prepared. It also provides a crucial road map for the reader announcing major subject areas. Faculty some-times include brief summary statements on the importance and quality of their work and how their activities support the mission and vision of their institution.

Teaching

Typically five or six pages long, this section usually includes a statement of teaching responsibilities, which provides details on courses taught and average student enrollment. A chart or table is a useful way to present the information graphically. The section on teaching responsibilities also includes information on student advising and, where relevant, thesis mentoring. The sections that follow explain the topics typically included in the teaching section.

Teaching Philosophy, Objectives, and Methodologies

The focus here is on the philosophy of teaching and learning that drives the classroom performance of the professor. Following are some guiding questions to consider as prompts when preparing this section: What do I believe about the role of the teacher? The role of the student? Why do I teach the way I do? What does learning look like when it happens? Why do I choose the teaching strategies and methods that I use? How do I assess my students' learning?

Description of Curricular Revisions

This section concerns new or revised courses, material, and assignments.

Guiding questions as prompts: Have I introduced new applica-tions of technology? Changed course objectives? Used new mate-rials? Introduced new assignments? Have I added (or dropped) guest speakers? Field trips? Laboratory work? Have I developed a new course? Revised a course? Team-taught a course?

Selected Course Syllabi

Samples of syllabi are placed in an appendix file, but highlights are included in the narrative, and the two are cross-referenced.

Guiding questions as prompts: What does the syllabus say about my teaching and learning beliefs? What do I want it to say? Does it speak to the tools and information that I provide students to help them learn? Is it a learning-centered syllabus? What does it say about the course and my way of teaching it that is specific to me?

Documentation of Teaching Improvement Activities

Improvement efforts and professional development activities are highlighted here. These are especially important when framed within the context of institutional mission and priorities. Samples of certificates of attendance can be placed in an appendix file, but reference is made to them in the narrative, and the two are cross-referenced.

Guiding questions as prompts: Which faculty development workshops and seminars have you attended? When? Where? How are you applying what you learned from those programs in your teaching? What specific steps have you taken to improve your teaching? What evidence do you have of growth or change in your teaching? How have you responded to suggestions for improvement that have come from students?

Student Course Evaluation Data

Student course or teaching evaluation data, especially those that produce an overall rating of effectiveness or satisfaction, are included in the narrative section of the portfolio. All claims must be supported by evidence in the appendix. Often they are presented in a chart or table that includes course title, number of students, mean score, and, if available, the department or collegewide mean score on each question. When the portfolio is used for promotion or tenure, it is especially important to include ratings on each of the common core student rating questions that are considered to be pivotal by the institution's personnel committees.

Guiding questions as prompts: Are student evaluation data included from each class that is regularly taught? Are data from all common core questions included? From a summary question on overall effectiveness? Are all claims made in the narrative about student ratings supported by evidence in the appendix? Are there any special circumstances that have affected the student ratings? Is the vast majority of the student feedback current or from the recent past (three to five years)?

Classroom Observation Reports by Faculty Colleagues or Administrators

Some institutions use classroom observations for tenure and promotion decisions. Assuming the observations are characterized by careful planning, training, and trust, such reports can be a valuable addition to the portfolio. Excerpts from observation reports are placed in the narrative section and are cross-referenced to the complete report, located in an appendix file.

Guiding questions as prompts: Are there any special circumstances (for example, room too small, too large, too hot, too cold, too noisy) that interfered with teaching and learning during the observation? Is the observation report dated and signed by the observer? Are any excerpts included in the narrative that tie in with the professor's philosophy of teaching or selected methodology?

Research and Scholarship

Typically this section is five to six pages in length and has an especially important role, particularly when used for tenure and promotion purposes. It educates college or university personnel committee members (some of whom will be from outside the professor's discipline) about the importance and quality of the professor's research and scholarship and how it supports the mission of the department and the institution.

For that reason, it is particularly important that the section be written in clear, concise, easily understood language. Imagine speaking with your grandmother and explaining the essence of your research to her—in language she will understand. Avoid jargon and acronyms, and embrace brevity, clarity, and simple language. The sections that follow are frequently included in this part of the academic portfolio.

Nature of the Professor's Research and Scholarship

This is a brief (two-page) description of the purpose and focus of the faculty member's research and scholarship. Simplicity of language is vital.

Guiding questions as prompts: How would you explain your research to someone who knows very little about your discipline? What are your goals? Methods? Results? Why is your research significant? What impact has it had on your discipline? On your department colleagues? On your students? What are your short-term and long-term research and scholarship goals?

Statements from Others Commenting on the Professor's Research and Scholarship

Testimonials from experts in the field, either inside or outside the institution, that the professor has made original and substantive contributions to the field of research and scholarship (or creative specialty) can be useful qualitative indicators of performance. For members of personnel committees, especially those outside the professor's discipline, such testimonials can be particularly helpful in determining promotion or tenure. But they can also be helpful when used for grants, awards, travel funds, annual raises, graduate student assistants, and release time.

Excerpts are typically included in this section of the portfolio, and the complete testimonial letters are placed in the appendix.

Guiding questions as prompts: Have you included the original signed and dated letters and placed them in the appendix? Do the testimonial letters speak to your current research and scholarship? If such testimonial letters are not available, from whom might they be obtained? Does the institution have policies or procedures that govern solicitation of such letters—for example, who contacts the experts? Is a standard form with specific questions used?

Selected Sample of Books or Publications in Journals or Creative Works

Academic publishing is enormously important as professors build professional visibility and establish reputations. Books and articles are seen as valuable contributions to a discipline by an audience of peers. If editors and referees regard a manuscript as original and significant, they allow it to be published. And if colleagues then cite it in their own work and develop it further, the professor receives the reward of recognition.

Professors who excel in publishing their writing get hired and gain tenure and promotion more readily, of course. And they are often appointed to key positions (editorial boards, state or national committees), gain access to financial resources (grants, stipends, awards), and gain major gatekeeping roles (dean, chair).

This section of the portfolio includes a selected sample of books and other publications in refereed scholarly journals or creative works. Many professors include reference to just three or four items here and refer to the complete list of their publications in the appendix of the portfolio.

Guiding questions as prompts: Why have you chosen these samples of your publications or creative work? What is significant about each? In specific terms, what is the importance of each sample selected to your discipline? Have any of these activities made you a more effective teacher? In what specific ways? Are the highlighted samples consistent with the preferences of your institution or department as to books versus journal articles, applied versus basic research, publications versus creative work?

External Funding and Grants Obtained, Grant Proposals Under Review

Larger, older colleges and universities, especially those with strong graduate programs, often look with favor at faculty activity that results in outside funding. For those institutions, grants obtained are a critical measure of faculty performance, especially in the sciences, medicine, and engineering. As a result, much faculty time is devoted to preparing proposals for funding, along with a compelling program of work to the three main sources of outside financial support: government, foundations, and industry.

External funding is fiercely competitive. At one university, the grant pressure cooker propelled anxious professors at year's end to pile their rejection slips on the department chair's desk as evidence of their efforts to fulfill this obligation.

Guiding questions as prompts: Have you received funding from an outside source? For what project? When? Specifically from whom? Were you the principal or coprincipal investigator? If others were involved in the project, who were they? What was the outcome of the funded work? Did it lead to publications? Conference presentations? Symposia? Additional funding? Have you cited a sample of funded activities in this section and included a complete list in the appendix?

Editorial Appointments and Offices Held in Professional Societies

Some disciplines or institutions regard editorial appointments and offices held in professional societies as research and scholarship. Others categorize it as external service. Regardless of how it is labeled, this form of activity refers to discipline-based service to the broader academic community. Examples include serving as a special issue editor or on the editorial board of a journal; participating as an officer of a state, regional, national, or international professional society; or serving on the organizing committee of a state or national conference.

Guiding questions as prompts: Which of your editorial appointments or offices held in professional societies do you consider especially significant? Why? Have you cited a sampling of these in your portfolio narrative and provided evidence of them in the appendix? Have you edited conference proceedings? Reviewed proposals for external funding agencies or the federal or state government? Is cross-referenced evidence—in the form of letters of appointment or a thank you for professional service—included in the appendix?

Selected Sample of Conference Presentations, Readings, Performances, or Exhibits

Many colleges and universities look with favor on a listing of a professor's invited conference presentations, readings, performances, or exhibits. A large number of institutions also value accepted proposals for such professional activities, especially if they have been peer reviewed.

This section of the portfolio contains a selected sample of conference presentations, readings, performances, or exhibits. Many professors find it useful to include reference to just three or four examples here and provide a complete list in the appendix.

Differences from one discipline to another determine whether conference presentations or creative works are more appropriate to include in this section. For example, a professor of biochemistry would likely cite invitations to present research-based papers at conferences, while a professor of poetry would be inclined to stress readings, and a professor of modern art would probably emphasize exhibits.

Guiding questions as prompts: Why have you chosen these particular samples? What is especially significant about each? How does each relate to your discipline? Have you provided cross-referenced evidence (such as a conference program) in the appendix to demonstrate that you actually presented the paper at a conference, not just that your proposal was accepted? Are the selected samples consistent with the expectations of your department and institution as to the public presentation by faculty of an original intellectual, pedagogical, or creative contribution? Is a complete list of your presentations or creative activities included in the appendix?

Supervision of Graduate Students

This will not be a relevant subcategory of the portfolio for faculty at small liberal arts colleges and those at community colleges. But for professors who work at larger institutions, particularly those with strong graduate programs, this can be an especially important section of the portfolio.

Without question, the significance of supervising graduate students is discipline specific. For example, in medicine, the sciences, and engineering, where research is often team oriented and laboratory based, the ability to find and fund graduate students is of paramount importance. But that is a very different situation from that in the humanities, the creative arts, and business.

As a subcategory, supervision of graduate students is broad and refers to such areas as serving on master's or doctoral committees as thesis director or reader, overseeing graduate students as research or teaching assistants, guiding them as fellows or residents in medicine, and directing field placement activities.

Guiding questions as prompts: What is the nature of your graduate student supervision? How many students do you supervise? Are you responsible for selecting or funding them? For how long will you supervise them? What do you like (or dislike) about supervising graduate students? Have you included a representative list of some graduate students you supervised previously and indicated their career path or current employment?

Service

Virtually every college and university recognizes that some kind of institutional service is part of the responsibility of each faculty member. But the kind of service that is valued varies from institution to institution. Some institutions construe service as the professor's relationship, attitude, and behavior within the department or institution. Others see it as the professor's willingness to shoulder a heavy workload of less desirable courses. Still others recognize it in the discharge of extra administrative duties.

But across the country, the leading index of institutional service is participation on department or institutional committees. Most faculty allot a good deal of time to the service function. Sometimes it seems that they spend endless hours in endless meetings as they are assigned to such committees as institutional governance, promotion and tenure, student activities, parking facilities and regulations, athletics, student standing, and even campus security.

Because service is typically considered less important than teaching or research and scholarship by colleges and universities, it is given a less prominent role in the academic portfolio. Typically, most professors allocate just a few pages to it.

Selected Sample of Department and Institution Committees and Task Forces

Professors typically serve on a variety of departmental or institutional committees and task forces. In this section, a selected sample of three or four is cited. The complete list appears in the appendix.

Guiding questions as prompts: Why have you chosen these particular sample committees and task forces? Do they reflect the wide spectrum of your service contribution? The significance of your service activities? How often did they meet? In personnel decisions at your institution, are department or institution-wide service activities considered more important? Have you reflected that greater importance in your choice of samples? Provided information on the size, scope, and mission of committees? Included any published final reports in the appendix?

Description of Role and Contribution to Committees and Task Forces

Many professors join this portfolio subsection to the preceding one on committees and task forces. It makes good sense to do so since the faculty member preparing the portfolio can easily add references to his or her role or contribution to each of the selected committees and task forces previously cited.

Guiding questions as prompts: What was your role or contribution to each committee or task force mentioned? If you served as chair or director, how were you chosen for that position? Have you included any formal or informal feedback on your performance? If you carried out any special committee or task force assignment, either on- or off-campus, have you included it in this subsection?

Student Advising, Mentoring Junior Colleagues, and Service-Learning Activities

Although these activities may seem to be outside the essential triad of teaching, research and scholarship, and service, they are part of the professional life of some professors. As such, they can be included in their portfolios.

In truth, professors who take the time for thoughtful, constructive, informed student advising, especially on the undergraduate level, often seem to get little credit for it. The same is often true of professors who mentor junior colleagues and discuss what they need to know about the department and the institution, as well as the expectations and available resources for teaching, research and scholarship, and service. Moreover, little credit seems to go to faculty for using service-learning, a teaching method that combines organized community service with academic instruction.

For many faculty, the reward for advising students, mentoring junior colleagues, or teaching using service-learning is largely intrinsic. But in part, that is because these activities are frequently not documented. Where that occurs, chairs, deans, and members of personnel committees are simply not aware that they have taken place. They should be.

Guiding questions as prompts: Why have you chosen these activities to discuss in your portfolio? What is significant about them? Have you published articles or presented conference papers about what you do, why, and how you do it? Does your portfolio include information (for example, evaluation forms, e-mails, letters) that indicates your effectiveness as a student adviser, mentor, or faculty member who uses service learning in teaching?

Participation in Community Civic Groups, Agencies, and Organizations

Some professors engage in external community service. They participate in various civic groups, agencies, and organizations. To be valued by the college or university, though, the external service contribution must be closely linked to the discipline-based skills and expertise of the faculty member. For example, the accounting professor who chairs an ad hoc committee that examines the county budget will likely be applauded for his efforts. But if he coaches a Little League team, his efforts will probably not be recognized as valid community service.

Guiding questions as prompts: Which of your community service activities do you consider especially noteworthy? Why? How do they tie in with your discipline? Your institution? Have you provided a sampling of such activities in your portfolio narrative and included evidence of them (minutes, handouts, flyers, advertise-ments) in the appendix? Have any of your community service activities made you a more effective teacher? Which ones? In what specific ways?

Integration of Professional Work and Goals

In their work as professors, faculty strive to integrate their teaching, research and scholarship, and service. When the professional puzzle forms a coherent puzzle, the nexus is exhilarating, even inspiring. But when there is little or no connection among the array of respon-sibilities, commitments, hopes, and dreams, the nexus is overwhelm-ing, even discouraging (J. Zubizarreta, personal communication, February 5, 2008).

Happily, many professors do find the interrelated threads that bind together their professional activities. Their teaching and research and scholarship are intertwined, and both contribute to their service activities. For example, a professor of management does research in the area of leadership innovation, discusses the findings in her graduate organizational behavior class, and applies them in a campus workshop on effective leadership for depart-ment chairs. Another example: working with two doctoral stu-dents, a professor of environmental engineering does research in the area of drinking water contamination, assists her graduate stu-dents in preparing a conference presentation on the findings, and uses the research results to help her university redesign its system to ensure institutional water quality. A third example: a professor of American history teaches a seminar on the Revolutionary War, takes his students on a three-day field trip to several important battlefields, and chairs the department curricu-lum committee, which is considering adding a field experience to certain history courses. Finally, a professor in nutrition, whose research focuses on eating disorders, has her students do a service-learning project with local elementary school students about making healthy food choices and conducts a workshop for faculty on feminist teaching methodologies.

In each example, the professor's teaching, research and schol-arship, and service were linked and contributed to his or her professional growth and development. The professor gained new knowledge, had new experiences, and found new opportunities to apply what he or she had learned.

A related point is that failures, if used as learning experiences, can be a positive addition to a portfolio. For example, a teaching practice that did not work at first can be a powerful asset if a professor shows that he identified a problem or issue, dealt with it, and learned from the experience. A manuscript rejected for publication by a major discipline-based journal can be a portfolio plus if the professor shows that she corrected the weaknesses, resubmitted it, had it accepted for publication, and learned from the experience.

Guiding questions as prompts: In what specific ways have your teaching, research and scholarship, and service contributed to your professional growth and development? Have you provided appropriate examples? What has been the impact of your teaching or research and scholarship on your institutional service? Your community service? How have students contributed to your professional growth and development? How have failures contributed?

Three Professional Accomplishments and Why They Are Noteworthy

Faculty members typically have many professional accomplishments. Some are likely to be in teaching, others in research or scholarship, and still others in service. But regardless of which segment of faculty life they are in, some accomplishments are more important to the professor than others.

This section of the portfolio asks faculty to consider their many accomplishments and select three that are especially noteworthy to them. In that process, professors typically choose items that are consistent with the mission and scope of their department and institution. This is particularly important if the portfolio is being prepared for purposes of personnel decision.

This example is from a professor of English at a small liberal arts college: "I am especially proud to have been given the 2008 President's Award for Teaching Excellence. Selection was on the basis of student ratings, classroom observations, alumni reports, and department chair evaluation. This honor is especially welcome as the president has repeatedly said that we are a teaching institution and that excellence in the classroom is why we exist."

Another example is from a professor of bioscience at a large research university: "I am particularly proud of the $4 million grant I received in 2008 from the National Science Foundation. As Principal Investigator of the project to research biocontamination threats, I work with a team of academics from the University of Michigan, University of Texas, and Harvard University. This grant is especially noteworthy because our institution is committed to achieving national status as one of the top ten U.S. universities in grant money received."

Guiding questions as prompts: Why have you chosen these specific accomplishments? How do they fit in with the priorities of your department? Your institution? Who has been the primary beneficiary of each selected accomplishment: Students? The discipline? The department? The institution? What has been the impact of these accomplishments on your career? Have there been setbacks or disappointments that later served as the foundation of any of these accomplishments?

Three Professional Goals

Different institutions and different disciplines have different trajectories for an academic career. For that reason, professional goals are often scripted by the particular environment in which faculty members work. Others are determined by their personal preferences. This section of the portfolio asks professors to look ahead and identify three significant goals they still want to achieve. The thought process required to develop plans in teaching, research and scholarship, and service over several years forces faculty to crystallize thinking about possible projects and activities.

In doing so, some faculty are specific in identifying their goals—for example: "By spring, 2009, I want to learn to more effectively use PowerPoint so I can incorporate it into my teaching methods with genuine confidence." Others write in more general terms, such as, "I'd like to publish another article in a top-tier journal."

The initial goal of just about every faculty member is to attain promotion and tenure. Post-promotion and tenure goals might be found in such general areas as continuing one's development as a teacher, expanding a research area or creating a new one, publishing in a top-tier journal, or participating in institutional governance or discipline-based editorial service.

Guiding questions as prompts: What professional goals have you been unable to attain in the past that you would like to pursue now? Why are they important to you? What goals would your department like to see you attain? Your institution? Why are those goals important to them? How can your college or university help you achieve those goals? What kind of resource help (people? money? space? time?) do you need to achieve the goals that are important to you?

Appendix

The appendix material needs careful attention to be sure that all statements of accomplishments in the narrative are adequately supported. It is best not to engage in overkill.

Just as information in the narrative part of the portfolio should be selective, so too the appendixes should consist of judiciously chosen evidence that adequately supports the narrative section of the portfolio. If the appendixes contain nonprint media or items that do not fit within the portfolio three-ring binder—videotapes, journal articles, books, or CDs, for example—the professor may briefly discuss such materials in the narrative and make them available for review in a designated location.

Rather than offer a separate, isolated commentary for each appendix item, the vast majority of professors weave references to appendixes within the narrative portion of their portfolio (as an example, "See Appendix A for original student evaluation summary sheets"). Why? Because this approach strengthens coherence.

Which sorts of evidence might go into the appendixes depends on the requirements of the department and the institution, as well as the personal preferences of the individual professor. But many of the following items are often included: student ratings of instruction, syllabi, classroom observation reports, samples of selected publications and conference presentations, copies of external funding awards, letters of editorial appointments, and samples of department and institution committees and relevant community civic groups.

The appendixes must be of manageable size if they are to be read. For most professors, six to ten categories of appendix items are sufficient.

A word of caution: Sometimes faculty preparing academic portfolios fall into the trap of permitting the appendixes—the supporting documents—to determine the portfolio creation. In this case, the tail wags the dog. Should that occur, professors may find themselves focusing on a shopping list of possible portfolio items, determining which are easily obtainable, and then creating the reflective section of their portfolios around the evidence they have at hand. The result is that they end up focusing on the "what" rather than the "why."

A far better approach is to:

1. Reflect on your underlying teaching philosophy, the nature of your research and scholarship and your service activities, and most significant professional accomplishments.
2. Describe the strategies and methodologies that flow from that reflection (why you do what you do).
3. Select documents and materials that provide the hard evidence of your teaching, research and scholarship, and service activities and accomplishments.

Electronic Portfolio

Sometimes a professor decides to do an academic portfolio in an electronic rather than a paper version. A portfolio constructed in this way includes technologies that allow the developer to collect and organize the contents in many formats, including audio, video, graphical, and text. The electronic portfolio typically uses hypertext links to organize the material, connecting it to appropriate goals and standards.

For purposes of improvement, both electronic or paper formats work well. But for purposes of promotion and tenure—despite enormous advances in technology—the paper version is preferred by most colleges and universities. It has the important advantage of enabling committee members to easily be on the same page at the same time. That is more difficult to do with the electronic version because most personnel committees do not meet in rooms with a computer bank.

Whether electronic or paper, a typical academic portfolio table of contents might look like this:

Academic Portfolio

NAME OF FACULTY MEMBER

Department / College

Institution

Date

———————

Table of Contents

Purpose

Teaching

    Statement of Teaching Responsibilities

    Teaching Philosophy, Objectives, Methodologies

    Description of Curricular Revisions

    Selected Course Syllabi and Other Course Material

    Teaching Improvement Activities

    Student Course Evaluation Data

    Classroom Observation Reports

Research and Scholarship

    Nature of Faculty Research and Scholarship Statements from Others on the Importance of the Research Study to the Discipline

    Sample of Books/Publications in Refereed Journals or Creative Works

    External Funding or Grants Obtained and Proposals Under Review

(Continued)

Editorial Appointments/Offices Held in Professional Societies

Sample of Conference Presentations, Readings, Performances, or Exhibits

Supervision of Graduate Students

Service

Sample of Department/Institution Committees and Task Forces

Description of Role/Contribution to Committees or Task Forces

Student Advising, Mentoring Junior Colleagues, Service-Learning Activities

Participation in Community Civic Groups, Agencies, Organizations

Integration of Professional Work and Goals

Description of How Teaching, Research and Scholarship, and Service Contribute to One's Professional Growth and Development

Three Professional Accomplishments of Which You Are Especially Proud

Three Professional Goals

Appendix

Typical Portfolio Length

The typical academic portfolio has a narrative of approximately fourteen to nineteen double-spaced pages, followed by a series of tabbed appendixes that provide documentation for the claims made in the narrative. Information in both the narrative and the appendixes should be carefully selected.

Though disciplines and institutional requirements differ, professors often allocate pages to specific topics roughly as follows:

$\frac{1}{2}$ page	Table of Contents
$\frac{1}{2}$ to 1 page	Preface
5 to 6 pages	Teaching
5 to 6 pages	Research/Scholarship
2 to 3 pages	Service
1 to 2 pages	Integration of Work/Goals
TOTAL: 14 to 19 pages	

Some institutions put a ceiling on the number of pages or the number of pounds they permit in order to prevent data overkill in the portfolio. Others distribute a three-ring binder of perhaps two inches and insist that they will read only information housed in that binder if it is submitted for tenure or promotion decisions.

Portfolio Preparation Time

The answer to the question of how long it takes to prepare a portfolio is that it depends. Professors who prepare an annual report will probably already have a good deal of the material on hand. For example, they probably have a list of their teaching responsibilities, copies of syllabi, student rating data, samples of books and publications, letters regarding grant proposals, conference proceedings, and letters appointing them to committees. When they have that information on hand, preparation of the portfolio will probably take between fifteen and twenty hours spread over a number of days.

But if the professor does not currently do an annual report, the needed documents and materials are likely to be scattered and less organized. In that case, it will probably take between twenty and twenty-five hours, spread over a number of days, to put together the portfolio.

Whether the professor has on hand an annual report or not, some preparation time is spent in gathering, planning, and sifting the documentation. And even more time is spent in self-reflection.

| **Preparing the Portfolio**

Keys to the success of the academic portfolio are four crucial cornerstones: the value of self-reflection, the importance of collaboration, the need to discuss expectations, and gaining acceptance of the concept.

The Value of Self-Reflection

One of the most significant parts of the portfolio is the faculty member's self-reflection on his or her teaching, research and scholarship, and service. In truth, it is at the heart of academic portfolio development. It is individual strategic planning, articulation of philosophy and methodology of work, a road map to past achievements and future goals, and a bank of supporting documentation.

Preparation of the academic portfolio stimulates faculty to ponder an array of profound, value-laden *why* questions: *why* we teach as we do, *why* our syllabi are constructed in a certain way, *why* our student ratings are either affirming or disheartening, *why* teaching is more or less fulfilling than research or scholarship, *why* we focus our research and scholarship in a particular field, *why* we prioritize our time as we do, *why* we agree to serve on certain committees and turn down others.

It is in the very process of creating the portfolio that the professor is stimulated to (1) reconsider activities in teaching, research and scholarship, and service; (2) rethink strategies; (3) rearrange priorities; and (4) plan for the future. For many professors, the *process* of portfolio development is as important as—if not more important than—the final product: the portfolio itself.

Academic portfolios possess a special power to involve faculty in reflecting on their own professional practices and how to improve them. The level of personal investment in time, energy, and commitment is high, and those are necessary conditions for professional growth and development.

Consider these typical comments from professors on the benefits of reflection:

From a history professor in Connecticut: "Reflection is the heart of the portfolio process, an opportunity to think critically about one's responsibilities, philosophy, methods, goals. It invites self-analysis and understanding of one's areas for improvement. And it keeps us focused on professional identity, vision, and well-being."

From an educational psychology professor in Nebraska: "The most beneficial part of developing a portfolio is structured reflection. The process lends itself to deep, focused thought and self-analysis."

From an accounting professor in New Mexico: "The reflective component of the portfolio is critical since there are pieces that go into it that go well beyond my cv. It's the why I do what I do."

From a microbiology professor in Virginia: "Reflection is at the heart of my portfolio. I was forced to think hard about: What are my strengths? Where do I want to concentrate my post-tenure career? What will make me content professionally and personally?"

From a chemistry professor in Massachusetts: "The reflection process was critical to the creation of my portfolio. It provided a crucial lens through which I analyzed my academic career."

From a social work professor: "The reflection process was an opportunity to consider all of my activities and weigh which I enjoy and/or are helpful for my career, and which just take a lot of time. Since writing the portfolio, I am taking active steps to redefine my working self and reduce the time I spend in activities that turn out not to matter that much. This process of reprioritizing has made my personal life much better too, because—like most professional women who are also mothers—I am balancing many nonprofessional activities as well."

The Importance of Collaboration

Portfolios *can* be prepared by the professor working alone. But this isolated approach has limited prospects for improving performance or contributing to personnel decisions. Why? Because portfolios prepared by the faculty member working alone do not include the collegial or supervisory support needed in a program of improvement. And, importantly, there is none of the control or corroboration of evidence that is essential to sustain personnel decisions. Collaboration ensures a fresh, critical perspective that encourages cohesion between the portfolio narrative and supporting appendix material.

From mounting experience, we know that portfolio development should involve interaction and mentoring in the same way that a doctoral dissertation reflects both the efforts of the candidate and the advice of the mentor (Miller, 2005).

Who might serve as a mentor? A department chair, a colleague, or a faculty development specialist could fill the role. The mentor discusses with the faculty member guiding questions: Which areas of teaching, research and scholarship, and service are to be examined? What kinds of information do they expect to collect? How will the information be analyzed and presented? What is the significance of their accomplishments? Why are they preparing the portfolio? (This is especially important because the purpose drives the content. So does the audience who will read it.)

Consider these comments from professors whose portfolios were prepared under the direction of a trained, experienced mentor:

> *A medical school professor in Georgia:* "Mentoring is one of the linchpins that make the portfolio a powerful tool for honest, rigorous, shared assessment of professional performance. I can envision producing a good portfolio in isolation, but the coaching and challenging perspective of a mentor who helps generate new avenues for improvement and supportive approaches to accountability are critical in achieving the full potential of portfolio work."

> *A physics professor in Arizona:* "It was invaluable to work with a mentor, to have other eyes evaluate my drafts, especially eyes from outside the department to ensure that my portfolio was understandable to those outside my discipline."

A management professor in Oregon: "The mentor was incredibly helpful. She forced me to get beyond retelling 'war stories' into a higher-level analysis of what I had gained from the various battles. I don't think I could have been as introspective without the support and encouragement of my mentor."

An architecture professor in New York: "The mentor helped me organize my thoughts and got me to be less shy about documenting my accomplishments. He gave me constructive advice on the structure of the document and provided valuable insight into how I came across to an audience outside of my discipline. He was very encouraging at every step of the process."

A geology professor in Pennsylvania: "The mentoring process was essential as she asked me 'why' questions that forced me to think about the underlying reasons driving my teaching and research."

A philosophy professor in Colorado: "The mentoring process was absolutely crucial in the creation of my portfolio. The guidance and encouragement of my mentor were invaluable. Asking questions of someone with so much experience in the process and explaining what I do to someone outside my field forced me to see things in a different way."

A religion professor in Maryland: "Thanks to the mentoring process, I am now more aware of the need for guidance of younger professors. I have already informed my younger colleagues to keep track of their significant accomplishments and activities as they evolve, as well as to organize and archive their career information."

To be effective, the mentor must have wide knowledge of procedures and current instruments to document effective faculty performance. But having such content knowledge alone is no guarantee of effective mentoring. The mentor must also have the interpersonal skills and attitudes necessary to develop the relationship needed for mentoring.

A caution: to be effective, the mentor must remember that the portfolio is owned by the faculty member who prepares it. Decisions about what goes into it are generally cooperative ones between the mentor and the professor. But the final decision about what to include, its ultimate use, and the retention of the final product all rest with the faculty member. No matter how tempting it might be, the mentor must refrain from imposing his or her purpose, form, style, and assumptions. The mentor role is that of guide, not director.

Self-Mentoring

Sometimes there are no willing and able mentors available. In that case, even though the important collaborative aspects of portfolio development will be lost, it is still possible to prepare a portfolio. The guiding questions as prompts in this chapter should help. So should the self-assessment questions that follow:

- What is your purpose in creating the portfolio?
- Who are your primary readers?
- What evidence will they expect to see?
- What types of evidence will be most convincing to those readers?
- What weight will review committee members give to teaching? To research and scholarship? To service? What criteria will be used?
- Will reviewers expect to see actual copies of publications?
- Will they expect to see testimonial letters from internal or external reviewers?
- Which are the "valued" publications in my discipline? The "valued" professional conferences?

Discussing Expectations

Whether the academic portfolio is prepared by a faculty member working with a mentor or working alone, it will have genuine value only when personnel decision makers and faculty members learn to trust the approach. Important to the development of trust is the periodic exchange of views between the department chair and professor about teaching, research and scholarship, and service responsibilities, ancillary duties, and specific items for the portfolio.

The discussion between the department chair and professor should address expectations and specifics of what and how faculty performance is to be reported. Otherwise there is a danger that the chair may erroneously conclude that the data submitted overlook areas of prime concern and may even cover up areas of suspected weaknesses. Such possible misunderstanding is largely eliminated by open discussion, especially when accompanied by an exchange of clarifying memos. When used in this way, the portfolio attains the status of an important, trusted instrument.

Since there is no guarantee that the current department chair will be in that position when the faculty member is being considered for tenure or promotion, it is a good idea to also talk with recently tenured faculty and to respected, older, straight-shooting professors who can give solid, realistic advice. Such conversations are likely to yield insights into what happens in actual practice so they can be measured against the official version of what happens.

The topics of conversation with the chair and with others are the same:

- What does the institution expect of faculty in terms of teaching, research and scholarship, and service?
- What is the relative importance of each of the three professional activities and their weight and influence in the distribution of rewards?
- What evidence of successful performance—both quantity and quality—is considered appropriate for each activity?
- How much evidence is enough?
- What are appropriate and effective ways to report the evidence?

Caution: If answers to these questions are not obtained in advance, the process of constructing an academic portfolio can be hollow and disappointing. In truth, institutional expectations are of great importance even in the case of a portfolio created for improvement and personal growth instead of personnel decision. The balance of teaching, research and scholarship, and service at a given institution must still be considered.

It is not enough for faculty to perform well. In a resource-limited academic environment, faculty must perform well on the "right" things, including the "right" things from the perspective of the department and institution.

Ideally, the institution and the department must enunciate their goals, objectives and values. This sets the stage for faculty performance expectations. Otherwise faculty risk performing successfully on low-priority criteria. For example, a department or institution that values top rankings for research is more likely to define faculty research excellence as publishing in top-tier refereed journals and receiving large external funding grants. Another department or institution with less research focus might define faculty research excellence as simply publishing in refereed journals, with less concern for external funding. A different department or institution with even less research focus might define it as any publishing in any journal with no concern for external funding (Curry, 2006).

Gaining Acceptance of the Concept

Even on campuses of higher education there is an indecent amount of xenophobia toward strangers bearing new ideas. The academic portfolio is no exception; some faculty have taken to the barricades to resist the incursion of the portfolio. Their antagonism grows out of uncertainty and a tinge of fear that somehow they are threatened. Other faculty say they are not comfortable as self-promoters, don't need to raise "defensive" documentation, and have neither the time nor the desire to keep a record of their teaching, research and scholarship, and service achievements.

But these concerns can be disposed of by pointing out that in this age of accountability, professors (1) must produce better evidence of contributions, (2) need positive documentation to support accomplishments, (3) must convey those accomplishments clearly and persuasively to third-party inspection outside their immediate discipline, (4) need to be selective about what they provide readers who have limited time and energy to review their documentation and evidence, and (5) must provide meaningful reflective evidence that provides direction and rationale for past accomplishments and future growth and development.

If the academic portfolio approach is ultimately to be embraced, an institutional climate of acceptance must first be created. How can that be done? The following guidelines should be helpful in this regard:

- The portfolio approach must be presented in a candid, complete, and clear way to every faculty member and academic administrator.
- Professors must feel, with justification, that they "own" the program. That will occur only when they have a significant hand in both the development and the operation of the portfolio program.
- If portfolios are used for tenure or promotion decisions, every professor must know the criteria and standards by which portfolios will be evaluated. Those who evaluate portfolios must also know the criteria and standards and must abide by them.
- The institution's most prominent teachers and researchers should be involved from the outset because their participation attracts other faculty to the program. It also signals the value of portfolios and the willingness of faculty leaders to go public with their teaching, research and scholarship, and service performance data.
- The portfolio approach should not be forced on anyone. It is better to use faculty volunteers, who take part willingly in the portfolio development process.
- Sufficient time—a year, even two years—should be allowed for acceptance and implementation. Use the time to modify procedures, standards, criteria, and techniques. But keep moving forward. Don't allow the portfolio concept to stall in a futile search for perfection.
- It is wise to allow individual differences in developing portfolios. Disciplines differ, and so do teaching styles, research interests, and career points.
- Top-level administrators must give their active support to the portfolio concept. They must be publicly committed to the program and provide whatever resources are necessary to ensure that it operates effectively.

- Encourage collaboration. A mentor from the same discipline can provide special insights and understandings as well as departmental practices in dealing with portfolios. Also, a mentor from a different discipline can often help clarify the institution's viewpoint—the big picture. That can be significant since portfolios submitted for personnel decisions will be read by some faculty and administrators from other disciplines.
- Remind every professor that the portfolio should include selected information. It is not an exhaustive compilation of all of the documents and materials that bear on teaching, research and scholarship, and service. Instead, it presents selected information on professional accomplishments and activities.

The academic portfolio concept has now gone well beyond the point of theoretical possibility. More and more institutions—public and private, large and small—are emphasizing, nurturing, and rewarding excellent faculty performance based on portfolios.

Chapter Four

Suggestions for Improving the Portfolio

Whether a portfolio is used for improvement or personnel decisions, the following list of suggestions should be helpful to faculty members in preparing their portfolios. Some of these elements are minor and may even go unnoticed. But in mentoring scores of faculty in different colleges and universities as they developed their academic portfolios, we have found that these items are frequently overlooked.

House the Portfolio in a Binder with Tabs for Appendixes

A $2\frac{1}{2}$-inch, three-ring binder with sleeves on the front and spine is a useful and inexpensive way to secure material and make it easy to add or delete items. The tabs serve to organize and neatly separate the appendix items. Experience suggests it is best to (1) label all loose items, (2) three-hole-punch everything, (3) not use sleeves for materials inside the portfolio (they slip out easily), and (4) use tabbed dividers with computer-generated stick-on labels.

Include the Date of the Portfolio

Putting the date on the portfolio enables the professor to establish a baseline from which to measure development in performance. That growth can be gauged by the degree to which the portfolio demonstrates improvement in teaching, research and scholarship, or service performance.

Include a Detailed Table of Contents

A table of contents enables portfolio readers to see the breadth and flow of responsibilities, philosophy, objectives, strategies, and priorities in an academic life. Built on reflection and evidence, it serves as a road map to the portfolio narrative and appendix.

Add a List of Appendix Items

Positioned either on the table of contents page or on the first page of the appendix itself, the list makes it easier for readers to find specific evidence for claims made by the professor in the narrative.

Include Specific Information, Not Generalities

Avoid generalities, and be specific. Include dates, names, programs, titles of courses taught, and citation references to articles and books. Instead of saying, "My student ratings are generally high," it is better to say, "Ninety-seven percent of the 120 students in my Introduction to Economics course (Fall 2008) stated that they would recommend that their friends take my class."

Explain the Evidence in the Portfolio

Unexplained evidence is difficult for readers to understand and interpret. For example, a journal article provides evidence of research and scholarship. But the significance of the article to the department and institution may not be readily apparent, especially to readers from outside the discipline. That is why the addition of a commentary explaining why the journal is significant (top-tier journal that accepts just 10 percent of submitted manuscripts, for example) as well as reaction of readers (e-mail comments included in appendixes) provides more convincing evidence of the professor's accomplishments.

Enhance the Narrative Section

Reading eighteen pages of straight text can be tedious. Bolster reader interest by the judicious use of boldface type, italics, bullet points, charts, and graphs. Avoid long paragraphs.

Cross-Reference the Narrative to the Appendix

Every item in the appendix should be cross-referenced in the narrative text. For example, at the end of a discussion of one's syllabi, reference would be made to evidence in the appendix: "See Appendix A for copies of syllabi." Another example, at the end of a discussion on one's most important research presentation, reference would be made to evidence in the appendix: "See Appendix B for copies of the conference program."

Limit the Number of Student or Colleague Comments

Some professors assume that the greater number of favorable student or colleague comments they include, the better. But that is a mistaken assumption. Generally just two or three comments each from students and from colleagues are sufficient. Those comments should be specific and tied to the professor's methodology. An example from a student: "The case method used by Professor Jones was especially effective in engaging us in the material." An example from a colleague who observed a class: "Professor Smith's use of the case method was effective, engaging, and appropriate for the Introduction to Clinical Psychology class."

Number the Pages in the Portfolio

Though this may seem self-evident, our experience as mentors of scores of faculty as they prepared their portfolios proved otherwise. Numbering pages in an academic portfolio is just as important as it is in a student term paper.

Make Bulky Portfolio Items Available upon Request

Some items do not lend themselves to being placed in an appendix because they are unwieldy or too large and can be easily lost. Examples are musical scores, sculptures, large photographs, oversized manuscripts, and videotapes. For that reason, if the appendixes contain items that do not fit within the portfolio covers, the faculty member may briefly discuss these materials in the narrative and make them available for inspection on request.

Revise the Portfolio Each Year

Thinking of the revision as a complete reshaping of all the fundamental components of the portfolio is both intimidating and unnecessary. Certain things are not likely to change. One's teaching philosophy and methodology, for example, rarely undergo dramatic changes. But there will be new student rating data, perhaps new courses taught, new research areas and publications, new funding proposals, new conference presentations, and new committee assignments.

Recommended is an annual updating, perhaps at the end of each academic year. The process should take no more than one day. If the professor maintains a file and stores new evidence on professional opportunities, assignments, and achievements, all of the information needed for the portfolio update will be in one location, and the revision will be an uncomplicated or time-consuming task. One reminder: when new material is added, older, less relevant items are deleted. The portfolio size remains constant.

Chapter Five

Evaluating the Portfolio for Personnel Decisions

Deciding what to evaluate is one of the most difficult problems in personnel decisions. Small wonder that evaluating a professor's performance can be perplexing, when one considers how quickly a football fan concludes that a team's quarterback is a poor player because several of his passes have been intercepted.

An objective appraisal of the quarterback would raise the following questions: Were the passes really bad, or did the receivers run the wrong patterns? Did the offensive line give the quarterback adequate protection? Was the quarterback recovering from an injury? How good is the vision of the fan? Was he talking to a friend during the game? How many beers did the fan drink during the game?

In comparison with a barroom judgment of a quarterback's performance, the evaluation of a professor's performance is far more complex and consequential. Experience suggests that most professors prepare their portfolios for purposes of personnel decisions, such as tenure, promotion, retention, and hiring. For that reason, this chapter addresses the question of "what personnel committees should look for when they evaluate teaching, research and scholarship, and service performance from an academic portfolio."

In truth, the evaluation of academic performance from portfolios or any other instruments is unavoidably an exercise in subjective judgment. Of course, tenure, promotion, retention, and hiring decisions should be based on objective data. This does not suggest that the judgments cannot be systematized and sanitized. On the contrary, if the evaluation process meets key requirements, the likelihood of making more accurate personnel decisions is greatly enhanced.

Key Requirements

Certain key requirements are especially relevant to the evaluation of faculty performance through academic portfolios.

Acceptability

This requirement is critically important. Unless the portfolio program has won unqualified support of both the evaluators and those being evaluated, it will be on shaky ground. Support is built by focusing attention not just on the technical soundness of the portfolio but also on its attitudinal and interpersonal aspects. Frank and open discussions are vital to building acceptability of the program. There is no substitute for the active support of faculty in the efficient operation of a portfolio assessment system.

Practicality

It is essential that portfolios be easily understood and easily put to use by personnel committees. Reading and evaluating them should not take an inordinate amount of time or energy. One way to ensure this is to put a page limit on the length of the narrative in the portfolio. Whatever the limit—twenty pages, perhaps—the figure should be clearly known by professors and committee members and adhered to.

To put teeth in that page limit, committee members at some institutions are instructed to read and review only the narrative material that fits within the page limit. Information on additional pages is not read or considered. In the same way, some institutions put limits on the size of the appendix by distributing a standardized three-ring binder and informing faculty that any information submitted by professors in additional binders will not be considered.

Relevance

There must be clear links between the goals of the department or institution and the performance standards and criteria used to evaluate performance through portfolios. Put another way, relevance can be determined by answering the following question, "What really makes a difference between excellence and mediocrity, between success and failure, in teaching, research and scholarship, and service?" For example, a college that has a goal of being a stellar teaching institution should not expect faculty members to produce a scholarly book every year or two. Or a university that has a goal of being a premier research center should not expect faculty to teach four different courses each semester.

Overcome Obstacles

Although the potential obstacles to effective evaluation of faculty performance through portfolios are considerable, several are significant enough to warrant special mention:

- Standards and ratings are mercurial and tend to fluctuate widely, and often unfairly. Some evaluators are tough, others lenient. Thus, the less competent in one department can potentially be awarded a higher rating than the more competent in another department. This is true whether their performance is evaluated through portfolios or other means.
- Derogatory publicity about the portfolio and misinterpreting the popularity of professors with their colleagues and their students for real worth can undermine the evaluation of faculty performance through portfolios.
- Excessive emphasis is sometimes placed on numbers: number of journal articles, number of conference presentations, number of committees, number of students who rate the professor as "excellent." A portfolio evaluator who has a numbers fetish venerates numbers, which actually are the equivalent of subjective judgments, as though they were hard, objective facts.

- In truth, portfolios do not lend themselves to a simple count of publications on a curriculum vitae. Their primary virtue is that they reflect the complexity, individuality, and interrelatedness of all teaching, research and scholarship, and service activities.

This is a daunting list of potential obstacles and can give pause to any college or university contemplating the introduction of portfolios. Yet it is no solution to decide *not* to institute such a program. Off-the-cuff evaluations of faculty performance will always be made by some. It is better to use a portfolio program that assists evaluations to approach uniformity, fairness, and accuracy.

The point bears repeating: the portfolio is built on meaningful faculty reflection—the "why," not just the "how" and the "what." It includes vital information on the significance of faculty work and the context in which it was done. These factors are the crucial lens through which numbers must be viewed.

Establish Criteria

To encourage the adoption of academic portfolios, faculty must have an opportunity to generate ideas on how best to represent certain types of work such as research and scholarship. Lynton (1993) has suggested criteria for reviewing faculty work represented within portfolios:

- The work is reasoned and reflective.
- It demonstrates expertise in making choices in a given context.
- It reflects responsiveness to unanticipated developments and creativity in developing a scholarly approach.
- The work results in new knowledge from a scholarly situation and demonstrates its validity and significance.
- It involves communication of new knowledge or fresh variations of the content.

For colleges and universities, these criteria and the list that follows can be a useful starting point for judgments of portfolio quality in peer review deliberations.

Checklist of Items for Evaluating Portfolios

This list of suggested items for evaluating portfolios was developed from detailed discussions with more than 150 members of personnel committees at colleges and universities of varying sizes, shapes, and missions:

1. All claims made in the portfolio must be supported by evidence in the appendixes.
2. Evaluators must focus attention on the evidence supporting teaching, research and scholarship, and service effectiveness and ignore an elegant cover or attractive font.
3. Evidence of accomplishments—not just a reflective statement—must be present in the portfolio.
4. The degree of documentation in each of the three areas of teaching, research and scholarship, and service must be consistent with the expectations and requirements of the department and institution.
5. Evidence must be presented to show that academic institutional goals, for example, development of student critical thinking skills, are met.
6. The vast majority of data in the portfolio must be current or from the recent past, perhaps the past three years.
7. Evidence must be presented to show the significance of faculty work and the context in which it was done.
8. The portfolio must meet established length requirements for the narrative and for the appendix.
9. It must reflect consistency between the professor's reflective statements and his or her actions in teaching, research and scholarship, and service.
10. Efforts of improved performance over time must be reflected in evaluation reports.
11. The portfolio must demonstrate that professional activities and resulting levels of performance are consistent with departmental and institutional strategic priorities and missions.
12. Some evidence of peer evaluation of teaching, research and scholarship, and service must be presented unless this would be inconsistent with the institution's culture.

13. The sections on teaching, research and scholarship, and service responsibilities must be consistent with the department chair's statement of the professor's responsibilities.

14. The portfolio must contain information from the professor and others who can offer a diverse and objective evaluation of his or her academic performance—for example, students, peers within the discipline, peers in other disciplines, administrators, and alumni.

15. The portfolio must profile individual style, priorities, and achievements within the academic discipline.

16. The reflective statement of what and why professors teach as they do must be consistent with the syllabus and with student and peer evaluations of their teaching.

17. The ratings on all common core questions on student rating forms (the ones that personnel committee review most closely) from several courses and several years must be included in the portfolio.

18. Review committees must not assume that every faculty member must teach, engage in research and scholarship, and serve on committees in the same way. It is better to allow individual differences in styles, techniques, preferences, and priorities as long as they can be tolerated by the department and institution. In general, it is best to develop criteria within the smallest possible unit. At times, it will be the entire institution. More often, it will be a department or group of departments with dominant similarities.

19. Review committees must avoid relying too heavily on any one source of evidence. No personnel decision—for promotion, tenure, retention, hiring, or even merit pay—should be made on the basis of a single rating or other source of evidence. Such decisions should rest on a holistic examination of the professor's portfolio. The focus should be not on a single stone but rather on the mosaic formed by all of the stones.

Chapter Six

Answers to Common Questions

In recent years, we have discussed the academic portfolio concept at dozens of colleges and universities of differing sizes, shapes, and missions. We have talked with countless faculty groups and administrators about the portfolio and its place in the evaluation of academic performance. And we have served as mentors to numerous professors across disciplines as they prepared their portfolios.

In the course of this activity, certain questions were raised by professors or administrators with much greater frequency than others. This chapter is devoted to answering those questions.

Is the Academic Portfolio Concept in Use Today?

In truth, it has gone well beyond the point of theoretical possibility. More and more institutions—public and private, large and small—are nurturing and rewarding academic performance through portfolios. Some colleges and universities use them to improve performance. Others use them in tenure and promotion decisions. Still others use portfolios for both improving performance and personnel decisions.

Can an Impressive Portfolio Gloss Over Terrible Teaching, Research and Scholarship, or Service Performance?

That is a contradiction in terms because the weak performer cannot document effective performance. The evidence is just not there. An elegant cover, fancy graph, and attractive typeface cannot disguise weak performance. The portfolio is an evidence-based document. Every claim made must be supported by hard evidence. For example, a professor who claims that student evaluations rate his overall teaching performance as "outstanding" must provide numerical rating data that bear out this claim. A professor who claims to have published an article in a top-tier journal must provide a copy of that published article.

How Much Time Does It Take to Prepare a Portfolio?

Most faculty members construct the portfolio in fifteen to twenty hours spread over several days. Most of that time is spent thinking, planning, and gathering the documentation for the appendixes. Updating the material is made easy and can be accomplished in a single day if the professor maintains a file of everything relating to teaching, research and scholarship, and service so that all of the evidence needed for a portfolio update is in one location. A gentle caution: When new material is added to the portfolio, older, less relevant material is removed. The size of the portfolio remains about the same.

How Long Is the Typical Academic Portfolio?

The typical portfolio is fourteen to nineteen pages, followed by a series of appendixes that document the claims made in the narrative. Often a three-ring binder holds the portfolio, and tabs identify the different appendixes. Just as information in the narrative should be selective, so should the appendixes consist of judiciously chosen evidence. If the appendixes contain nonprint materials or items that do not fit within the portfolio cover—such as books, videotapes, or CDs—the professor may briefly discuss these materials and make them available for inspection on request.

How Does the Academic Portfolio Differ from the Usual Faculty Report to Administrators at the End of Each Academic Year?

First, the portfolio empowers faculty to include the documents and materials that, in their judgment, best reflect their performance in teaching, research and scholarship, and service. It is not limited to items posed by administrators. Second, the portfolio is based on collaboration and mentoring rather than being prepared by faculty in isolation. Third, in preparing the portfolio, professors engage in structured reflection about why they do what they do as academic professionals, and for many faculty—almost as a product—it produces an improvement in performance. Fourth, professors describe the nature and significance of their work in clear, simple language, and that is of enormous help to members of tenure and promotion committees, especially those not in the professor's discipline.

Why Do Portfolio Models and Mentors Need to Be Available to Professors as They Prepare Their Own Portfolios?

The models enable them to see how others—in a variety of disciplines—have combined documents and materials into a cohesive whole. Some institutions have found it helpful to make available locally developed portfolio models of exemplary, satisfactory, and unsatisfactory quality. At the same time, since most faculty come to the academic portfolio with no previous experience with the concept, the resources of a mentor with wide knowledge of the ways to document teaching, research and scholarship, and service should be made available to them.

Can a Portfolio Be Prepared by a Professor Working Alone?

An isolated approach to portfolio preparation has limited potential to contribute to tenure and promotion decisions or to improve performance. Why? Because portfolio entries prepared by a professor working alone provide none of the controls or collaboration of evidence that may be needed to sustain personnel decisions. It also enlists none of the collegial or supervisory support needed in a program of performance improvement. In practice, the portfolio is best prepared in collaboration with another person, who serves as portfolio mentor. A department chair, a colleague, or a faculty development specialist can talk to the professor about such guiding questions as why she is preparing the portfolio, what sources of evidence she will include, why she needs balance among the portfolio sections, and what the portfolio must include in order to be in line with current department and institution mission and goals. In short, the portfolio mentor helps the professor separate the wheat from the chaff.

Must the Mentor Be from the Same Discipline as the Professor Who Is Preparing the Portfolio?

The process of collaboration is not discipline specific. True, a mentor from the same discipline can provide special insights and understandings as well as departmental expectations and practices. But a mentor from a different discipline can often help clarify the institution's viewpoint, the "big picture." That can be a significant help since portfolios submitted for personnel decisions are read by faculty and administrators from other disciplines.

Because the Role of the Mentor Is So Crucial, How Are Mentors Recruited?

Once faculty have been taught about the portfolio and coached by trained mentors from outside the institution, a core group of faculty emerges as experienced leaders who can help others in developing their portfolios. A faculty development administrator may facilitate the process by educating both faculty and administrators about academic portfolios, sponsoring in-house workshops, helping faculty members connect with mentors, and setting up a library of reading materials, forms, and sample portfolios. The cost is nominal, and the payoff is better performance in teaching, research and scholarship, and service.

Who Owns the Portfolio?

Without question, the portfolio is owned by the professor who prepared it. Decisions about what goes into the portfolio are generally cooperative ones between the mentor and the professor. But the last word, the final decision on what to include, its ultimate use, and retention of the final document all rest with the professor.

Should Administrators Develop the Portfolio Program and Then Tell Faculty to Prepare Portfolios?

Absolutely not. Imposing a portfolio program on faculty is almost certain to lead to strenuous faculty resistance. Far better is to involve faculty in both developing and running the program. It makes no difference if portfolios are used for tenure and promotion decisions or for improving performance; either way, the program must be faculty driven.

The Portfolio Concept Is Undoubtedly Useful for Junior Faculty, But Why Would Senior Faculty Want to Write One?

All academics stand to benefit from writing a portfolio. At institutions where post-tenure review is required, the portfolio can play a major role in describing and documenting a professor's ongoing commitment to academic excellence and professional integrity. Portfolios can also be instrumental in determining salary increases, merit pay, awards, grants, fellowships, and release time.

Moreover, because improvement in performance is a primary motive for engaging in the reflection and documentation that comprise a portfolio, senior faculty can prepare portfolios to sharpen their teaching, research and scholarship, and service skills or set the stage for experimentation and innovation.

Are the Time and Energy Required to Prepare a Portfolio Really Worth the Benefits?

In the view of the writers, and in the views of virtually every one of the scores of faculty members we have personally mentored as they prepared their portfolios, the answer is a resounding yes. It usually takes no more than a few days to prepare, and the benefits are considerable. The portfolio allows professors to describe their strengths and accomplishments for the record, a clear advantage when evaluation committees examine the record in making promotion and tenure decisions. But the portfolio does more than that. Many professors report that the very process of reflection and collecting and sorting documents and materials that reflect their performance serves as a springboard for self-improvement and a reexamination of priorities.

What Guidelines Would You Suggest for Getting Started with Portfolios?

Perhaps the best way to get started is for a group of faculty to develop general standards of good teaching, research and scholarship, and service. Guiding the group should be the emphasis on the institution's strategic plan, and the need to develop an institutionwide evaluation system with common elements and procedures, yet have enough flexibility to accommodate diverse approaches to teaching, research and scholarship, and service. The following guidelines should be helpful in doing so:

- Start small.
- Involve the institution's (or department's) most respected faculty members from the start.
- Rely on faculty volunteers, and don't force anyone to participate.
- Obtain top-level administrative support for the portfolio concept and an institutional commitment to provide the necessary resources to launch the program successfully.
- Field-test the portfolio process.
- Keep everyone—faculty and administrators—fully informed about what is going on every step of the way.
- Permit room for individual differences in portfolios. Styles of teaching, research and scholarship, and service differ. So do disciplines.

It is important to allow a year, even two years, for the process of acceptance and implementation. During this period, draft documents should be carefully prepared, freely discussed, and modified as needed. And keep in mind that all details of the program need not be in place before implementation. Start the program incrementally, and be flexible to modification as it develops. Remember that the quest for perfection is endless. Don't stall the program in an endless search for the perfect approach. The goal is improvement, not perfection.

President John F. Kennedy was fond of telling a story about the French marshal Louis Lyautey. When the marshal announced that he wished to plant a tree, his gardener responded that the tree would not reach full growth for a hundred years. "In that case," replied Lyautey, "we have no time to lose. We must start to plant this afternoon." Colleges and universities thinking of using academic portfolios for improvement in performance or personnel decisions have no time to lose. They must get started now.

Chapter Seven

Sample Portfolios from Across Disciplines

This section comprises eighteen sample academic portfolios from across disciplines and institutions. They have been prepared by faculty at Columbia College (South Carolina); Concordia University (Canada); Drexel University (Pennsylvania); Texas Christian University (Texas); Loyola College in Maryland; Parsons The New School for Design (New York); The New School for Jazz and Contemporary Music (New York); the University of Alabama at Birmingham; University of Georgia (Athens); and the University of Massachusetts Amherst.

There is a noticeable difference among the portfolios, reflecting a diversity of purpose, research disciplines, teaching methodologies, length of service, career trajectories, philosophies, personal preference, and university contexts. Because each portfolio is an individualized document, varying importance has been assigned by different faculty to different items. Some faculty discuss an item at length; others dismiss it with a sentence or two, or even omit it. These models reflect both the individuality and the richness that the academic portfolio can capture.

The appendix material referred to, although part of the actual portfolios, is not included because of its cumbersome nature.

Important note: Readers are urged to remember that there are differences among the disciplines in terms of both faculty practice and methodology. And there are differences in the weight that institutions give to teaching, research, and service. Specific settings do vary. Yet virtually all of the faculty whose portfolios appear here, regardless of discipline or institution, are held accountable as professionals for demonstrating achievement and growth in teaching, research, and service, the universal trio of domains in faculty evaluation systems. For that reason, readers are urged to bear in mind that sample portfolios from other disciplines and institutions often provide helpful information and insights applicable to your own position.

The portfolios are arranged alphabetically by discipline:

Biomedical engineering: Timothy M. Wick

Bioscience and biotechnology: Shivanthi Anandan

Child and family studies: Lynda Henley Walters

Education: Robert M. Maninger; Clement A. Seldin

English: John Zubizarreta

Environmental engineering: Charles N. Haas

Foreign languages and literature: Sheri Spaine Long

Geology and environmental science: Ranjan S. Muttiah

Jazz and contemporary music: Reginald Workman

Mathematical sciences: Lisa A. Oberbroeckling

Nutritional sciences: Gina Jarman Hill

Pastoral counseling: Kelly Murray

Pediatric emergency medicine: Annalise Sorrentino

Political science: Carrie Liu Currier; Marlene K. Sokolon

Product design: Robert Kirkbride

Psychology: Pamela A. Geller

Biomedical Engineering

Timothy M. Wick

Department of Biomedical Engineering
The University of Alabama at Birmingham
Fall 2008

Table of Contents

Sample Professional Accomplishments
    Chair and Organizer of the Phillips Petroleum/C. J. "Pete"
        Silas Program in Leadership and Ethics
    Career Development of BME Faculty
    Faculty Recruiting
    Department Staffing
    Successful Interactions with the BME External
        Advisory Board
Appendixes

Introduction to the Portfolio

Purpose

The purpose of this portfolio is to document my responsibilities, organize my priorities, and develop methods for effective leadership as I grow into the position of Chair of the Department of Biomedical Engineering (BME) at the University of Alabama at Birmingham. In addition to department chair, I am considered a regular faculty member and expected to lead an externally funded research program as well as contribute to the academic mission of the department. Thus, I must balance teaching, research, and administrative responsibilities. My goal as Chair is to grow the reputation of the department within UAB and relative to similar programs at peer institutions while maintaining an active and successful research program. I am also committed to teaching undergraduate and graduate students. I will use this portfolio to develop goals, document accomplishments, and develop assessment and reflective methodologies to improve my performance as a teacher, research director and administrator.

Teaching

Teaching Philosophy, Objectives, and Methodologies

Engineering is by nature interdisciplinary—engineers seek to apply fundamental knowledge from science disciplines such as chemistry, biology, mathematics, and physics to create new technology for the benefit of society. Engineering education is fundamentally teaching students to solve problems that address the technical needs of society. My objective is to teach students how to use fundamental knowledge along with an intuitive understanding of the physical world to solve engineering problems. For undergraduate courses, I teach problem-solving strategies in addition to fundamental concepts. In graduate courses, the course structure facilitates deeper understanding of advanced concepts and improvement of problem solving skills. I bring enthusiasm to the classroom and try to engage students, not only on the course material, but also on the social and ethical ramifications of engineering accomplishments.

My teaching style uses lectures, small group discussions, and in-class problem sets to demonstrate how to apply new knowledge to solve engineering problems. I am most interested in developing critical thinking skills so that each student can solve many different problems of a given class (transport phenomena, dynamics, biomechanics, reaction engineering, etc.). Analytical skills are learned and honed by making students solve problems—in class and outside of class in homework sets. I make time for students to solve problems in class in groups. These interactions with me and classmates are important for students to learn how to apply knowledge.

Course Responsibilities at UAB

BME 350 Biological Transport Phenomena

This course uses fundamental principles of momentum, mass, and energy transport to establish equations that describe biological transport and reaction processes in living systems. This is a lecture-based course with a number of homework and small group projects. It is a new required course in the Biomedical Engineering curriculum. I developed this course because I believe that students who master the material will have important tools in their repertoire to address relevant biological transport problems. I am comfortable teaching the concepts—I really enjoy the material. Typically, this course will have 15–20 students, almost exclusively BME majors. I have included the course objectives, administrative information and syllabus in Appendix A.

BME 3XX Biomedical Engineering Ethics

In addition to teaching students the fundamentals of Biomedical Engineering, I provide opportunities for students to engage in professional development. The purpose of this course is to provide each student with tools and relevant experiences in a learning environment so that if a complex moral dilemma arises during the course of professional practice, the student has resources to navigate the situation in a way that accounts for competing obligations and maintains his or her professional integrity. I envision this to be a BME elective course with enrollment of approximately 15 students per year. I have included the course objectives, administrative information, and syllabus in Appendix A.

Undergraduate Student Mentorship

I am an academic and professional advisor to approximately 15 percent of the BME undergraduates. I meet with each advisee at least twice per year to learn of each student's academic progress, plans for the next term, and professional aspirations. I try to dispense with the nuts-and-bolts of scheduling courses early in the meeting so I have time to learn how the student is doing in his or her courses. I provide useful information on academic programs (minors, the UAB Triple Threat Program, etc.), internships, study-abroad opportunities, and co-ops and encourage students to explore the opportunities of interest that match their long-range plans. I also learn what the student plans to do after graduation and provide guidance on how to prepare for graduate school, professional school or industry. Beyond the required semiannual meetings, I stress to the students that I am available by appointment at other times when necessary. I enjoy interacting with them outside of class and make every attempt to be available to my advisees as needed.

Graduate Student Mentorship

I believe the primary role of the faculty mentor is to provide each graduate advisee the resources and intellectual environment needed to become a successful independent investigator. In addition to maintaining a well-funded lab with state-of-the-art scientific equipment, I spend enough time with each student to learn of his or her interests and passions and to provide appropriate guidance. Early in their career, I encourage students to build up their knowledge of the relevant literature and to develop good habits to keep up with advances in their field. Students are expected to begin experiments immediately, even if they do not fully appreciate their significance. Within a few months, the student understands the methodology and can explain the significance of any new laboratory results. By encouraging each student to guide the direction of his or her project, the student takes ownership of the research and pushes to succeed. Throughout the student's career in my lab, I treat him or her as a peer-in-training. We are collaborators on the research project. In the beginning, I am primarily responsible for guidance on the research project. However, after a period, the student assumes much of the responsibility for the project. This transition ensures that the student can become a truly *independent* investigator.

Documentation of Teaching Improvement Activities

Since most of my courses teach engineering problem-solving skills, I have found it most useful to schedule "in-class" problems at the end of each section of new material. The problems I pose are diagnostic and intended to be solved in small groups during the class period. I walk through the classroom listening to each group develop their approach to solve the problem. I interact with the group to determine their level of mastery of the new concepts. Near the end of the class period, I regain the students' attention and go over the correct solution, pointing out the areas where students made incorrect assumptions or developed an erroneous approach. Student feedback for these problem sessions is positive, and I have observed that student performance on midterms is higher when I incorporate these problem sessions in my classes.

In addition to the in-class problems, I have developed a number of anonymous surveys that I use to gauge the level of student learning during the term. The simplest is the two-question survey that asks, "What do I have to do to improve my performance in the course?" and "What does Wick have to do to improve his performance in the course?" The first question challenges the students to think about their approach to the course. Are they taking advantage of all of the resources available to succeed (office hours, TA office hours, supplemental material, and their peers)? Are they devoting the time necessary to succeed in the class? After these surveys, I consistently observe more students starting homework assignments earlier, coming to office hours more frequently, and generally being better prepared and more involved in lectures and classroom activities. The second question prompts students to reflect on how well my teaching style matches their learning tendencies. From this feedback, I learn where I provide too little (or too much) instruction and know immediately how to adjust my style and the pace of the course to better match the ability of the students in the class.

Evidence of Student Learning

I have taught a number of graduate and undergraduate courses as a faculty member. I have included a sampling of courses that I have had a significant role in developing or improving in Appendix B. Student evaluation of my teaching is in Appendix C. I have trained 32 students (10 M.S. and 22 Ph.D.) as primary adviser or coadviser. I have also provided research mentorship for 10 undergraduate students. The table provides information on the position held by each student whom I advised in recent years. A comprehensive list of advisees is in Appendix D.

Name	Degree and Date	Thesis Title	Current Position
Chantal Jouret	M.S. 1997	Culture of Fibroblasts Under Extreme Hemodynamic Conditions: Hemodynamic Studies to Aid Tissue-Engineered Heart Valve Design	Research Scientist, Procter & Gamble, Belgium
James P. Siano	Ph.D. 1998	In Vitro Studies Characterizing Sickle Erythrocyte Adherence to Lung Vascular Endothelium: The Effects of Endothelial Injury Induced by Biochemical Factors on Sickle Erythrocyte-Pulmonary Endothelial Cell Interactions	Analyst, Andersen Consulting, Atlanta, GA

(*continued*)

Name	Degree and Date	Thesis Title	Current Position
Stewart McNaull	Ph.D. 1999	In Vitro Studies of Sickle Erythrocyte Adherence to Vascular Endothelium: Contributions of Hemodynamic Attachment Conditions and Erythrocyte Heterogeneity to Adhesion Strength	Principal Associate Process Development Scientist, Bayer Corporation, Research Triangle Park, NC
Richard Montes	Ph.D. 1999	Physico-Chemical Modulation of Sickle Cell Adherence: A Different In Vitro Model	Research Scientist, Global Biologics Supply Chain (GBSC), LLC, Malvern, PA
Sunil Saini	Ph.D. 2001	Bioreactor for Production of Tissue Engineered Cartilage: Defining Operating Parameters for Optimal Construct Growth	Research Scientist, Therics, Inc., Princeton, NJ
Crysanthi (Sandy) Williams	Ph.D. 2003	Perfusion Bioreactor for Tissue-Engineered Blood Vessels	Staff Scientist, EnduraTec, Minneapolis, MN
Padmini Rangamani	M.S. 2005	Bioprocessing Conditions for Improving Material Properties of Tissue Engineered Cartilage	Ph.D. Student, New York University
Lola A. Brown	M.S. 2005	Effect of Sickle Erythrocytes on Vascular Pathobiology	Core Laboratory Technician, Center for Biomedical and Behavioral Research, Spelman College

(*continued*)

Name	Degree and Date	Thesis Title	Current Position
Amanda R. Owings Amos	Ph.D. 2006	Regulation of Cytokine-Induced Adhesion Molecule Expression and Sickle Erythrocyte Adhesion to Microvascular Endothelial Cells by Intracellular Adenosine 3',5'-Cyclic Monophosphate and Nitric Oxide	Currently seeking employment
Matthew C. Wagner	Ph.D. 2006	Histamine Stimulation Promotes Sickle Erythrocyte Adherence in a Shear-Dependant Manner	Postdoctoral Fellow, Division of Pulmonary, Allergy, and Critical Care Medicine, Department of Medicine, Emory University School of Medicine
Ingrid Menegazzo	Ph.D. Student 2006–present	Effect of Low Oxygen Tension and Dynamic Mechanical Loading on Cartilage Development	Department of Biomedical Engineering, UAB
Katherine Sinele	M.S. Student 2006–present	Tissue Engineering Model to Characterize Dynamics of Tumor Cell Adhesion and Migration under Physiological Flow Conditions	Department of Biomedical Engineering, UAB
Carlos Carmona Moran	Ph.D. Student 2007–present	Bioreactors for Cartilage Tissue Engineering	Department of Biomedical Engineering, UAB

Research and Scholarship

Introduction

Whether I am engaged in formal classroom teaching or informal interactions with students, I strive to enable them to master the fundamentals necessary to succeed as a Biomedical Engineer. Similarly, the goal of my research program is to train students to become independent investigators while solving important research problems. My professional goal is to work with students, colleagues, and collaborators to educate Biomedical Engineers, discover new knowledge, and improve the reputation of the faculty, staff, and students in the BME Department.

I have maintained an active and productive interdisciplinary research program as a faculty member for more than 17 years. My main research areas are tissue engineering and blood cell adhesion. Along with students and collaborators, we apply knowledge to solve clinical and medical problems. I have competed successfully for funding from government agencies, private foundations, and industry. I have received over $2.2M in research funding in my career. A sample of my funding sources is listed below.

Funding Agency	Period
American Heart Association—Georgia Affiliate	1988–1989
Kimberly Clark Corporation	1991–1993
The Whitaker Foundation	1991–1994
National Institutes of Health (various)	1991–2004
Telios Pharmaceuticals, Inc.	1992–1993
Allelix Biopharmaceuticals, Inc.	1993–1994
CytRx Corporation	1995–1997
National Science Foundation	1998–2012

I have published in clinical and engineering journals. My work has been presented in seminars to industry, academia, and various scientific organizations. A partial list of research presentations is listed in Appendix E. Below is a summary of my research approach and accomplishments from my lab.

Description of Research

Development of Bioreactors for Tissue Engineering

The potential promise of tissue engineering is development of regenerative matrices and living tissue constructs to replace damaged or diseased body parts such as bone, cartilage, tendon, ligament, blood vessel, heart valve, and other tissues and organs. Tissues are complex three-dimensional structures that perform multiple metabolic and mechanical functions. Proper tissue function in the body requires that tissue architecture and function be replicated prior to implantation. Bioreactors are devices engineered to regulate the mechanical and nutrient environments to optimize tissue growth. Our combined experimental and numerical approach to bioreactor development and growth of tissue engineered constructs will result in industrial bioprocesses to engineer human tissue in a reproducible manner on an industrially relevant scale. These bioreactors are described in peer-reviewed journal articles in Appendix F. I have also included letters from collaborators that address the relevance of our bioreactors to the field of tissue engineering (Appendix G) and a sample research proposal (Appendix H).

Biophysics of Sickle Cell Adhesion to Endothelial Cells

Blockage of blood flow in tissues is a frequent complication for patients with sickle cell anemia. In microvessels, adhesion of sickle red blood cells to blood vessel wall endothelial cells promotes blood vessel blockage and inhibits oxygen delivery, leading to severe pain. Therapies to prevent these complications are limited. To better understand how sickle red blood cells stick to the blood vessel wall, we have developed culture models that mimic the cellular milieu and flow environment of human small blood vessels. Our studies have identified specific factors on the sickle red blood cell and the blood vessel wall that enhance cell sticking. These studies have identified novel targets for development of therapeutics block sticking and the attendant tissue damage. Examples of the combined biological and engineering approach to understanding the dynamics of sickle cell adhesion to the blood vessel wall are detailed in articles and expert commentary in Appendix F. I have also included letters from collaborators that address the relevance of our dynamic cell adhesion studies to clinical complications in sickle cell anemia (Appendix G) and a sample research proposal (Appendix H).

BioMatrix Engineering and Regenerative Medicine (BERM) Center

One goal I have is to develop a broad research vision and the ability to lead multidisciplinary research teams that develop important technologies to improve human health. Toward this goal, I was appointed Co-Director along with Dr. Joanne Murphy-Ullrich, Professor of Pathology, of a new University-Wide Interdisciplinary Research Center at UAB. The BioMatrix Engineering and Regenerative Medicine (BERM) Center's *mission* is to develop tissue engineering products and regenerative medicine technologies for orthopedic trauma repair and musculoskeletal tissue regeneration, craniofacial reconstruction, and matrix scaffolds for cardiovascular tissue repair and translation of these technologies to industry and patients. The Center is well positioned to compete for resources from funding agencies, industry, and private foundations to develop and deploy technologies to repair or replace tissues damaged by disease, trauma, burns or battlefield injuries. Selected BERM Center proposals, letters of support from UAB administrators, intellectual contributions and extramural support are included in Appendix I.

Administration and Service

Introduction and Responsibilities

I have provided active service to my universities and my profession in a variety of different ways. I have held a number of leadership positions at Georgia Tech and UAB. Samples of service activities are listed in Appendix J. As Chair of the Department of Biomedical Engineering, my major leadership responsibilities are strategic planning and strategic assessment; resource management; research development; faculty recruiting; fundraising; outreach to alums, industry, and other constituencies; curriculum development; and professional development of faculty and staff. As Chair, I work with the faculty, staff, and administration to nurture our strengths and focus on activities that grow the reputation of the department. I estimate that these duties consume more than

70 percent of my activities. It is particularly important to me that each member of the department has opportunities for professional development consistent with their needs and the departmental objectives. The Chair leads efforts to develop, implement, and revise the BME strategic plan. The Chair must provide the leadership necessary to develop the department's vision and communicate that vision to our constituencies. Additional duties include faculty and staff recruiting, development and retention, faculty and staff evaluation, and the departmental budget. Recently, I was named Co-Director of the BioMatrix Engineering and Regenerative Medicine (BERM) Center. The BERM Center directors are responsible for developing the Center's vision and mission and implementing the programs necessary to achieve the Center's goals.

Context

Prior to being appointed Chair in September 2005, an interim chair led the BME Department for nearly 5 years. During that time, the department was operating in a search mode with apparently less focus on other aspects of departmental administration. Thus, I inherited a department that was not focused in formal ways on community. This manifested itself as a group of faculty and staff who discharged their duties independently. Although I felt welcome on the faculty, I recognized that I had to address this culture in the department and implement strategies to improve departmental communication and collegiality.

Biomedical Engineering is a highly interdisciplinary field with strong representation in engineering, basic sciences, and clinical sciences. The medical and dental schools at UAB are a strong resource for the BME academic and research programs. Most BME faculty members collaborate effectively with other faculty members in Engineering, Medicine, Dentistry, Natural Sciences, and Mathematics and other units at UAB as well as at other universities. The institutional culture at UAB that encourages interdisciplinary and multidisciplinary research and training programs facilitates the ability of BME to meet our research and teaching goals.

Administrative Philosophy

In my opinion, the primary goal of an academic institution is to develop people—mainly by expanding the intellectual capacity of the undergraduates, graduate students, and faculty. I believe that departmental governance should be shared among the faculty, and where appropriate should include the staff. My personal administrative philosophy is to value the abilities and support the development of the students, colleagues, and staff in the department. Recognizing that inspiring people to achieve their professional goals is paramount to the success of the department, I believe that developing a culture of consensus is important. I inherited a culture—a set of formal and informal rules, values, and practices that govern Departmental operations. I work to understand these rules and practices. Where they work and there is consensus, I do not try to implement changes. However, where no best practices exist or where the current practices appear ineffective, I work with the appropriate constituencies to develop effective consensus procedures and practices.

Methodology

My leadership style is to develop a shared vision and value system for the department. I pursue excellence, and I appreciate working with others who work hard to succeed. I am an intuitive leader; I value positive interactions that result in us being prepared in advance to succeed. This is not unreasonable since the academic year is a cycle, and the upcoming events are fairly predictable. I give people latitude to meet their position requirements without a lot of "hovering." I do not follow up regularly because I expect that when I am told that a person understands the assignment or responsibility, it will be completed correctly and on time. I am available for discussion should a problem arise. I expect to be consulted regarding uncertainty or changes. I have difficulty accepting failure.

One of the most important things for me as a leader is that my constituencies understand and take on our goals, value system, evaluation procedures, etc. I develop practices to promote widespread productive input from the major constituencies—faculty, staff, students, alum, the Advisory Board. I believe in open, honest communication and respectful listening. I will always strive for unanimity, but recognizing that this is not always possible, I will try to support the majority. Also, I recognize that as department head, I have additional rights and responsibilities that may require me to overrule the majority when that seems prudent to achieving larger goals.

This shared vision is developed through extensive communication between me and the faculty (individually and as a group). Since my arrival at UAB, I have implemented monthly faculty meetings that were expanded this year to include all BME faculty and staff. Included in Appendix K are minutes of recent faculty meetings. It is expected that each faculty member engage in administration of the programs in the department. I organized the BME Department around three committees responsible for departmental governance—Undergraduate Program, Graduate Studies and Faculty Search. I am pleased that each faculty member is an active member of one of the departmental standing committees. The committees are active in their area of responsibility and provide helpful guidance to the department. The committees bring thoughtful recommendations to the departmental meetings. Faculty and staff engage in careful evaluation of recommendations that often leads to changes that improve our effectiveness. In this manner, the entire faculty is involved in changes to policies, procedures or practices.

This year I created the BME Student Advisory Council (SAC) charged with facilitating communication between BME students and the BME leadership as well as representing the needs of the BME students to the BME leadership. I hope to contribute to development of student leaders in the BME department. The charge to the SAC and the current roster are included in Appendix L.

Recently I have initiated a strategic planning initiative in the department. Again, recommendations for strategic change in the department come from a committee of BME faculty. However, all faculty and staff members are involved in developing a strategic plan with goals and milestones *consistent with our mission* that will serve as a basis to recruit and develop faculty and students, identify synergistic interactions, and grow the reputation of the department within UAB and the profession. In this way, each member of the BME department has ownership in development and implementation of strategic goals and milestones.

Sample Professional Accomplishments

During my first year as chair of the Department of Biomedical Engineering at UAB, I worked hard to share my vision of success for the department with department faculty, students, staff, administration, alums, and constituents. We have worked hard to improve our undergraduate program, and as a result we had a positive outcome the first time we sought accreditation from the Accreditation Board for Engineering and Technology (ABET) in October 2006. The ABET evaluation team found no deficiencies, weaknesses, or concerns and cited departmental leadership, outstanding faculty, excellent undergraduate laboratory facilities, and the high quality and diversity of the undergraduate biomedical engineering student body as program strengths. We have invested considerable time recruiting graduate students and improving the quality of our graduate program. The recently funded BERM Center will provide additional opportunities for BME faculty to collaborate across campus, develop intellectual property, and compete for external resources to further the research and graduate education goals of the department. Finally, we spent much of the year engaged in faculty recruiting and successfully added five new members to our faculty. Some of the accomplishments that I believe best reflect my professional contributions are described below.

Chair and Organizer of the Phillips Petroleum/C. J. "Pete" Silas Program in Leadership and Ethics

The Phillips Petroleum/C. J. "Pete" Silas Program in Leadership and Ethics was established in the School of Chemical Engineering by an award from the Phillips Petroleum Foundation in recognition of the outstanding career achievements of Georgia Tech Chemical Engineering Graduate C. J. "Pete" Silas. I chaired this symposium from its inception in 1995 until I left Georgia Tech in 2005. My contributions to the program were a 3-credit-hour Engineering Ethics course and a symposium series on Ethics and Leadership presented by recognized leaders in industry. The ethics course was taught 5 times from 1998–2005 with an average enrollment of 25 engineering students.

The symposium spotlights the importance of ethics and leadership by focusing on technical and business decisions that have ethical ramifications and culminates in an interactive discussion between students, faculty, and invited speakers. I arranged eight visits from leaders of large multinational companies to share their views and experiences on the importance of strong leadership and integrity on their success and that of their company. Their personal accounts and concrete examples provided valuable discussion about the importance of personal ethics to professional success.

Career Development of BME Faculty

My goal is to work with each faculty member to help improve his or her professional reputation and satisfaction. It is important to me that each faculty member receives appropriate feedback and support to meet his or her career objectives, including earning promotion and tenure in a timely manner. I am committed to aiding all Assistant Professors and Associate Professors in the Department to earn tenure and promotion to the rank of Professor. Where appropriate, I provide resources for development—attending a grant writing workshop, a professional meeting. I also funded a pilot research project with the expectation that the results will lead to external publications and sustainable research funding. In one instance, this support has led to a successful industry-funded grant with the BME faculty member and a collaborator in the Department of Medicine as co-investigators. In another instance, I facilitated collaboration between a BME faculty member and a faculty member in the Cardiology Department. This collaboration is ongoing, and I expect it will lead to additional external funding for their research programs.

Faculty Recruiting

When I arrived at UAB, the BME department had no junior faculty. The department recognized the need to add new faculty with emphasis on those at the rank of Assistant Professor. In my first year, I spent significant time and energy recruiting the best junior faculty we could identify. I am proud that we were able to add four tenure-track and one research-track faculty members to the department in my first two years as chair. This demonstrates my ability to convey my vision for the department to others—both to people at UAB and at other institutions.

Department Staffing

To assemble an effective staff, I spent much of my first year learning each staff person's responsibilities as well as their job skills and interests. My goal was to understand their strengths and motives so that I could write job descriptions that maximized job satisfaction and productivity for each person. Within the first year, I was able to develop position descriptions that would work with expanded job duties and complement the skills of the department personnel. I was also able to share a complete vision for the department to the Program Manager when she was hired and was able to provide advice on how each staff member would best contribute to the mission of the department.

Successful Interactions with the BME External Advisory Board

Having inherited a department that was searching for a Chair for five years, one of the overlooked activities was the regular meetings of the External Advisory Board (EAB). The EAB is composed of diverse national leaders from industry, academia, and government who have professional expertise in biomedical engineering and related disciplines. The External Advisory Board meets periodically with students, faculty, staff, and administrators and provides impartial expert guidance, strategic direction, and management advice. The Board appraises the mission, strategic plan, research goals, and academic programs of the BME Department. Upon my arrival at UAB, I reconstituted the Board with members who had expertise in the various areas in which the Department of Biomedical Engineering has influence—academia, industry, entrepreneurship, regulatory agencies, and economic development. Over three meetings in the first two years, the Board has contributed significantly to the growth of the department. I can rely on the Board for positive guidance as we continue to the BME Department's reputation and prominence.

Appendixes

Appendix A: Sample Course Syllabi

Appendix B: Sample Syllabi for Courses That I Developed or Revised

Appendix C: Student Evaluation of My Teaching

Appendix D: List of Undergraduate and Graduate Student Advisees, Thesis Titles and Employment

Appendix E: Representative Research Presentations to Academia, Industry, and Professional Meetings

Appendix F: Sample Peer-Review Publications That Illustrate the Success of Interdisciplinary Research Focus

Appendix G: Assessment of Research Significance from Collaborators

Appendix H: Sample Research Proposals

Appendix I: BERM Center Letters of Support, Intellectual Contributions, and Extramural Support

Appendix J: Sample Significant Service Activities

Appendix K: Recent BME Department Meeting Agendas and Minutes

Appendix L: BME Student Advisory Council Charge and Roster

Bioscience and Biotechnology

Shivanthi Anandan

Department of Bioscience and Biotechnology

Drexel University

Fall 2008

Table of Contents

Abstract

My purpose in writing this document is to use it as a tool to document my evolution from a tenure-track faculty member into a leader at this institution. Therefore, this document contains evidence that showcases my continued development in three key areas: research, teaching, and service to the community. At this time, this document also serves as a reminder of past accomplishments, and as a promise of future goals.

Teaching Responsibilities and Teaching Philosophy

a. Teaching Responsibilities

As part of the faculty in the Department of Bioscience, I teach several undergraduate and graduate level courses. At the undergraduate level, I teach a required freshman-level Cells and Genetics course (Bio 122) and several other elective courses—Microbiology (Bio 221), Biotechnology (Bio 312), Mechanisms of Microbial Pathogenesis (Bio 320), and Genetically Modified Foods (Bio 212). I also teach two required courses at the graduate level, Microbial Genetics (Bio 530) and Issues in Scientific Research (Bio 680), and an elective course, Medical Microbiology (Bio 670). Enrollment for Bio 122 is approximately 200. For the other courses it is generally 25–30.

A comprehensive list of all the courses I have taught at Drexel University can be found in Appendix A, together with the syllabi for these courses.

b. Teaching Philosophy and Methodologies

My role, as I see it, is to bring the field of biology to students and help them learn and understand the basic tenets of the discipline. In doing so, I aim to illustrate the uses and applications of basic concepts in biology in the real world. I work hard to foster my students' ability to learn and think critically while building their problem-solving skills. I believe that the classroom is the ideal setting for instructors to discuss ethical issues of conduct with their students.

To achieve this goal, there must be good rapport between teacher and students. This includes being accessible to students, both within and outside the confines of the lecture hall. To build rapport, it is also necessary to be accessible in attitude: to be open to hearing their questions, comments, and opinions. I try to foster an environment conducive to discussion and encourage my students to ask questions both in lecture and in lab.

This is particularly important when discussing ethical conduct with students. When teaching issues in scientific research, I use case studies to illustrate key points. In this way, the students and I are part of a team that comes up with solutions/strategies for dealing with instances of professional misconduct. I make the atmosphere as relaxed as possible, so that we can have an open discussion.

The success of my teaching philosophy and methodology can be seen from student comments and from the numerical scores on my student evaluations. Selected examples and comments are given below. A student in my microbial genetics course describes the impact of the application-oriented nature of this course.

> Microbial genetics was by far the best course I had this term. The material was relevant to anybody who does any genetics lab work. Dr. Anandan made the class work interesting and lively with her energetic teaching method. The student interaction through in-class questions/experiment "design," weekly presentations, and occasional group huddles really helped to keep me thinking and focused, which is saying something in a 5 hr class.

The following comments from students in my Biotechnology course also address this aspect of my teaching philosophy: "I enjoyed this class very much, I especially like the book *Mutation* and the discussions on genetically modified foods." Another student wrote, "Made me think about all the issues on both sides of the arguments of Biotechnology." Comments from a student in my freshman Genetics course also refers to the application-based nature of my teaching style. "Dr. Anandan is one of the best teachers I ever had. She always brings current applications into the material being taught, making it more interesting."

Copies of student comments from all of my courses taught in recent years can be found in Appendix B, and my complete set of student evaluations since I arrived in 1997 are available upon request.

Standardized Student Evaluation Scores
for the Freshman Genetics Course

The scores are for the "overall rating of the instructor." This is question 12 on the student evaluation form, which can be found in Appendix C. Rating scale: 5 = excellent, 1 = poor.

My freshman course in Genetics has an enrollment of 150–200 students per year. I am using the scores from my student evaluations in this course as representative of my performance as an

Table 1. Summary of Student Evaluation Scores

Year	Overall Rating	Enrollment
Winter 98/99	4.11	119
Winter 99/00	4.08	133
Winter 00/01	4.87	132
Winter 01/02	4.55	130
Winter 02/03	4.9	150
Winter 03/04	4.85	165
Winter 04/05	4.4	202
Winter 05/06	4.74	188

instructor. As these scores in Table 1 demonstrate, my average scores for the freshman genetics course have always been higher than 4 on a 5-point scale. This indicates that my overall rating as an instructor has consistently been very good. It addition, these scores reflect my own growth and improvement as the instructor of this freshman course.

c. Curriculum Development

I have developed four courses in this department: Molecular and Cellular Genetics (Bio 117/122), Biotechnology (Bio 212), Genetically Modified Foods (Bio 312), and Issues in Scientific Integrity (Bio 480/680) for senior-level undergraduate and graduate students. These courses reflect not only my discipline-specific areas of expertise, but also reflect those areas of science that I find personally interesting.

Academic Research Program
a. Primary Research Focus

My research background is in two similar fields that complement each other: plant molecular biology and microbial genetics. The common theme has been my interest in photosynthesis and photosynthetic organisms. I have worked with plants and cyanobacteria, both of which are photosynthetic. My primary research interests center on how photosynthetic organisms sense and respond to environmental cues like light and nutrition. Photosynthetic organisms are by far the greatest natural biological resource that we possess. They are the primary producers in the food chain because they possess the unique feature of photosynthesis. The process of photosynthesis allows plants and some bacteria (like cyanobacteria) to make their own food using the energy of sunlight and the gas carbon dioxide present in air. Animals do not have this ability and must rely on the food synthesized by plants, algae, and cyanobacteria, either directly or indirectly, for their nutrition.

As a postdoctoral researcher at Texas A&M University, I identified a gene, *orfG,* in the cyanobacterium *Synechococus elongatus.* This gene has been the central focus of my research, which has shown that this gene is implicated in cell growth in this organism. I am using this gene as a model gene to determine what external factors (like nutrient deprivation etc.) affect cell growth in this micro-organism.

b. Collaborative Research Projects

My research background with two different model experimental systems (plants and cyanobacteria) allows me to collaborate in research studies that need expertise in either area. These collaborative research projects are described below.

Microbiological and Molecular Characterization of Mexican Soft Cheeses

This collaborative project with Dr. John Luchansky, at the USDA Eastern Regional Research Center, focuses on characterizing the microbial content of raw milk Mexican soft cheeses by testing the survival of the pathogen *Listeria monocytogenes* on Mexican soft cheeses formulated and prepared in this country. The emphasis is on inhibiting the growth of *Listeria monocytogenes* and extending the shelf life of these cheeses. See Appendix D for a copy of this project proposal.

Examination of Impact of Socioeconomic Factors on Food Quality and Safety

In keeping with my interest in food microbiology and food safety, this collaborative project with Jennifer Quinlan, Ph.D., investigated the socio-economic factors that impact food safety. We examined perishable foods like fruits, vegetables, and meat, purchased from grocery stores in both high- and low-socio-economic areas for the presence of microbes causing food-borne illnesses. In this project, my role was that of the microbiologist who trained and supervised the graduate student. See Appendix E for a copy of the project proposal.

Examination of Biotechnologies to Assess the Effect of Training Activities at Military Installations on Endangered Species and the Environment

This collaborative project with Drs. Spotila, Avery, and Lee required my expertise in plant science and molecular biology. We evaluated the use of DNA-based technologies, particularly DNA microarrays, to diagnose the ill effects of munitions and training activities at Army training sites on the surrounding fauna and flora. My role in this project was to train and supervise a graduate student. A description of this project and my role in it are in Appendix F.

Drexel University Major Research Initiative: "PLASMA BIO-MEDICINE"

I am part of a group of researchers in this university that are exploring the use of plasma arc devices for anti-microbial purposes in the sanitizing and cleaning of food and surfaces. This proposal is one of two that has been recently funded by the Drexel University Major Research initiative. Appendix G contains a description of the project and the award statement.

Selected publications that showcase my research activities are in Appendix H.

Research Funding History

Table 2 lists the grants that I have successfully obtained. A complete list of all grants that I have submitted can be found in Appendix I.

Table 2. External Research Funding

Title	Year	Agency	Funds Awarded
Examination of Impact of Socioeconomic Factors on Food Quality and Safety Jennifer Quinlan, Ph.D. PI^ Shivanthi Anandan, Ph.D. Co-PI*	2004	USDA-NRI	$100,000
Examination of Biotechnologies to Assess the Effect of Training Activities at Military Installations on Endangered Species and the Environment. James R. Spotila, Ph.D. PI Shivanthi Anandan, Ph.D., Harold Avery, Ph.D. and Jeremy Lee, Ph.D. Co-P Is.	2004	US Army	$420,000
Enhancing Safety, Shelf Life and Quality in Ethnic Cheese. Shivanthi Anandan, Ph.D. PI	2002	USDA-ERRC	$165,000
An Internet-Based Predictive Microbiology Portal to Assist Small and Very Small Food Processors in Meeting Food Safety Regulations Workshop held January 12, 2007 Shivanthi Anandan, Ph.D. PI	2006	Rutgers University	$33,991

^Principal investigator; *Co-principal investigator.

Department/Institutional Committees

a. University Biosafety Committee

The University Biosafety Committee has the charge of overseeing the safety of all research activities in this university, from the perspective of compliance with mandatory government regulations on chemical and biological safety. My role draws on my expertise with recombinant DNA techniques, and I am responsible for reviewing submitted research protocols for their compliance with recombinant DNA safety guidelines. Appendix J contains my letter of appointment to the University Biosafety Committee.

b. Chair, Undergraduate Curriculum Committee

As a member of the undergraduate and graduate committees in this department, I have participated in revising curricula at both levels. In the last two years since tenure, I have chaired the Undergraduate Curriculum Committee. In the 2006–07 academic year, the committee carried out extensive revision of the Bioscience curriculum for majors, and received Academic Senate approval to put the new curriculum into practice starting the 2007–08 academic year. A copy of the documents filed with the Academic Senate are in Appendix K.

Mentoring Activities

a. Mentoring of Undergraduate and Graduate Students in Research

I believe that my mentoring role does not stop in the classroom, but extends into my research laboratory. Therefore, I have undergraduate students carrying out independent research projects in my lab. I find that those undergraduate students who are drawn to my research program are motivated, very interested in the scientific process, and technically extremely competent. Generally, the experimental concept is mine, but the undergraduate students carry out the day-to-day research.

Two years ago, one of my exemplary undergraduate students generated sufficient data to present her results in the form of a poster at the annual national meeting of the American Society for Microbiology. She had worked in my research laboratory for four years. I mentored her through this time, teaching her laboratory skills and honing her analytical abilities by giving and discussing with her appropriate scientific articles. This is another avenue by which I motivate students. This particular undergraduate student, Jennifer Uram, is now in her second year of graduate school at Johns Hopkins University. Appendix L contains a copy of the abstract for this poster presentation and the peer-reviewed journal article that resulted from this project.

Another excellent undergraduate student, Jennifer Hillemann, has been invaluable on the *orfG* project. She has extended some initial results obtained by my last graduate students, and a poster of her work was presented at the Drexel University Research Day in 2007. I find students to be an invaluable component of my research laboratory. The table in Appendix M describes the undergraduate students who worked in my research laboratory and the graduate students who carried out research with me.

b. Mentoring Junior Colleagues

I have mentored two auxiliary faculty, such that each of them is now a junior tenure-track faculty member. One of them, Venu Kalavacharla, and I taught a plant genetics and genomics course together a few years ago. We also applied for funding from the Strategic Education Initiative at Drexel University for a mini-grant to institute this plant-based course with an accompanying Web site. I also suggested that he enroll in the University teaching portfolio workshop, which he did. This portfolio was a large part of his applications for faculty positions. He is now a tenure-track faculty member at Delaware State University. A letter from him is in Appendix N.

The second person is Jennifer Quinlan. She and I received funding from the United States Department of Agriculture-National Research Initiative to support a pilot project on assessing the impact of socioeconomic factors on food quality and safety. This research was carried out in my research laboratory. Jennifer is now a tenure track faculty member in this department, and this grant and research were key in her achievement of this faculty position.

c. Mentoring Junior Colleagues in Teaching

About four years ago I took on the role of instituting a teaching circle in the department to mentor junior and auxiliary faculty in the practical aspects of teaching. The idea of the teaching circle arose because the department had hired several new junior faculty, and a method for the mentoring of these junior faculty in all aspects of teaching, big and small, was clearly needed. Participants in the weekly meetings include Rita Berson, Laura Duwel, Liz Gardner, Cecilie Goodrich, Phil Handel, Blanche Haughton, Mark Lechner, Peter Oelkers, Jennifer Quinlan, Lynn Riddell, Aleister Saunders, and myself. In the meetings, we discussed issues in teaching. I also scheduled outside speakers from the University to talk to us on matters related to teaching students. We had speakers from the Learning Center, Student Life, Drexel Study Abroad, the Office of Disabilities, and the International Students office. In addition, we discussed topics dealing with the everyday teaching of students, including the use of homework, grading policies, and mentoring graduate teaching assistants.

d. Mentor, Teaching Portfolio Workshop

Since last year, I have been a mentor in the teaching portfolio workshop. I have mentored several faculty on their teaching portfolios for tenure. Some of them have successfully been awarded tenure. I have enjoyed working with them to bring out the best of their teaching styles, and have really felt fulfilled in giving back something of what I have learned in the past few years. In sending out this year's letter to the teaching portfolio workshop participants, Teck-Kah Lim, the organizer, asked them to read my teaching portfolio in the third edition of Peter Seldin's book *The Teaching Portfolio*. I really felt honored and proud, and realized that this has been one of my best achievements! A copy of the email from Teck-Kah Lim is in Appendix O.

e. Faculty Adviser, TriBeta Biological Honor Society

I serve as the faculty adviser to the TriBeta Biological honor society in the Bioscience department. An integral goal of TriBeta is to foster within its members academic interest in the biological sciences through the sponsoring of several fun-filled/academically enriched social activities. Such activities range from Research

Seminars presented by eminent Faculty to Faculty Bake Sales and Popcorn & Movie Nights. The members are also involved in outreach activities to the West Philadelphia community.

Contribution from Teaching, Research, and Service to My Professional Growth and Development

Simply put, my research informs my teaching, and both my research and teaching keep me current in my discipline in Biology. I believe that I can offer advice in only areas that I have gained expertise. Therefore, I try to choose service opportunities that play to my strengths and experience: those that involve mentoring students in research and junior faculty in the practice of being a faculty member. I find that since being granted tenure, I have been put into more leadership roles in the department, which encourages and validates my own growth and development as a faculty member in areas outside the laboratory or classroom. I am now chairing committees rather than just being a member. This allows me to use my experience in teaching and research to plan and execute revisions in curricula, and be a better mentor to students and faculty.

Three Significant Professional Accomplishments

Three major professional accomplishments of which I am especially proud follow. They have defined and validated my work as a researcher and mentor. These accomplishments have also satisfied my personal goals for success.

a. Achieving Tenure at Drexel University

This is of great significance to me personally and professionally. I have worked very hard in both research and teaching to achieve tenure. It is significant to Drexel University since this now allows me to innovate my research. Until I was granted tenure, I was very focused on certain research projects that would ensure my research productivity for tenure. I now am able to collaborate with other scientists on joint ventures where my expertise is needed. I can also open my own research up to follow paths that may not in the short term be profitable, but in the long term will allow us to understand a fundamental biological process. This allows me to explore avenues of research that will allow me to fully understand the workings of a basic process in microbiology.

b. Mentoring My First Doctoral Student for a Fulbright-Hays Award

This award was recognition of my effectiveness as a mentor. I have always maintained that any doctoral student of mine would have to seek federal graduate fellowships, not only for financial independence but also for experience in grant writing. This student, Adrienne Dolberry, applied to every single federal predoctoral fellowship sponsor and was unanimously turned down by all. A year later, I brought the Fulbright-Hays award to her notice, since I knew that she was fluent in the German language, and thought that this might be a very good opportunity for her. We were both ecstatic when the awards were announced. There had not been a Fulbright-Hays awardee at the graduate level in Science in this university for the past ten years, at least. My student's welfare is of importance to me, and this award gave her prestige and the acknowledgment that she can compete on a national (or international) level in scientific research. She is currently a post-doctoral associate at Massachusetts Institute of Technology, Cambridge, Massachusetts.

c. Chairing My First Committee at Drexel University

The first committee that I chaired at Drexel University is the Undergraduate Program Committee in this department. This is noteworthy to me because it signifies that I have crossed that invisible boundary between junior and tenured faculty. It also signifies that the department head trusts that I can carry out this function. It is significant to Drexel University because this role allowed me to oversee and execute a revision of the Bioscience curriculum, so that it is now more appropriate for our current students.

Three Professional Goals That I Want to Accomplish

a. Promotion to Full Professor

In the next few years I will work hard to get promotion to full professor. This would be a validation from my peers at this university of my expertise in both teaching and research. I understand that this is the hardest step for a faculty member in academia.

To become full professor, I would need the university to give me some release time or be more flexible about the time I spend on campus. It would also help if the university recognized and rewarded the time and effort I spend on teaching undergraduate students, with appropriate release time for research. These decisions would be up to my department head and dean. Achieving this step would also require systematic mentoring and encouragement from the institution.

b. Leadership in Curricular Issues

Since joining Drexel University, I have gained a great deal of knowledge and expertise in curricular matters. I would like to put all of this experience to work at the University level and become a leader for curricular development. This goal plays to my strength as a teacher and makes use of my past experience in curricular development.

For this goal, the rewards to this university would be an increase in the retention and recruitment of students. To achieve it, my expertise in curricular development would have to be recognized. I would then have to be appointed to an administrative position where I could fully utilize my expertise in this area. Again, some release time from teaching would be necessary to free up time to work on projects of curricular development.

c. Gain Expertise in Offering Online Courses

I want to become expert in offering online courses. Online course delivery is an innovative new method of teaching, one that requires expertise in new areas of course content presentation. Gaining expertise in this area allows me to reach a population of older/nontraditional students whom I do not have access to right now. This is important to me, since I feel that the needs of older students are not well looked after on traditional college campuses. It would be of importance to this University, since increased emphasis on online learning would be a significant source of revenue.

Again, release time would be needed for me to acquire this expertise. Otherwise, the time that I would spend to gain this expertise would take away from my time in research, and be counter productive to accomplishing the goals of this university and myself.

Appendixes

Appendix A: List of Courses Taught and Relevant Course Syllabi

Appendix B: Student Comments from Courses Taught

Appendix C: Course Evaluation Form

Appendix D: Project Proposal for Microbiological and Molecular Characterization of Mexican Soft Cheeses

Appendix E: Project Proposal for Examination of Impact of Socio-Economic Factors on Food Quality and Safety

Appendix F: Project Proposal for Examination of Biotechnologies to Assess the Effect of Training Activities at Military Installations on Endangered Species and the Environment

Appendix G: Project Description and the Award Statement for Plasma Bio-Medicine

Appendix H: Selected Publications That Showcase My Research Activities

Appendix I: A Complete List of All Research Grants Submitted

Appendix J: Letter of Appointment to the University Biosafety Committee

Appendix K: A Copy of the Documents Filed with the Academic Senate for Revision of the Bioscience Undergraduate Curriculum

Appendix L: A Copy of the Abstract for the Poster Presentation and the Peer-Reviewed Journal Article Written with Jennifer Uram

Appendix M: Table Listing the Undergraduate Students Who Worked in My Research Laboratory, and the Graduate Students Whom I Mentored

Appendix N: Letter from Venu Kalavacharla on My Mentoring Skills

Appendix O: A Copy of the Email from Teck-Kah Lim to the Teaching Portfolio Attendees, 2007

Child and Family Studies

Lynda Henley Walters

Department of Child and Family Development

College of Family and Consumer Sciences

The University of Georgia

Fall 2008

Introduction

The purpose of this legacy portfolio is for me to reflect on my professional life. I earned my first graduate degree not because I wanted a graduate degree but because I wanted to have more knowledge and I wanted to teach in order to widen my net (I directed a child care center that was for low-income children and families, and I was frustrated that I could impact so few). With my first graduate degree in hand, I began teaching child development and early childhood education. It was satisfying and exciting for at least two years, when I began to feel the frustration of needing to know more and to know how to conduct my own research. The driving force for my need for education has always been people and their situations. However, graduate education may have removed me further and further from my roots. I substituted the needs of university and graduate students for the needs of low-income children and families. I became committed to the processes of higher education and the place of research in education.

I was never able to commit to a program of research that built upon itself (possibly regrettable) because knowing one thing always propelled me into another. Today, I work hard to help others avoid that trap, but for me it was a *gift*. Without it, I would not have gone to Moscow and embarked on nearly twenty years of work in Russia and Poland. It expanded my perspective to the world. I was invited to collaborate with Michael Matskovski on a study of families in Soviet Russia, Soviet Georgia, and Poland because I had been working to be the best researcher I could be. I believe that I cannot always know what my opportunities will be, but the way to prepare for them is to be as good as possible at what I am doing now. I have worked with a passion that seems to apply to whatever I am doing at the moment. I have evolved toward greater interest in art and philosophy, possibly out of need to touch the lives of others in another way. Still, my passion for understanding human development and the human individual remains strong, along with the need to engage the minds and hearts of others in an effort to create the world as we wish it.

Teaching

My academic career has been a bit backward compared to others. For the first ten years, I served as Associate Dean for Research and Instruction in the College of Family and Consumer Sciences with an academic appointment in the Department of Child and Family Development. While I served in this position for ten years, I went through the academic ranks to Full Professor. I carried a full administrative load and a full academic load. After ten years, I chose to move to a full-time faculty position. Thus, I left administration about one-third of the way through my career and concentrated on teaching and research.

The move to full-time faculty gave me more time to serve as a mentor for students. During my last 20 years, I have served as major professor for 14 masters of science students and eighteen doctoral students (See Appendix A for a list of students). In addition, I have served on at least one hundred student committees and closely mentored many, many others. I consider my work with graduate students some of my most gratifying. It has been rewarding to work with students, and it is exciting to see them move into positions of responsibility after finishing their degrees.

On the other hand, I have been delighted by undergraduate students who have just understood something important about their own development or the development of others. I love it when students get "hooked" on human development and begin to use it as a lens in their daily lives. I relish the opportunity to talk with students about how to use this knowledge in the work they choose after graduation. I find that students are hungry to try out their ideas on an interested ear, and they can always find one in me.

In my thirty years of experience, I have taught nearly every course that has been offered by my department. I have, however, evolved into teaching mostly courses on human development. Occasionally I teach a quantitative methods course, something I did quite a lot of ten years ago. I have also developed an interest in diversity and, as a result, I have taught our undergraduate course on diversity in human development and family relations for the last five years. Most recently I have taught the following courses:

Course/Course Number	Level	Enrollment/Semester
Introduction to Child Development CHFD 2950	Undergraduate	200
Development of Adolescents and Young Adults CHFD 3700	Undergraduate	40–50
Diversity in Human Development/Family Relations CHFD 4330	Undergraduate	40–50
Quantitative Research Methods CHFD 8800	Doctoral	4–6
Seminar in Adolescent Development CHFD 8950	Doctoral	10–12
Theories of Human Development CHFD 6100	Master's	10

I use a combination of lecture, discussion, and problem solving in my classes. A copy of some of my course syllabi can be seen in Appendix B.

Philosophy

I teach because I want to share knowledge. I believe that knowledge is an essential building block for competence in children and adults in our culture. I believe that our culture is better when people are educated. I do not believe that education solves all of our problems. I do not believe that the education of any single person will change much of anything. I do, however, think it is better when education pervades.

I am passionate about the subject matter I teach and about the students who are in my classes. I believe that teaching is not a neutral enterprise and that my passion inspires those who might otherwise not attend. Perhaps passion is a part of the process of challenging the long-held attitudes and beliefs of learners. Learning something new requires changing an existing idea or creating a new one. When students are inspired, they are more interested in exploring and they are more comfortable behaving as learners. As learners accept the challenges to their existing ideas, they build more complex mental structures and ideas that make it possible to think at higher levels.

The final point that I would like to make in my philosophy of teaching is that I believe that it is important to trust students to learn. I present information, I work at inspiring students, and I try to make my class interesting so they will want to attend. In the final analysis, I cannot learn *for* them. I must trust them to want to learn and to learn. I find this trust to be powerful.

Objectives

Even as I want students to be challenged to think at higher levels, I want them **to be able to apply their knowledge.** I believe that application is the most difficult form of thought. I want my students to get in the habit of applying their knowledge of human development throughout their day no matter what they are doing. I tell them stories of application; I show movie clips and ask them to interpret them; I ask them to tell me stories of things that have happened to them in the last few days and to include their assessment of the role of human development in those events. I want them **to be immersed in the excitement of knowing.**

Teaching about diversity is a bit more of a challenge. The long-held attitudes and beliefs of students are accompanied by values communicated to them by their parents and/or their churches. These values often contain messages of entitlement and discrimination, but the rhetoric has been washed clean of political incorrectness. Students approach my challenges cautiously and often silently. Thus, it is important to find ways to reveal the silent reluctance about or outrage toward some of the ideas that are presented in class. Creating an environment in which **students feel safe** and can separate their ideas from those of their respected elders enough **to explore their own ideas** is difficult. Some students need to express their ideas, but that can make other students feel more vulnerable. I have found that my ideas and beliefs need to stay in the background. I need to encourage exploration that can lead to ideas that I believe are wrong, but I must accept them. It is feeling safe in the process of exploration that is the most important goal of this course rather than some specific knowledge. This means that I must be able to trust students to keep using the tools they develop in class. In the end-of-semester evaluation, one student said,

> Dr. Walters' lectures are very intriguing and I love how she challenges us to think from all different angles.

Methods

Online Quizzes

I want students to be prepared when they come to class because they will get more from the lecture if they know what to expect. To that end, students have the opportunity to take quizzes online for extra credit before a chapter is covered in class (see Appendix C). Students appreciate the quizzes and they appreciate the opportunity to earn extra credit, for example:

- "Quizzes help to get me motivated to study."
- "I really enjoyed having the extra credit quizzes. Reviewing the chapters before discussing them in class was very helpful—it made it easier to understand the concepts."

PowerPoint Notes Online

I also want students to be able to pay attention and think in class rather than rushing to write down everything. When they are trying to write everything, they do not have time to think. I encourage students to print the outline of my notes before they come to class. It makes it easier to be sure that they are following me, and if they miss something, they know what to ask about or look up in the text. Using this procedure, I also find that students will discuss more in class, even in a class of two hundred. Some student comments were as follow:

- "I liked the PowerPoint Notes and especially the incorporation of the videos that related to topics we were discussing in class."
- "The online notes/slides available on WebCT were helpful so that I could pay attention to the lecture vs. concentrating on note taking."

Curricular Revisions

Every time I teach a course, I revise it. Sometimes revisions are quite large, particularly when I first teach a class or when I am moving large parts of it to online access. However, most of the time revisions reflect new knowledge in the field, new videos, or new activities. Looking at my syllabi, it is difficult to see that a course has been revised. The basic structure of my human development courses stays the same. My lectures, videos, activities, and examinations change. My class on diversity has changed in terms of readings and the order in which concepts are considered, but it is remarkably the same in its basic structure.

Choosing from all the knowledge that can be included in any one class is a challenge. Most of it seems important to me, but I have to remember that I am adding on to my knowledge, and my students are just building their basic knowledge. It seems to me that this is one of the biggest challenges faced by teachers in higher education.

Course Syllabi

I want to make my syllabi clear and easy to use. It is a fundamental tool for students, and they should not have to ask for additional interpretation about material in a syllabus. Everything that they must know to get through the course is in the syllabus: purpose of the course, course objectives, schedule of what will be covered and when, explanations of assignments, the grading scheme, my expectations for use of online communication, and the expectations of the University for academic honesty. Following the suggestion of a faculty colleague, I give students in my large classes a quiz on the syllabus. They may use their syllabus while they take the quiz because they need to find all the elements of the syllabus and read them. If they complete the quiz, I give them 1 point (out of 1000) of extra credit. I do this because I think the syllabus is so important, and I have found that students who would not otherwise read it are more familiar with it.

Evaluation of Teaching

Feedback from students regarding their perceptions of my teaching and the course are very helpful to me. Of course, I take advantage of the college Survey of Student Opinion of Teaching.

This survey is used by the entire faculty in my department. I like it because there are eight questions used by all faculty and twelve more questions may be selected from a bank of about forty questions. These additional questions are for individual faculty feedback and diagnosis. These questions can change with each course depending on the needs and interests of the faculty member— and these questions are not considered for any administrative evaluation of faculty. The eight common questions are used by department heads to monitor teaching and as part of the input on teaching awards.

Recent student perceptions (last two years) are based on one of the questions I most highly value: *"I learned a great deal from this class."*

Course	Number of Students[a]	Average Rating[b]
CHFD 2950	About 125 of 200 students each semester	4.3
CHFD 4330	About 35 of 50 students each semester it is taught	4.0
CHFD 3700	About 35 of 50 students each semester it is taught	4.5
CHFD 6100	9 of 10 students in the class	4.6

[a]Numerical evaluations are not conducted in classes with fewer than 10 students unless requested by the professor

[b]Scale is based on 1 as Strongly Disagree and 5 as Strongly Agree

A list of the eight common questions and a few of the possible feedback questions included in student evaluations can be found in Appendix D. In this evaluation system, students also respond to two open-ended questions requesting their opinion about the things they liked best in class and what they think should be done to improve the class. Some student evaluation narratives from the past two years can be seen in Appendix E.

In addition, I ask my students to write "minute papers." These papers are written at the end of class one day of each week. Some are anonymous so that students can say things that they might otherwise hesitate to say. On others, names are used. With these papers, students can reflect on what we are discussing in class, relate other experiences to the class, and let me know what is going well and what is not. The minute papers also give me an opportunity to find out what students have misunderstood and clarify concepts in class. In their end-of-semester comments, students mentioned the minute papers as follows:

- "I like the minute papers because it makes me think and open up on paper."
- "I found that when you responded to minute papers it was helpful to better understand the topic."

Teaching Achievements

In my years of teaching I have been awarded the Outstanding Teacher of the Year in my college twice. I have been selected as a Senior Teaching Fellow and to the Instructional Technology Leadership Program. Also, based on student nominations, I have been included in *Who's Who Among America's Teachers* for two years. However, the greatest rewards for me are found in anonymous student comments like these:

- "I like this class so far. I like the way tests are done and appreciate having the quizzes for extra credit/review of topics. I think the physical development paper was graded a lot harder than I expected, but oh well, I've learned a lot so far!"
- "This class was very interesting. The debates were aggravating, but they encouraged me to think about issues I wouldn't normally think about."
- "I love how caring she seems. She comes off as *really* caring about her students and their success which is much more than most other professors! I love this and greatly appreciate it!"

And from an email on October 1, 2007:

Many years ago, 1983 I recall, you worked with me on my dissertation committee as chair of the reading committee and stats guru! . . . When I talk with folks about my dissertation experience, I tell stories about how you were so gracious, helpful, smart, and gifted in working with me on my research. I do so to underscore the importance of getting wonderful people like you on their committees. For me, the dissertation was the highlight of my doctoral study and working with you was a very significant factor in that enjoyment.

Research

I fell in love with research in the mid-1970s. It provided a way to create new knowledge in ways that were much more systematic than organizing my thoughts into logical wholes. It was seductive. I began by studying **adolescent sexuality and pregnancy.** I was able to demonstrate that the old view that early, unintended pregnancy was a function of income and race was not true. I could see the **advantage of using statistics in order to conceptualize** at higher levels. I found ways to use statistics to represent highly complex concepts related to individuals and families. Papers that represent my research can be seen in Appendix F.

I also recognized that it would be necessary to understand the **cognitive processes** that organize our attitudes, beliefs, and behaviors if I was ever going to understand adolescents. Toward that end, I began studying cognition in adolescents with several students. Each one brought me to a new level of understanding; it was my students' enthusiasm that helped me maintain interest. It culminated in, for example, one student's paper that was accepted for publication without revisions and two papers that won "top three paper" awards from national and international communications associations.

As those students moved on, I went back to a topic that is dear to me. I gave rein to my interest in law, and searched for rhetoric in United States Supreme Court decisions about the position of **children and families in the law.** I studied and wrote about parenthood and sexuality from the perspective of case law. A new world of thinking was opened and I worked in it for years.

International Work

In 1989, I met a sociologist from Moscow, USSR, who wanted to do a **comparative study of families** in the Soviet Republic of Georgia and the state of Georgia, USA. I was enchanted with the opportunity and went to Moscow to develop a team of researchers in the Soviet Union (Russia and Georgia) and Poland to work with my team in Georgia. With our cultural and language differences (there was never one person in the room who spoke all the languages in the room), it took us two years to develop a questionnaire. We collected our data (approximately two thousand couples) over a one year period, organized and cleaned it over a year period, and began the process of presenting and publishing at a meeting in Germany. I met one of my best friends during this process. I still work with colleagues in both Russia and Poland (all of our Georgian colleagues died before the dawn of the twenty-first century). I am now studying poverty with my colleague and friend in Poland.

It was my work on this project that cultivated my **interest in diversity.** That seems like such an obvious statement, but I learned what we all know but rarely really think about: there are more differences within countries than between countries; the similarities in people across countries are quite great. There were, of course, differences, but it was necessary for me to go back to my old interest in statistics to find them. Teasing out differences that were relevant was an exciting process.

Personally, my life was changed by this research. I sat for hours with colleagues trying to get the nuances of concepts from their perspective. After so many hours, we continued to find discrepancies in our assumptions. We began to understand each other more than we understood those who were not in our group. We were an interesting example of the concept of an in-group: the similarities and differences of people within the group are much better understood than are people in other groups.

Editorial Work

In addition to my experience with research, I have served as Assistant to the Editor of *Family Relations* for six years, and I served as a referee for about ten journals. A list of these journals can be seen in Appendix G. In my view, editorial work is important for at least three reasons: it teaches you to write, it helps you stay abreast of new thinking and new issues in your field, and it provides insight into who are the best resources on relevant topics in the field. I have found that not only was my research improved by editorial work, so was my teaching! I was aware of new views as they were being formulated, and working with authors helped me make abstract, jargon-filled articles more personal and more interesting for students.

Professional Organizations

I belonged to, attended conferences, and presented papers at six professional organizations over my career. Most notably, I spent years working with the premier organization for the study of families, the National Council on Family Relations. I served as the Chair of the Research and Theory Section, on the Board of Directors, as Secretary of the Board of Directors, Chair of the Strategic Planning Committee, and **finally as President.** It was some of the most challenging and engaging work I have undertaken. **I believed that the organization made a difference in the quality of research that was done on families. I still believe it.**

A list of organizations and my involvement in those organizations can be found in Appendix H.

Service

University

A lot of my service time has been spent in service to the university. Primarily I spent time on computing, curriculum, international development, and an emerging Women's Studies Program. I served on the Computer Advisory Committee from its inception in the early 1980s. For most of those years, I was the only woman on the committee and the only person with an end-user perspective (as opposed to a programming or technical perspective). Similarly, I was instrumental in writing the grant proposal for the Agency for International Development (AID) Title XII Strengthening Grant. This was the beginning of campus-wide development of international programs and activities. There had been international activities for years, especially in agriculture, but this grant was the beginning of the push to involve all colleges and departments in international programs. Looking at international programs today and the support for such programs is amazing. In the early days, deans often believed that supporting international programs would drain resources and weaken existing programs. I repeatedly heard this argument as I worked with them to consider international programs to be integral to their colleges. Currently, international involvement is important for the credibility of colleges, and it is expected and valued as an indicator of excellence for tenure and promotion.

In the same period of time, the UGA Women's Studies Program has grown from a few affiliated faculty to an institute that is respected across campus for its scholarship. Although not as directly instrumental in its growth, it was my pleasure to play a supportive role to several program directors, to serve on and/or chair the Steering Committee and the Curriculum Committee for about six years.

Reflecting on these activities, I think some of my best work was done here. These were times and efforts that needed vision and hard work. I felt strongly that I could make a difference with these colleagues, and I worked hard with them. Some of my closest professional friends were developed in this work.

In addition to these efforts, there were years of work with the University Curriculum Committee where we dealt with all aspects of managing curriculum on a large, complex campus. Although it took a lot of time, because of the centralized nature of the university during those years, this committee was central to the academic mission of the university. But this work also helped me because I learned about programs all over campus and met faculty associated with those programs.

Also, in my work as an Associate Dean, I was very active in what is now the American Association for Family and Consumer Sciences. I worked with accreditation for four years as a member of the Council for Accreditation, and I chaired the Accreditation Appeals Committee for two years. At the same time I was very active in the Association of Administrators of Home Economics. The work I did in these two organizations I consider to be some of my best contributions to my field.

Community

In the community I worked with educators in mental and physical health on problems of adolescent sexuality and pregnancy. We then worked to convince community agency administrators of the need for services for adolescents, we designed services, and we worked with schools on the development of sex education. It has been awhile since I was involved in that work, but recently I came full circle and began working with a Board of Education task force that is redesigning the sex education curriculum in our public school system.

A more detailed list of University committees and community activities can be seen in Appendix I.

Integration

To me, teaching is an important part of scholarship. It involves academic detective work that I enjoy so much, but it has the added advantage of working with people who appreciate me. Please do not misunderstand; I have encountered many students who do not like me. They are critical of me, often seem to hear the opposite of what I say, and seem to interpret what I do very differently from other students. I worry about this. It is much more reinforcing to watch as understanding dawns in a student's eyes and passion for the subject gains a toehold. I plant seeds. I love to see them grow. But whether I can see them grow or not, I trust that some good will come for them. I cannot imagine anything that I could have done that would have been more rewarding.

As I reflect on my years of research, I am both enthralled and disappointed. I wish I could have conformed to a program of study; I know now how important that is for contributing to a body of knowledge. At the same time, I have loved my journey.

I have been enthusiastic about my own work, and I have been flexible enough to facilitate the work of students whose ideas do not match mine. I think my greatest contribution has been through my students who have carved their own niches both because of me and in spite of me.

As I reflect on my years of service, I am most proud of my work in the National Council on Family Relations and the Association of Administrators of Home Economics. I think my commitment to those organizations was important, but I think my dedication to maintaining openness to new ways to conceptualize old and emerging issues was even more important. Sometimes I got ahead of myself—and everyone else—but my loyalty to that approach was valuable.

Three Goals I Accomplished

So what have I accomplished? I have lived a very full life of complex good times and complex bad times. All have served me well. Many involved mentoring students. Helping students think more clearly about whom they are and what they wanted from what they were doing has been a theme in my life. Recently, a former student reported to me that another student said to her as their Ph.D. commencement was ending, "I am so sad. No one will ever care about my thinking the way that Lynda does." I regret her sadness, but her comment is an excellent summary of what I have tried so hard to do throughout my life.

Belonging to the National Council on Family Relations and working with colleagues there so that they eventually had the confidence in me to elect me as their president was a great accomplishment for me. Being president was great, but being elected president was amazing and so very reaffirming!

My research in the former Soviet Union and in Poland is another accomplishment that I value. That I ever got involved is an overwhelming thought. My first trip to Russia was made by myself at the behest of a man I had discussed a project with in a bar in Philadelphia. It was 1989; if he had not met me at the airport in Moscow, I would have had no recourse but to get on the next flight back to the States. But I felt confident—perhaps not reasonable, but confident. This unrestrained action lead to what is now eighteen years of work with colleagues in Russia and Poland and some of my best friendships.

The notion of an accomplishment is thought provoking. Accomplishments are neither pinnacles nor singular events. They are inherent to action; they are embedded in a body of work and take their importance from the whole. It concerns me when accomplishments are viewed out of context because the value of an accomplishment is in the process of getting there.

The Future

I am retiring soon, but I expect to continue mentoring new faculty and graduate students in the Department of Child and Family Development. I have a couple of students who will not finish until some time during the year after I retire. Also, I have close relationships with new faculty that I expect to continue for many years.

A related goal is my interest in inspiring curiosity about everything in life, including academics. I would also like to work with child care center personnel to encourage them to talk with children. I do not mean guiding them or telling them what to do; I mean chatting, the kind of talk that is so important for structuring the brain for learning. I also want to foster a focused curiosity about children so that workers will be less likely to rely on "common wisdom" regarding appropriate practices with children.

I intend to continue writing, but not academic writing. I want to use my knowledge to write poetry that will challenge the assumptions of readers. What a surprise to me! I found that the best way to tell a student what he or she had meant to me was to write a poem about the person. Now, when one of my graduate students completes a degree, I present them with my photograph of a flower that reminds me of them and a poem that describes both the flower and the person.

Reflections

I spent the first ten years of my post-Ph.D. career as Associate Dean in the College of Family and Consumer Sciences. During those years, my mind was flooded with work, and it was difficult to stretch beyond the daily expectations. The thing I am most proud of from those years was the development of the computer laboratory in my college. We started with my personal computer, a used Osborne, the first truly "portable" computer, and a half-time statistical programmer. We became a model laboratory on campus. We began with a clear vision of computers as a tool for faculty and students, not a new career for them. To my great pleasure, that position has been upheld since my tenure as Associate Dean.

Thinking of the "flowers" in my life, occasionally I hear from a former student. I am amazed at what they do. I love remembering my time with students: learning how to think as they did so that I could edit their papers effectively, helping them hone their ideas into researchable questions, challenging them to do things they never believed possible, helping them find humor in their/ our personal craziness, helping them hold on to their souls, recognizing what they cared about. People have always exhausted me, but they are also exhilarating. I am grateful to know that these relationships will never end and that new ones will continue to form.

I have written all of this without mention of my family. I am grateful for all of my family, but especially my daughter Anna. She has taught me (maybe demanded) that I am human and that it is okay. We know together the importance of holding on.

I would also like to mention that the process of writing this legacy portfolio has brought a different but welcome focus to my professional and personal life. I deeply appreciate the invitation to write it.

Appendixes

A. List of Graduate Students

B. Examples of Course Syllabi

C. Explanation of Extra Credit Quizzes

D. Questions Used in Course Evaluations

E. Student Evaluation Narratives

F. Publications and Presentations

G. Editorial Work

H. Professional Organizations and Involvement

I. University Committees and Community Activities

Education

Robert M. Maninger

College of Education

Texas Christian University

Fall 2008

Table of Contents

Purpose

The purpose of this portfolio is to outline and document the evidences of my professional career, at TCU and otherwise. I believe that it will provide confirmation that my teaching, scholarship, service, and professional development are worthy of tenure. I spent my first year at TCU as a Visiting Lecturer, and have been tenure-track since the 2004–2005 academic year. I have made progress in all areas of my faculty activities and this is but a highlight of these activities. Herein readers will find not only the "what" but also the "why" to my journey at TCU.

Teaching

Teaching Responsibilities

The following chart describes the course load that I teach. The name and catalogue number of the course, typical enrollment, required/nonrequired status, and the level of the course are provided. This illustrates that a "full load" is normal for my teaching.

Title	Number	Average Enrollment	Type	Graduate or Undergraduate
Technology Applications in Education	EDUC 50253	15–26	Required/ Elective	Graduate
Critical Investigations: Teaching and Learning	EDUC 20003	75–130	Required	Undergraduate
Trends and Issues in Educational Administration	EDAD 60133	30–45	Elective	Graduate
Early Childhood: Social Studies	EDEC 30234	60–70	Required	Undergraduate
Educational Psychology	EDUC 30123	30–45	Required	Undergraduate
Principal TExES Exam Seminar		10–15	Elective	Graduate

Undergraduate Advising

I serve twenty-five undergraduate students as their adviser. We meet as needed and determine their progress toward their degree, or their quest to become accepted into the College of Education. I utilize all of the TCU forms and the opinions of my colleagues to meet the advising needs of individual students.

Philosophy and Objectives

I truly do wish to pass the torch to the next generation of educators, to generate a group of uncommon thinkers, and to arm them to ask questions of everything they know. I fully intend to improve the instructional methods of preservice teachers. I enjoy introducing preservice teachers to the profession that I love and encouraging them from the outset to strive to be passionate about what they do as a teacher. I feel that this passion will drive them to be teachers who wish to improve the methodology of their instruction. Then, when I have the opportunity to teach them software packages and applications, they will see the advantages and use this understanding wisely in their future careers.

This is more than just rhetoric because my colleague in the College of Education, Dr. Sue Anderson, and I have substantiated statistically significant improvement in students' abilities, value beliefs, self-efficacy, and intentions to use software. I also have the same approach with the EDAD [educational administration] students in that one of my primary goals is to exhort them to become campus level instructional leaders who have a passion for what they do. It is my desire to inspire students to think, to question their thinking, and to plan for their future.

I have several objectives for the courses that I teach. I want preservice teachers to:

- Know about the profession on at least a minimal level.
- Make educated decisions on whether or not they want to teach. I then want them to evaluate their journey and decide the level to which they are best suited.
- Understand the history, policies and laws, ethics, and unwritten rules of education in order to form a foundation on which they can build.

- Have a working knowledge of a variety of educational software and understand how to best integrate the use of these software packages into their future classroom.
- Understand and apply to their best ability the common theories of psychology, especially as they relate to children.

Methodology

A variety of methodologies are used to accomplish these objectives. I use a teacher-centered method of instruction such as lecture when there is a large group, or when there is new and unknown information that must be communicated. My preference is to use a more Socratic method of lecture in which I ask questions and engage the audience in discussion, rather than the lecture models that call for simple recitation of information. In this I also utilize a variety of technologies including PowerPoint, the Internet, and handheld remote devices. The goal is to model the kind of behavior I expect from them when they are in the classroom.

A number of small group tactics are utilized. I use research-based cooperative learning strategies that require participation by everyone in the group. Small group instructional methods are used for groups ranging from four to twenty. I also use paired groupings of two or three students with some situations.

Case studies are used in group settings to stimulate students thinking about real-world problems that they will one day face. The use of hands-on instructional methods is very important to me, and I use this style of teaching often. Being a risk taker when it comes to methodology, I am willing to try new things if I see the relevance to the students' ability to grasp concepts and make connections. Feedback is one of the critical junctures of teaching that allows me to celebrate their knowledge or redirect their thinking as they form valuable analysis of the material. Student engagement itself is critical, and I try different methods in order to maintain their attention and their engagement in the lesson.

eCollege as a Companion

eCollege is used extensively in my teaching. Student reading assignments are posted, they conduct threaded discussions (an asynchronous style of conversation), helpful information is posted, students have access to their grades, and the dropbox is used for their assignments to be turned in—and returned. I really value writing with my students, and this gives me the opportunity to do that. Utilizing the "track changes" tool in MS Word, we can insert comments and talk back and forth to each other and do it all electronically. I think this helps me establish a deeper professional relationship with my students, and it allows me the opportunity to develop their critical thinking skills.

Curricular Revision

I have not come to the end of a semester in which I did not make changes in the courses I will teach for the next semester. One way that I have consistently revised course work is through eCollege. I stay current in my own reading so that I can update case studies and examples so that they will be fresh and relevant. I made changes in some classes to improve the rigor and the content to better fulfill the objectives set for each course.

At the request of faculty and administration, my colleague in the College of Education Sue Anderson and I developed EDUC 50263 Cybercommunication in Education to be offered opposite the English department offering of Cyber-Literacy. We found that even though the secondary English/language arts majors were required to take this course, it was not being offered in a timely manner for their degree progress. This course has passed through Undergraduate Council and is now scheduled.

Course Syllabi

What I do that differs from other faculty is to require students to make a connection with the school community and celebrate the diversities that lie therein. Usually this is accomplished through a field-based component that is attached to all my courses. An excerpt from the final observation report for the EDUC 20003 course is as follows: "Final Report Description: This must include an overall reflection on and evaluation of the field-based component of this course. This exercise will allow you to analyze diversity within and across cultures. You will also be able to demonstrate an interconnectedness of society and the public schools." Hands-on activities and online activities are highlighted in EDUC 50253 as follows: "Online discussion questions can be found on eCollege. Approximately once a week there will be new questions posted for you to discuss with your classmates online. Competencies: These assignments are designed to give you a minimum level of hands-on experience and practice with the computer applications covered in class." See Appendix A for more detailed course syllabi.

Evaluation of Teaching

The following chart describes TCU Student Perceptions of Teaching (SPOT) course evaluation samples for Spring 2007. The four questions highlighted are drawn from the survey based on what the Dean of the College of Education, Sam Deitz, signifies as the most relevant.

Prompt (Judged on a Likert-Style 1–4 Scale)	Department Average	EDUC 20003 (N = 97)	EDUC 50253 (N = 19)
The instructor provided an intellectually stimulating environment.	3.54	3.77	3.77
The instructor encouraged active student participation.	3.64	3.55	3.85
The instructor treated me with courtesy and respect.	3.74	3.81	4.00
The instructor did a good job in this course.	3.61	3.77	3.92

Student comments often reflect the course objectives, "This course helped me decide that I really wanted to teach, and that I want to teach middle school math." Another student commented, "I better understand how to use software, and that gives me the confidence I need to use it in my own classroom some day." One student said, "I feel challenged to perform at my best when Dr. Maninger puts us in smaller groups."

One of my peer review letters (see Appendix B) is from Dr. Janet Kelly. In her review of my teaching, she comments favorably on my ability to reach out to a large class, keep things motivational and lively, and engage students in the class. There is a peer review conducted by Dr. Elizabeth Taylor in Appendix C. In this review, she comments on my "excellent teaching style and approach to students." Her review of my teaching is very positive, and she highlights my organization, student-centered approach, and multiple modalities of teaching.

I utilize a variety of instructional methodologies, but I always search for more. I offer my students the option to complete a mid-term evaluation, and from this I try to make adjustments in the course if needed to better suit the objectives I have set forth. Through the TCU Koehler Center for Teaching Excellence I have had the opportunity to plan and participate in many developmental workshops. Through these often intimate settings, I have gained understanding and wisdom from colleagues here at TCU as we discuss our course delivery. I have used many tips from PowerPoint delivery to eCollege strategies that I gained from these workshops.

Research and Scholarship

Publications

I have published seven refereed articles, and two more have been accepted and are scheduled to be published this year (See Appendix D for a complete list). The overall themes of my research agenda are technology and educational leadership. My writing centers on several themes. Do technological gadgets improve student achievement? Does a stand-alone technology course serve a purpose in a teacher preparation program?

I am driven to answer the question: "Does this (insert whatever gadget is new/next) improve student achievement?" My practitioner side knows that gadgets are fun, but worthless to instruction if they do not assist students in learning and performing. I have written several articles in pursuit of this question:

- Maninger, R. M. (2004). Test scores of at-risk students enhanced by technology. *Texas Study of Secondary Education, 4,* 28–30. This article is important to me because it was my first publication and because the audience was Texas administrators. If one can impact instruction in the schools, administrators have to be knowledgeable about the innovation.
- Maninger, R. M. (2006). Successful technology integration: Student test scores improved in an English literature course through the use of supportive devices. *TechTrends, 50*(5), 37–45. This publication is meaningful to me because it is my first article that was in a nationally renowned technology journal. (See Appendix E.)

I am also interested in the argument that persists in academia concerning the stand-alone educational technology course. Dr. Sue Anderson and I have conducted two studies to answer the question, "Over the course of the semester what are the changes in, and factors related to, students' abilities, beliefs, and intentions to use technology in their future classrooms?" This research will expand in the future to include a longitudinal study of not only what they intend to do, but what they actually do.

- Maninger, R. M. (2006). A stand-alone technology applications course in preservice teacher preparation. *Journal of European Teacher Educators Network, 2*(1), 3–10. This article is significant to me because it was published in an international journal.
- Maninger, R. M., & Anderson, S. (2007). Beyond skills: Evaluating the impact of educational technology coursework. In Kari Kumpulainen (Ed.), *Educational technology: Opportunities and challenges.* Oulu, Finland: University of Oulu Press. (See Appendix F.)

My research and writing also include an interest in publishing case studies and articles for professors to use in graduate educational administration course work. This writing comes from experiences I have personally had, or from situations I find in the schools now. (See Appendix G for an example article.)

Presentations

Below are two selected presentations. (See Appendix H for a complete list.)

My presentation at the European Teacher Educators Network Conference (February 2006, Leiden, The Netherlands) was titled, "Technology Applications in Preservice Teacher Education." It was a discussion of the research that Dr. Anderson and I have done in our technology applications course.

I copresented with a doctoral student, Mark Bloom, and our topic was "Examining Handheld Technology in Biology Labs." This presentation was for the International Society for the Scholarship of Teaching and Learning in Washington, D.C., November 2006.

Grant Support Received

- Maninger, R. M. (2004). Student Success Through Handheld Remote Technology. Instructional Development Grant Fund, TCU. (funded, $610)
- Maninger, R. M. (2002). Celebration of Teaching. Kappa Delta Pi International Education Society. (funded, $500)

Doctoral Candidate Advising

I supervise two doctoral candidates. I am the major professor for Doug Funk, a candidate for an M.B.A./Ed.D. He is currently entering into the dissertation phase having completed his course work. I serve on Shawntel Landry's doctoral committee and advise her on the direction that her technology-specific research is taking. Shawntel is approximately halfway through her degree plan.

Service

The highlight of my service to the TCU campus is my association with the Koehler Center for Teaching Excellence. The primary position that I held during the 2006–2007 school year was to serve on the committee charged with the Koehler Center Director Search. During the year and a half of our successful search, I also served as a Koehler Center for Teaching Excellence Faculty Consultant. In this position, my co-consultants and I planned and conducted: New Faculty Workshops, and *On-Line Insights* magazine.

I served as a committee member on the Adams Chair Search Committee that hired my peer, Dr. Molly Weinburgh, for the position. I take great pride in the fact that we looked at many respectable candidates and were able to see that one of our own was better qualified and already making the relationships necessary to succeed in this position. (See Appendix I for a complete list.)

Service-Learning

I have been a member of Kappa Delta Pi International Honor Society in Education (KDP) since 2000, and since coming to TCU I have been a co-sponsor for three years. In the 2006–2007 academic year, I became the sole sponsor of Kappa Delta Pi. I chose this avenue for service primarily for the opportunity to enrich relationships with students and as a sentiment of what I owe to the society for the things KDP has done for me personally. It is through KDP that I have started to have an impact on the TCU community through service-learning. KDP accomplishes at least two service-learning projects in a year. These projects include fundraising on campus and then using the money raised to provide resources to a local elementary school.

Integration of Professional Work and Goals

Professional Accomplishments

1. I am especially proud of my role of contributing to the leadership of the Koehler Center and have participated in planning, directing, scheduling workshops and conversation communities,

and emceeing the events. In doing so I developed important relationships across the TCU campus.

2. College of Education Dean Sam Deitz sending me to The Netherlands to speak at the international ETEN conference is an accomplishment that gives me great pride. This activity resulted in not only a presentation, but also built several relationships that resulted in an article publication and a book chapter publication. The fact that this was on an international scale is very important to me.

3. My work with master's degree students who are participating in my seminars to prepare for the state TExES exam for certification as a principal has given me a considerable sense of pleasure. To date, 95 percent of my students have been successful.

Professional Goals

I want to further develop the doctoral studies program in Educational Administration for the College of Education at TCU. I see the opportunity to make a significant impact on the education of tens of thousands of schoolchildren through these efforts. This includes the growth of the program and the attainment of grant money to provide resources. I see this taking several years to accomplish.

With colleagues, I am working on a book of case studies. We envision this book being different in stylistic approach from the normal educational administration-type case study collections. We expect to have the book completed by the end of 2008.

I want to collect statements from peers and administrators commenting on the importance of my research to the discipline and expect to do so in the spring of 2008.

Through my contacts in four professional societies, I want to pursue an editorial position in a major publication of at least one of them.

Appendixes

Appendix A: Course Syllabi Examples

Appendix B: Observation Letter by Dr. Janet Kelly

Appendix C: Observation Letter by Dr. Elizabeth Taylor

Appendix D: List of Publications

Appendix E: TechTrends Article

Appendix F: Educational Technology Coursework book chapter

Appendix G: Lincoln Middle School EDAD Case Study

Appendix H: List of Presentations

Appendix I: List of Service Activities

Education

Clement A. Seldin

*Department of Teacher Education
    and Curriculum Studies*

*School of Education, University of Massachusetts,
    Amherst*

Fall 2008

Table of Contents

Introduction

My academic career differs from most faculty. I was initially employed as a staff assistant at the University of Massachusetts in 1976. Within three years, I was promoted to Lecturer/Staff Associate and served as Director of Administration for Field-Based Programs. In this role, I gained greater understanding of administrative systems while working closely with School of Education deans to provide support and management for off-campus graduate programs. During this period, I conducted two national studies focused on off-campus in-service activities. Both were published in professional journals (see Appendix A, Scholarship).

Along with my administrative responsibilities, I taught one undergraduate course every semester, served on faculty committees, and advised many students. My dual role of administrator and faculty member provided a full and dynamic university career. However, after many years, I decided to pursue a professorial role full time. I was appointed Lecturer and a few years later, in 1991, the position became a tenure track Associate Professorship. In 1994, I was awarded tenure and promoted to full professor in 1998.

My thirty years of teaching and concurrent thirteen years as an administrator at the University of Massachusetts have afforded me with a unique perspective. My knowledge and understandings have scope and dimension, which provides a broad foundation from which to teach, research, and serve my program, department, school, and the university.

Teaching
Responsibilities

In recent years, I have taught the following courses:

Course	Level	Enrollment	Status
Social Foundations of Education[a]	Undergraduate	25–30	Elective
Social Foundations of Education: Honors	Undergraduate	10–14	Elective
Controversial Issues in Education	Undergraduate	25–30	Elective
Foundations: An Urban Perspective	Undergraduate	20–25	Required
Field Experience[b]	Undergraduate	22–28	Elective
Controversial Issues in Education	Graduate	25–30	Required

[a]Two sections each fall and spring.
[b]With graduate assistant.

As noted, my teaching responsibilities are primarily focused on undergraduate education. Teaching assignments are centered broadly on foundations of education and provide appropriate academic background for the Collaborative Teacher Education Program (CTEP), a master's licensure program in elementary and early childhood education; the Elementary Teacher Education Graduate Program; and the general Minor in Education. My courses are framed on a vigorous knowledge/research base and I use a blend of lecture, discussion, and problem solving.

Philosophy

Eight principles provide fundamental structure for me as teacher and learner. They serve as a strategic filter through which I shape my courses and advising, research, and service activities.

For decades, they have helped maintain my sense of balance and professional direction.*

- Growth is developmental and requires time and patience. We are the agents of our own growth.
- Teachers must focus on strengths and use positive feedback to help learners grow academically, socially, and emotionally.
- Critical thinking helps students internalize learning.
- Structure and shared decision making are significant to the learning process.
- Success stimulates further success.
- Teachers must strive to meet all learner needs and be keenly aware of social, emotional, and physical variables that affect the learning process.
- Teachers and learners must value diversity and seek unity in a multi-cultural nation.
- All teachers must seek continuous renewal and growth.

The Socratic dialogue is used in my classes—a method of argument and proof using a question and answer approach. I developed a series of case studies to encourage debate and critical thinking. These multifaceted case studies focus on contemporary problems to which students can easily relate. Given their diverse backgrounds, students bring unique perspectives to class that create a fertile environment to explore various issues represented in the case studies. I want them to appreciate the complexity of every issue. My aim is to illuminate the conclusion that being an absolutist on controversial issues undermines children and education.

Curricular Revisions

Every academic field is dynamic. Change and growth are often paced and evolutionary—yet sometimes dramatic. In terms of my courses, I strive to incorporate the most up-to-date data and professional perspective. Every semester, I seek new material to modify and/or supplement my courses. This growth is well-illustrated when comparing **Social Foundations** syllabi for spring 2004 to spring 2007 (see Appendix C, Course Syllabi).

---

*Based on the "Belief System" developed by Professor Emeritus R. Mason Bunker.

I also seek new ways to improve the delivery of courses. Perhaps the best example is the use of computer technology in the classroom. Students today are active consumers of technology. Their daily lives are often structured around the computer— a powerful tool to communicate, research, and understand information. Importantly, in the past twenty years, I have steadily increased use of computer technology in my teaching. Currently, it is a fundamental *tool* in all of my classes. Regular use of the Internet and several integrated computer programs (Microsoft PowerPoint, Adobe Dreamweaver Web Development, Adobe Premiere Elements, and Adobe Photoshop Elements) provide a multimedia learning experience. In both informal and formal written student evaluations, students point to my skillful and creative use of technology in classes.

> Professor Seldin's use of technology in the class was outstanding. Kept me on my toes and I learned so much! Concepts and theories of Essentialism, Progressivism, Perennialism all became visually alive.

> I heard that his PowerPoints are amazing. It was so true! He presented important info with colors, music, animations, and humor. Every class made me smile and the technology really helped me learn.

In recent years, I have also significantly expanded evaluation strategies in my courses. Rather than relying on one measure to assess student learning such as testing or research papers, I now include an array of ways for students to demonstrate their learning (see Appendix C, Course Syllabi). In addition to traditional examinations and research papers, I also weigh group and individual presentations, participation, reflection papers, small group interaction, and large class debate. When discussing the grading system in classes, I aim to empower students and guide them to academic success. Extra credit work is offered in all classes. Importantly, I emphasize that quality is more important than quantity. I press students to think and examine underlying rationale for their perspectives. In student evaluations, they commonly describe my grading system as *fair, consistent, and student friendly*. The following quotation from a senior reflects many student comments.

> I was so impressed by your grading system. You used varied approaches and different types of questioning—multiple choice, matching, true/false, short and long essay questions. You carefully evaluated our group work, both large and small. You graded on project work and the quality of participation in class. I know it was a great deal of work for you but you should know how much we all appreciated it. Thank you!

I overheard a former student telling a friend about my Social Foundations course.

> Seldin's "Foundations" is tremendous. You learn so much, it's really fun, but it's very hard to get an A. I wouldn't miss a class for anything!

Course Syllabi

My comprehensive syllabi include course descriptions, specific academic requirements and expectations regarding course organization, examinations, and papers as well as a grading rubric. Required and recommended readings are identified. A detailed weekly breakdown of topics and readings is presented (see Appendix C, Course Syllabi).

I believe that a comprehensive syllabus is a fundamental teaching tool. For students, it provides essential information and expectations about the course on the first day. For the teacher, it is a formal vehicle that conveys a blueprint for the course and expectations for student learning and academic performance. For the academic department, comprehensive syllabi collectively describe the department's curriculum, its scope and focus, and its academic rigor and standards.

Evaluation of Teaching

Student evaluations are vital to me as a teacher. I rely on a two-prong approach to gaining student feedback. I regularly administer the university's Student Response to Instruction (SRTI) evaluation form that focuses on both the course and the instruction. In addition, I routinely request anonymous written student assessments at both the halfway mark and the conclusion of courses. This approach provides longitudinal statistical and descriptive data focused on both presentation and content.

Evaluations are consistently at the highest levels in all categories (see Appendix D, Student Evaluations—SIRI). Illustrative of my very positive student evaluations are the ratings by 850 undergraduate and graduate students in all courses taught during the past five-year period. Mean student ratings on scale from 1 (*almost never*) to 5 (*almost always*) follow:

Instructor was well prepared for class	4.95
Instructor explained course material clearly	4.96
Instructor used class time well	4.93
Instructor inspired interest in the subject matter	4.92
Instructor provided useful feedback	4.88
Instructor stimulated useful participation	4.93
Overall rating of instructor's teaching	4.95
Overall rating for course	4.92

Anonymous student evaluation narratives reveal significant strengths of my courses and instruction (see Appendix E, Student Evaluations—Narratives). Representative examples from different classes in the past five-year period follow:

Throughout our amazing semester, you have repeatedly pointed out my academic strengths, gave me superior critical feedback on my work, and helped me to become more knowledgeable and confident. Thank you for your commitment and dedication to education and your students.

———————

Simply the best course at UMass! I had no idea there was so much to learn but you made every class fascinating. The lectures, discussions, readings, and debates were outstanding. I never missed a class. See you in the spring for another course!

———————

Dr. Seldin is by far the most dynamic and captivating professor I have ever had. It is eminently clear that he loves teaching and is genuinely concerned with each and every one of his students. My only regret is that I will not be able to take another class taught by Dr. Seldin and that there aren't more professors like him.

Administrator and Colleague Comments

> The evaluations of his teaching have been routinely superlative. The monotonous regularity of these exemplary evaluations is a part of the lore of our school of education.—Professor Ernest Washington, Chair, Department Personnel Committee

---

> I know of no one in the School of Education who cares more about his students or expects more educational growth from his students than Clement Seldin.—Former Academic Dean Ronald Fredrickson

---

> In my more than thirty-five years of involvement as a professional educator at both the public and university levels, I have not met an individual that I hold in higher regard professionally than I do Mr. Seldin.—Former Division Chair William J. Masalski

Teaching Honors

Over the years, I have been honored to receive many teaching awards at the University of Massachusetts including the **Order of Omega Teaching Award,** the **College Outstanding Teacher Award,** and the **Mortar Board Award for Outstanding Teaching.** But I am most proud of the **University of Massachusetts Distinguished Teaching Award** (DTA) which I received early in my career. This prestigious award is presented each year to only three faculty members (of 1400) at the university (see Appendix F, Teaching Awards).

Reflective Statement

I often reflect on how fortunate I am to have found a profession that provides a multitude of personal and professional rewards. I feel elated when I receive letters from former students who express genuine appreciation for my teaching, advising, and general support. I derive great pleasure from the challenge of designing a new component to a course and witnessing the nods and expressions of understanding on the faces of my students.

On the first day of every class, I tell my students, "You are my priority." They are. My responsibility as teacher is profound. I strive to improve content and delivery and to teach at my highest level every day. John F. Kennedy said, "The exemplary teacher instructs in realities and suggests dreams." That is my mission.

Research

For most of my academic career, my research agenda has focused primarily on problems in American public education. Specifically, I have worked to examine authentic problems that affect the lives of students and teachers. I explore the complexity of these problems, make connections, and suggest realistic solutions. This research focus is evident in my scholarship and in presentations to colleagues in higher education, teachers and parents.

Scholarship Reviews

Virtually all of his work [Dr. Seldin] is directly related to the work of the school of education, to his teaching, and to changing conditions in schools. In my view, that is exactly what a professor of education ought to be studying and publishing.—Director Richard Wisniewski, Institute for Educational Innovation, The University of Tennessee, Knoxville

---

It is this sense of social responsibility that seems to be thematic throughout his works. Yet, in Dr. Seldin's commitment to social responsibility, his work is never self-righteous or rigid. It provides criticism and constructive alternatives. His accurate criticism is balanced, well conceptualized, and has a logical framework that makes his writing appealing to academe or to public school educators. This unique ability is rarely found.—Professor Raymond L. Calabrese, Wichita State University, Kansas

---

His work truly exemplifies Ernest Boyer's definition of scholarship in *Scholarship Reconsidered*,". . . the work of the scholar . . . means stepping back from one's investigation, looking for connections, building bridges between theory and practice, and communicating one's knowledge effectively to students."—Professor Constance M. Perry, University of Maine

For three decades I have engaged in many research projects, published research in approximately thirty refereed journals, written several book chapters (see Appendix A, Scholarship), and many magazine and newspaper articles in the popular press. A sample of journals includes:

- *Educational Research Quarterly*
- *Kappa Delta Pi Record*
- *Curriculum Report*
- *Capstone Journal of Education*
- *Phi Delta Kappan*
- *High School Journal*
- *Journal for Middle Level and High School Administrators*
- *Bulletin of Educational Research (England)*
- *Journal of Educational Media & Library Sciences (China)*

Approximately forty research papers have been presented at numerous local, state, regional, and national conferences, including the New England Educational Research Organization and the American Educational Research Association (see Appendix B, Presentations).

In recent years, two research involvements have emerged as most significant and satisfying: the Schools of Education Research Project directed by Arthur Levine, Former President of Teachers College, Columbia University; and The Teaching Portfolio Program at institutions of higher education in the United States.

Schools of Education Research Project

As stated by Dr. Arthur Levine, the goal of this four-year study funded by Annenberg, Ford, and Kauffman Foundations is to "cut through all the rhetoric and criticism about schools of education and to look at the underlying reality. We plan to describe education schools, to look at what they do well, to discuss what they could do better, and, where useful, to make recommendations for future direction."

In addition to serving on site-visit research teams to almost every region of the country, I prepared monographs and contributed to three major reports (see Appendix G, Schools of Education Research Project Executive Summaries):

Educational Leadership: http://www.edschools.org/reports_
leaders.htm

Teacher Education: http://www.edschools.org/teacher_report.htm

Educational Research: http://www.edschools.org/
    EducatingResearchers/educating_researchers.pdf

Special Note: This research project provided the unique opportunity to work closely with a remarkable professional, the late
Alvin Sanoff. Al was Project Manager for this four-year research
program. He was the former managing editor of *U.S. News and
World Report*'s "America's Best Colleges" and "America's Best
Graduate Schools" and a valued consultant to many colleges and
universities. Al was my mentor. I learned every time I was with
this extraordinary man.

The Teaching Portfolio Program

This unique program has provided the opportunity to spend
intensive days at many colleges and universities in the United
States including Emory University, Miami University, and Brigham
Young University. As a member of on-site academic teams, I mentor professors who are developing their teaching portfolios, an
invaluable documentation in tenure, promotion, or reappoint-
ment reviews. For some senior faculty, portfolios have been
designed as "legacy portfolios" to help departments address future
personnel and programmatic needs. This is an exciting opportunity to work at a national level with other professionals as they
develop their teaching portfolios.

The Schools of Education and Portfolio projects have provided rare opportunities to engage in professional activity at a
range of institutions in all regions of the country, from prestigious small private schools to large state institutions. I consider
these to be peak experiences of my academic career.

Service

As a member of the faculty, I have actively engaged in both professional public service and university service. I have sought
opportunities to serve on various committees from department
level to the larger institution and to extend my professional activities beyond the university campus.

Department of Teacher Education and Curriculum Studies

I have served on and chaired both the Academic Matters Committee and the Personnel Committee. Meetings range from weekly to monthly depending on the nature of the tasks.

School of Education

I have served on and chaired an array of School of Education committees including the School Personnel Committee, Academic Matters, Undergraduate Task Force, and the Outstanding Future Educator Award Committee. Meetings range from weekly to monthly depending on the nature of the tasks.

Kappa Delta Pi International Honor Society

For twenty-five years, I have served as the faculty adviser to the UMass chapter of Kappa Delta Pi (KDP). Under my direction, the UMass Chapter has designed workshops, sponsored events, managed scholarships, and given awards to School of Education faculty and students. Our annual May Initiation Dinner generally attracts over 100 students, parents, and guests. I built the KDP Web site and manage it with the Executive Board (http://people.umass.edu/caseldin/kdp2/index.html). Executive Board meetings are generally monthly in the fall and biweekly during the spring semester.

Collaborative Teacher Education Program

In recent years, I have become fascinated by the power and impact of the World Wide Web. After course work in Web design and graphic imaging at the Office of Information Technologies at UMass, and extensive work with the Instructional Media Lab on campus, I designed a personal Web site (http://people.umass.edu/caseldin/) as well as a comprehensive Web site for the Collaborative Teacher Education Program (CTEP) (http://www.umass.edu/ctep/). I have been very gratified by the student and faculty response to the CTEP site. It has been described as *very professional, user-friendly,* and *enormously helpful.*

The University

I have served on the University Committee on Admissions and Records, University Career Center Furcolo Award Committee for Outstanding Internships, University Career Center and Experiential

Learning Faculty Advisory Board, and the Undergraduate Council of the Faculty Senate. I am also a Judicial Hearing Officer. Most university committees meet monthly, although subcommittee work has been more frequent.

Each year, the UMass Center for Teaching sponsors a TA Orientation Program. I have regularly presented a workshop titled, Course Design, the Syllabus, and the First Day of Class, every August/September since 1989.

In addition to serving on School of Education doctoral committees, I have served as an outside member of doctoral committees in other departments such as the Clinical Psychology Department, where I have had the opportunity to assist the academic development of clinical research at the advanced level.

New England and Beyond

At a regional level, I served as a board member and Massachusetts Representative to the **New England Educational Research Organization** (NEERO), which sponsors annual conferences in New England states. NEERO is a regional research organization with approximately two hundred members from institutions of higher education, public and private schools, state and local educational agencies, health and social service agencies, and private education firms. And at a national level, I serve on the **Editorial Advisory Board** for the **Northeast Foundation for Children,** which is the developer of the Responsive Classroom approach and offers professional development, services, and materials for educators. As a board member, I help review publication goals and marketing for publications, as well as consider manuscripts for publication. Finally, like many other faculty, I have regularly reviewed manuscripts for publication for publishing companies such as Allyn and Bacon, McGraw-Hill, and Harcourt School Publishers.

Integration of Professional Activities
Growth and Development

Reflecting on my academic career at the University of Massachusetts, I feel fortunate and honored: fortunate because the School of Education has provided encouragement to grow and pursue avenues of professional opportunity, and honored because I have had the pleasure to work with many talented students, teachers, and researchers.

Personal and professional growth provides the underpinning for a successful academic career. The courses I have taught, the research projects in which I have participated, and the service arenas I have pursued are dynamic, creative, and stimulating. The fundamental academic responsibilities of teaching, research, and service exist symbiotically. Often one area will stimulate another and lead to a third. For example, teaching Social Foundations of Education courses required a comprehensive historical and philosophical understanding of teacher training in the United States. This knowledge base led to a serious investigation of how teachers are trained in different states. Research and writing followed that resulted in articles that stressed the importance of selectivity and rigor in teacher training, which appeared in both professional journals and the popular press. This also led to presentations at research conferences (see Appendix A, Scholarship, and Appendix B, Presentations). Finally, the national Schools of Education Research Project, focused on schools of education, included a major examination of teacher training. This informed my teaching and provided support for my writing.

Special Accomplishments

It is exceedingly difficult to select professional accomplishments that are emblematic of a career as a professor. Focusing on the past five-year period facilitates this effort to identify three special accomplishments.

1. Student Development

"Mary," a twenty-two-year-old senior, admitted she was a mediocre student (2.2 GPA) who did not focus on her studies, yet she wanted to enroll in Social Foundations. From her first writing assignment, it was clear that she sorely lacked basic writing skills. After three weeks, I suggested that Mary and I talk. This was the beginning of weekly meetings throughout the semester during which we would carefully review course material, quizzes, exams, debates, and discussions with particular critical attention to her writing. These weekly hour-long meetings had dramatic impact. By the conclusion of the semester, Mary's writing had improved significantly; she appeared genuinely interested in the course and in learning; she smiled more and interacted in each class with students. Several weeks later, after she had received her well-deserved B grade, she e-mailed me.

> I cannot thank you enough. Your course and all the time you spent with me this semester have been so appreciated and helpful. For the first time in my life, I think of myself as a student with a future. I think of myself as capable of success. Meeting with me each week has changed the way I look at everything. Thank you for your amazing patience, great knowledge, and incredible support. I will always remember you.

2. Program Development

As described earlier, I have become intrigued by the use of technology in the classroom and as a fundamental vehicle for providing important information. Specifically, the Web has become an invaluable tool to describe academic programs, policy and procedures, standards, and key personnel. After six months of research and course work in Web design and graphic imaging and weekly consultation with the Instructional Media Lab at UMass, I built a comprehensive Web site for the Collaborative Teacher Education Program (CTEP): http://www.umass.edu/ctep/. I continue to receive appreciation for this Web work, which has served to educate, inform, and professionalize this academic program.

3. Profession Development

It has been a privilege to serve as a researcher for the national study of schools of education, directed by Dr. Arthur Levine, former president of Teachers College at Columbia University and now president of the Woodrow Wilson National Fellowship Foundation. Working closely with academics and nationally respected journalists was a powerful experience. Every site visit provided new knowledge and insights on schools of education. In addition, the reports I wrote following site visits and the rich information I could bring to my classes made this four-year experience unparalleled in my career.

The Future

Key goals will drive my work in the coming year.

- **Courses:** I plan to continue to customize my courses further and infuse new technology as well as new content perspectives using video production and editing, guest speakers, and case study development.
- **Program:** Serious Web development is a highly complex, professional activity. I would like to strengthen and expand my web skills through additional study at the Office of Instructional Technologies at UMass. During the year, I hope to improve my CTEP web work, personal web pages, and honor society web sites. I plan to consult with noted academic web developers as well.

Appendixes

Appendix A: Scholarship

Appendix B: Presentations

Appendix C: Course Syllabi

    351 Social Foundations of Education
    351 HO1 Social Foundations of Education: Honors
    492A Controversial Issues in Education
    351U Foundations: An Urban Perspective
    282 Field Experience I
    697R Controversial Issues in Education

Appendix D: Student Evaluations—"Student Response to Instruction" (SRTI)

Appendix E: Student Evaluations—Narratives

Appendix F: Teaching Awards

Appendix G: Schools of Education Research Project Executive Summaries

English

John Zubizarreta
Professor of English
Director of Honors and Faculty Development
Columbia College
Fall 2008

Table of Contents

Portfolio Preface and Rationale

Since the first draft of my teaching portfolio over fifteen years ago, I have invested a considerable amount of my personal and professional energy to the virtue of reflective practice. My effort has been an endeavor that challenges teachers and scholars to improve their influence on students and the academy by continually examining the core principles and practices that distinguish the nature and efficacy of their work.

This professional portfolio has the twin purposes of both improvement and assessment for annual review of my dual responsibilities as professor and administrative leader of the Honors Program and Faculty Development. It is an ongoing, updated tool for strengthening my roles as teacher, scholar, former Dean of Undergraduate Studies, program director, and academic citizen. The portfolio also serves as a frame for reflective analysis of my work with students, colleagues, my discipline, and the college. My primary focus is on how reflection and systematic documentation of my efforts can help me continue to learn and improve as a teacher-scholar and faculty leader in what has been a complex professional career path.

The portfolio contains many reflections and selective samples of evidence, but the following six narrative elements and accompanying appendix materials are essential to understanding the range of my professional achievements:

1. Multiple and diverse responsibilities   Appendixes A, D, G
2. Continual efforts to improve teaching   Appendixes B, F, J
   and learning
3. Emphasis on learning   Appendix J
4. Consistent awards and peer recognition   Appendixes E, K
5. Extensive and current scholarship   Appendixes G, H, I
6. Integrative professional engagement   Appendixes A, F, G

Reflections on Responsibilities

The standard load at the college is four courses each semester, but because of double administrative duties as Director of Honors and Director of Faculty Development, my teaching load is one course per semester (See **Appendix A** for annual faculty self-evaluation report). There have been semesters when, either by choice or by need, I have taught two or three courses in a term. Here is a sampling of my recent teaching loads: In fall 2006, I taught English 310: The Psychological Novel, an honors seminar I designed and taught for the first time. In spring 2007, I taught English 102 (H): Literature and the Mythology of the Hero, using in both classes a Web-based course shell to involve students in partial online course work and learning portfolio development. The main feature of our online engagement was an exciting and productive threaded discussion that received outstanding ratings by students when asked to reflect on their learning in the course. (See additional information about ratings and collected forms in **Appendix B**. Also, **Appendix J** contains samples of student work online, a compelling record of substantial learning and enhanced critical thinking and writing skills.) In 2007–08, my courses have included English 350: The Modern Short Story, an honors course I have taught several times before, and English 102 again as an honors section (see **Appendix F** for sample syllabi).

During recent semesters, I have also advised several English majors and served as co-adviser to many honors students across disciplines. See **Appendix C** for selective acknowledgments of my consulting with both majors and honors students on academic and personal issues, including e-mail and other correspondences from students and alumnae with whom I have worked as mentor and academic adviser this past year and before.

I realize as I reflect on my dizzying schedule and juggling of responsibilities that despite the numerous charges of director- and dean-level administration, I am a teacher by design and by calling. I cannot see myself *not* in the classroom, especially in my role as honors director. One of the facets of my work in honors that has made me and the program so successful is that I maintain an active and intimate connection to students in the classroom, always striving for the innovation inherent in honors education and effective teaching overall. For example, I have taught an interdisciplinary honors senior seminar that was instrumental in moving the institution forward in its mission of incorporating technology into the liberal arts curriculum; the course was linked to a live,

Web-based, interactive telecast. I have incorporated student-mediated midterm assessments, online threaded discussions, reflective learning portfolios, and other new methodologies into recent honors courses (see sample syllabi and assignments in **Appendix F**). Meanwhile, I have served as a first or second mentor to a number of honors senior projects, and I have collaborated frequently with students in making presentations at regional and national honors and disciplinary conferences (see **Appendixes G** and **I** for list and details).

Philosophy of Professional Engagement: Integrating Teaching, Scholarship, Service

Teaching

Philosophy

In my relations with students, I have learned that conscientious mentoring is a necessary dimension of transformative teaching and learning. Delivering information is a function of teaching that the competent teacher can perform. But the outstanding professor knows the value of working patiently with students on personal levels to help them achieve more significant learning. In a sense, the professor teaches more than content; he or she teaches habits of thinking, habits of being. Students discover in the process of engaged and active learning the rewards of controlled inquiry, the value of reasoned discourse, the delight of intellectual curiosity, and an earned respect for the process of questioning knowledge and moving freely among the linked components of learning that involve analysis, comprehension, synthesis, application, and evaluation—all underpinned by the power of reflection.

Methodologies and Outcomes of Student Learning

One example of my intentional focus in and out of the classroom on the value of such a process approach to teaching and learning is my use of self-styled RLMs (reflective learning moments) in my classes. An RLM is an opportunity to stop immediately whatever learning activity is in process—a classroom conversation, an online threaded discussion, an exam, a group project, a prewriting exercise, library research, a field experience—and ask directed questions about what, how, when, where, and why one has learned or not learned. Such recorded reflection deepens learning and makes it more meaningful, applicable, and durable. The impact of RLMs, combined with the use of learning portfolio strategies, has been powerful. **Appendixes B** and **J** include both formative and summative student assessments of the method and samples of student work in learning portfolios and other projects that reveal the positive effects of reflective practice on learning.

Additional details of the various methodologies I explore and use in my teaching to promote reflection, critical thinking, creativity, active learning, and strengthening of fundamental disciplinary skills are developed in my *Teaching Portfolio*. Such strategies include role plays, simulations, case studies, disciplinary exchanges, online threaded discussions, e-mail listservs, lecture, classroom discussion, group work, field experiences, journals, fishbowl observations, gallery walks, guest speakers, peer teaching, and more. The portfolio also documents the learning outcomes of my work by providing descriptions and reflective analyses of a variety of samples of student work in process stages, demonstrating the relationship between my teaching and student learning (see **Appendix F**).

Diverse Sources of Evidence

Such values have directed my commitment to teaching beyond my contractual obligations at the college, for teaching and learning are my core passions, my chief challenges, my greatest rewards. My complete philosophy of teaching, along with detailed evidence of effective practices and reflective analysis of disappointing teaching moments and efforts to improve, are documented in my *Teaching Portfolio*. The narrative portion of the portfolio is included in **Appendix F**, and the complete portfolio with appendixes is available for review on request in either hard copy or digital formats.

Student Evaluations

Because of the importance of both formative and summative feedback from students and peers in yearly professional improvement and evaluation, I emphasize for annual review the following information from student evaluations.

My student ratings continue to be excellent, though I recognize areas for improvement. Here is a summary of quantitative results on selected rating items relevant to my teaching philosophy and course goals. To attain sufficiently meaningful numbers from a contractually reassigned course load, I compile the information from the last two years of English 102(H), a course I teach regularly. The items represent areas that research on student ratings suggests are most appropriate for evaluating teaching performance. I have organized related items on rating forms into five simplified categories for more effective summative review:

Scale *(the lower the average, the stronger the rating)*	
1 Strongly agree *2 Agree* *3 Disagree* *4 Strongly disagree* *5 N/A*	
Item	*Average Rating*
1. Detailed, organized, clear syllabus, materials, and goals	1.64
2. Fair, timely, appropriate feedback and grading	1.68
3. Enthusiasm, increased interest, motivated and encouraged learning	1.08
4. Available, responsive, flexible	1.08
5. Challenging, rigorous	1.08

Qualitative comments on the rating forms include the following statements connected to components of the teaching philosophy I articulate fully in my *Teaching Portfolio* (**Appendix F**):

- "Dr. Z presented the materials to us with a certain personal passion that made everything we were studying seem important and relevant to our daily lives."
- "The whole atmosphere of the class was very welcoming."
- "Class and threaded discussions facilitated the process of applying concepts . . . to everyday life. The videos helped us explore common themes in different mediums. The midterm assessment was helpful, too."
- "I worked harder in this class than others because it was challenging and interesting."

Some student feedback has suggested areas for improvement. For example, in one class, after placing a great premium on the value of reflection, active learning, and how both classroom and online, asynchronous discussions help develop critical thinking and problem solving skills, I discovered through feedback that my use of objective exams—especially since questions tended to be designed more for basic knowledge than any other cognitive functions or levels of learning—seemed to contradict my stated philosophy and goals. Luckily, the feedback was generated at midterm, and I was able to alter my strategies, and students' evaluations at the end of the term revealed their appreciation of my taking their learning seriously; they also earned a new respect for themselves as engaged learners who take an active role in their success. (See **Appendix B** for record of student comments on midterm and end-of-term assessments.)

A compilation of additional midterm formative assessments using the student-facilitated "Critical Response" method innovated in honors at the college is included in **Appendix B**, along with documentation of student ratings and comments cited in the previous table and selected quotations.

Peer Review and Feedback

In **Appendix K**, I include various examples of peer review information from peer observations, feedback on teaching materials and methods, and written records of colleagues' responses to workshops and presentations on teaching and learning. Here are a few statements written by a variety of colleagues:

- "Thanks for your leadership in many areas, but especially in developing opportunities for student—and faculty—growth." —From colleague in my department
- "Ever since John arrived on campus, he has dazzled students and faculty alike with his engaging classes and individual attention to students and their needs."—From department chair in annual review
- "You have given the college wonderful leadership. . . . Your ideas about faculty development are known to be some of the best in the nation."—From provost in annual review

- "If I were wearing buttons, they would pop with pride! Thank you so much . . . for the wonderful work you do with these students."—From president, about teaching and mentoring of honors students

Awards

One of the features of my many teaching portfolio revisions of which I am very proud is the consistency of recognition awards over time. **Appendix E** lists and describes many lucky awards and nominations from sources such as the Carnegie Foundation/Council for Advancement and Support of Education, American Association for Higher Education, South Atlantic Association of Departments of English, South Carolina Commission on Higher Education, Conference on Christianity and Literature, and the college. I am a fortunate and perennial nominee on campus for our *Faculty Excellence* and other awards, and I am heartened that my performance continues to earn notice and reaffirmation from students and colleagues.

Scholarship

The professor must demonstrate competency and currency by actively engaging in the public, professional venues of publications, presentations, or creative work. I also believe that the "scholarship of teaching and learning" is an exciting change in academia that complements the traditional arena of disciplinary scholarship, professional work that validates expertise among communities of scholars.

Collaborative Scholarship and Undergraduate Research

I continually engage in different forms of professional scholarship and undergraduate research ventures to improve practice and contribute to a dynamic agenda in higher education. Here are some highlights:

Authors/Collaborators	Title of Research/ Presentation/Publication	Grant/Conference/ Publisher
Student: Jennifer Davis Mentor: Zubizarreta	"Iconography of Robert Frost"	South Carolina Independent Colleges and Universities Collaborative Undergraduate Research Grant
Student: Suzanna Edson Mentor: Zubizarreta	"Flannery O'Connor and the City of Spires: The Fiction Writer and Her Country"	South Carolina Independent Colleges and Universities Collaborative Undergraduate Research Grant
Coauthor: Larry Clark (Southeast Missouri State University)	*Inspiring Exemplary Teaching and Learning: Perspectives on Teaching Academically Talented College Students*	National Collegiate Honors Council, Monograph Series
Coauthors: Jimmie Cane (Middle Tennessee State University) and David Lavery (Brunel University, UK)	*Revisiting "Northern Exposure"*	Manchester University Press, Critical Studies in Television Series
Coauthors: Natalia Miteva and Gergana Yaneva (honors students, Columbia College)	"International Students and the Challenges of Honors," chapter contribution	National Collegiate Honors Council, Monograph Series

For more, see **Appendix H** for sample faculty projects and **Appendix I** for examples of grant-funded collaborative undergraduate research projects that demonstrate my activities with colleagues and students to enhance my own and others' professional development.

Appendixes G, H, and **I** provide evidence of current scholarship fostering a climate of faculty, student, and administrative reflective practice and collaboration. For example, the work included in the appendixes reveals collaborative publications, conference presentations, and professional workshops this year with students, peers, deans, and academic vice presidents at my own and other institutions worldwide. Such work, combined with my commitment to working with students in mentored undergraduate research, suggests the ways in which I try to integrate teaching, scholarship, and service.

Publications

In traditional scholarship, this year I have completed a coauthored volume on teaching and learning in honors for the National Collegiate Honors Council (NCHC, 2008), and I will soon finish a second edition of my book, *The Learning Portfolio: Reflective Practice for Improving Student Learning* (Jossey-Bass, 2008). I also have written a chapter collaboratively with two students on international diversity in honors programs for a National Collegiate Honors Council monograph (NCHC, 2008). My coauthored *Robert Frost Encyclopedia* (Greenwood Press, 2001) continues to be well used in disciplinary circles.

Presentations, Workshops, Keynotes

In 2007–08, I have presented numerous papers, workshops, and panel sessions at professional conferences such as the National Collegiate Honors Council, Lilly Conference on College Teaching, International Improving University Teaching, Professional and Organizational Development Network in Higher Education, and others. I have also consulted and served as keynote conference or faculty institute speaker on teaching and learning, academic leadership, academic program review, and other areas at several institutions internationally. Such opportunities have helped me apply my developing scholarly expertise in various academic arenas. My vitae in **Appendix G** contains a complete list.

Professional Activities

Externally, in professional venues, I hold several offices in academic organizations. I am Vice President and President-Elect of the National Collegiate Honors Council, a Past-President of both the Popular Culture/American Culture Association in the South and the Southern Regional Honors Council, and Co-Chair of the National Collegiate Honors Council's Teaching and Learning Committee. I also serve on editorial boards of peer-reviewed journals such as *The Journal of Excellence in College Teaching* and *Honors in Practice* (see **Appendix G** for complete details).

Service

The professor/academic leader is also responsible for meeting the obligations of academic citizenship, for engaging meaningfully in institutional priorities and goals. **Appendix D** contains a list of college, professional, and community services, including my various contributions to institutional program reviews, site visitations, faculty development consultations, convocation and keynote addresses, committee work, and more.

In addition to directing both honors and faculty development programs, I currently serve on four college and faculty committees, acting as chair of three, and on occasional ad hoc task forces for grant selections, academic and administrative searches, travel/study, and a start-up peer mentoring program. Currently, I serve on the college's Southern Association reaccreditation team for assessment of our institutional Quality Enhancement Plan. See **Appendix D** for a list of faculty and administrative service activities and **Appendix E** for faculty and administrative service awards, such as continuous nominations every year for different college, regional, national, and international teaching and disciplinary scholarship recognitions (see "Awards" for representative honors).

My *Teaching Portfolio* (**Appendix F**) also documents how I have lived up to my own values and performance standards in the full arena of the academy and its imperative of service. This more comprehensive yet concise academic professional portfolio adds another level of reflection to my professional growth, examining the interactions among my multiple roles and achievements in teaching, scholarship, and service.

Integration: Teaching, Scholarship, Service, and Leadership as Professional Nexus

I continually strive for integration in my professional endeavors. Sometimes, when the puzzle forms a coherent picture, the nexus is exhilarating and inspiring; sometimes I am overwhelmed and discouraged when I fail at making connections among the array of professional responsibilities, commitments, and dreams that pull me in different directions in a harried day.

Happily, I have mostly achieved a fair sense of balance, finding the interrelated threads that bind together my professional efforts. I have always believed that teaching, scholarship, and service should be intricately tied together in a healthy career. In my own case, teaching has repeatedly informed my scholarly endeavors and frequently determined the kinds of campus and community involvements I have chosen. For instance, dedicated to the power of reflection in enhancing teaching and student learning, my particular teaching strategies, materials, and assessment methods have fueled my presentations and publications on teaching and learning portfolios and reflective practice (see **Appendixes A** and **G** for records of achievements). My joy in working collaboratively with students in discovering and creating exciting learning experiences has moved me to engage in many collaborative undergraduate research projects and conference presentations with students, some leading to earned grants and publications (see **Appendixes A, I,** and **J** for evidence). My interest in faculty development and formative assessment processes that lead to stimulating improvement of teaching, learning, and institutional effectiveness dictated my choice to be a leader of our former reaccreditation self-study and our current initiatives for renewing our college accreditation. And the reason I continue to revel in my position as Director of Honors and Faculty Development is that both roles feed my enthusiasm for working with students and faculty to achieve academic excellence. Even in my narrower, disciplinary work, I have incorporated the work I do as a teacher by presenting and publishing on pedagogical issues in the field in addition to literary topics (see **Appendix G** for list).

Teaching, scholarship, service, leadership: a carnivalesque balancing act, indeed! But when they connect, the integration is professionally rich and rewarding.

Professional Accomplishments

I have been lucky to have had the inspiration and support to log accomplishments that may not be earth shaking to all but mean a great deal to me. I select three of which I am most proud:

- I am repeatedly touched by seeing students, year after year, move on to graduate or professional schools, strong careers, and joyful lives as a result of the rigorous academic experience, dedicated mentoring, and generous care they have received as undergraduates in the Honors Program. I have worked hard to build a program with a national reputation for excellence, and I revel in students' achievements when they distinguish themselves in regional and national honors conferences and through their impressive lives as alumnae.
- I puff up with peacock flourish whenever one of our faculty members celebrates an award, publishes an article, wins a grant, presents a paper or workshop—any achievement that has grown directly out of the effort I put into Faculty Development on our campus. We do not have many resources available for promoting, supporting, and rewarding faculty on a large scale, but our faculty do amazing things nevertheless, and I beam when their shine is a reflection of the positive influence, learning, and partnerships I try hard to foster in Faculty Development.
- My presentations and publications both in my field and in teaching and learning circles have opened up many wonderful opportunities for me, and I am grateful that I enjoy a good reputation among many colleagues in higher education. Professional accomplishments such as books on Frost, learning portfolios, teaching and learning in honors, as well as

other publications, presentations, workshops, and addresses have opened many doors for me. Besides the professional benefits of such recognition, the warm, life-long friendships I have made have been a special treat, bringing my professional and personal lives together in remarkable ways.

Professional Goals

1. Summer 2008: Develop a new team-taught, interdisciplinary honors senior seminar for spring 2009, culminating in a travel/study venture in May.
2. Summer 2008: As the organization's new Vice President and President-Elect, begin process of conference planning for the National Collegiate Honors Council's annual meeting in fall 2009.
3. Fall 2008: Work collaboratively with the college's reaccreditation team on our assessment plan for the Southern Association's required Quality Enhancement Plan.
4. Fall 2008: Consider application for major sabbatical project in spring 2010.

Appendixes

A. Annual Faculty Self-Evaluation Report
B. Student Ratings, Midterm Assessment, and Feedback
C. Advising Information and Acknowledgments
D. Faculty and Administrative Service
E. Honors, Awards, Recognition
F. Teaching Portfolio
G. Curriculum Vitae
H. Faculty Scholarship, Projects
I. Collaborative Undergraduate/Faculty Research
J. Outcomes of Student Learning
K. Peer Reviews and Feedback

Environmental Engineering

Charles N. Haas

Environmental Engineering

Drexel University

Fall 2008

Table of Contents

Teaching Responsibilities

Over the past ten years, I have taught a variety of graduate and undergraduate courses. Generally I teach one or occasionally two courses a term. The following table lists the courses I have most consistently taught:

ENVE 727 Risk Assessment	Grad, elective	Winter 1997	24
		Winter 1998	15
		Winter 1999	11
		Winter 2000	5
		Winter 2001	7
		Winter 2003	8
		Winter 2005	18 (team taught)
ENVE 662 Unit Ops: Biological	Grad, elective	Spring 1997	10 (team taught)
		Spring 2000	4
		Spring 2002	3
		Spring 2005	7
ENVR 480 Bioterrorism	One-time elective special topics course	Winter 2002	130
ENVE 302 Envir. Transport & Kinetics	UG, required for EnvE majors	Fall 1998	3
		Winter 2006	8
		Winter 2007	10
CIVE 360 Water Infrastructure (*)	UG, required for CIVE majors	Summer 1999	25 (team taught)
		Winter 2000	23
		Summer 2000	28 (team taught)
ENVE 300 Intro to Environ Eng	UG required for ENVE and CIVE majors	Spring 2001	6
		Spring 2002	16
		Fall 2002	6
		Spring 2003	8
		Fall 2003	17
		Spring 2004	37
		Fall 2004	39
		Spring 2005	32
ENVE 423 Water & Wastewater Design III	UG required for ENVE majors	Spring 2006	7
		Spring 2007	6

The undergraduate courses I have taught are mostly upper-division courses taken by those in the major or minor. The graduate courses have been primarily taken by those who have selected the particular area. In prior years, I have also taught more general graduate courses, for example, an Environmental Chemistry course (ENVR 401/501) and a Biostatistics course (ENVR 506).

In addition to formal courses, I have consistently supervised graduate students who are performing research for their theses under my direction. For the past five years, the following is the report of my M.S. and Ph.D. student supervision.

	M.S. Thesis Students	Ph.D. Students
2002/3	0	6
2003/4	0	7
2004/5	2	6
2005/6	1	6
2006/7	1	6
2007/8	1	7

Teaching Philosophy and Methodologies

In my intermediate-level undergraduate courses (ENVE 300, 302) I generally give students opportunities to succeed in different ways. This is exemplified in my teaching of ENVE 300, where I allow students to gain "points" toward their grades by exams, quizzes, homework, term papers, and group projects (an example syllabus for the ENVE 300 class is in Appendix B1). This has generally been popular with students who understand that this gives them incentives to learn at their own style as noted in student comments below:

"There are a lot of ways to get points. Students who don't mind putting in a TON of effort can get reasonable grades even if they don't understand the subject. Which is good for an intro course."

"Strengths: This course, and the instructors, helped to make the topic very interesting. It actually got me interested in wastewater treatment."

"Weaknesses: Not really a weakness, but an observation. There was a lot of information, but not a lot of time. The problem was solved by making the tests open book–open note."

"This course was by far the easiest course to get an A, since the system was based on points, not percentages of tests. This is really positive, because students don't feel as pressured. However, the students must not abuse this trust between them and the instructors. Thus, the point system means more responsibility to the students. The instructors are there to teach and help."

In my senior and graduate courses, which are generally smaller and taken by students who are more motivated to study the specific material, I encourage more interaction in several ways. In my ENVE 662 (Biological Unit Operations) course, which is taken by graduate environmental engineering students, I have had the advantage of working with a very good textbook rich in problems, and so my teaching style used in class uses student solution of selected problems in order to motivate a discussion. This is especially important in graduate classes, which are generally offered one night a week for three hours, in order to keep students engaged.

In my senior water treatment design class (ENVE 423), I have had a class of about ten students, and have used groups to go through a detailed treatment plant design over the course of a ten-week term. I assign students a specific geographical location, and as topics come up in the course of the class, I give assignments to the groups to apply that knowledge to the specific system that they are investigating in detail.

So, generally there is no one style that I universally employ. However, I have tried to break up the dull monotony of PowerPoint by incorporating unique twists in each of the courses that I have taught.

Research

I have been actively engaging in research since my doctorate. Figure 1 (from Web of Science) summarizes the rate of publication and rate that my work has been cited.

Figure 1

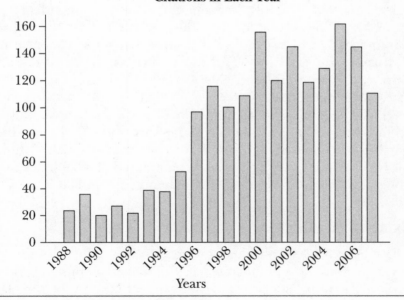

Published Items in Each Year

Citations in Each Year

Source: From Web of Science, Oct. 24, 2007

My general interests are in the area of human exposure to infectious microorganisms in the environment—estimation of their risk and design of engineering strategies and processes to reduce such risks.

My work has focused on two main areas. One broad area, which originated in the 1980s, was the development and application of methods to determine the risk that people incur when they are exposed (by ingesting or inhaling, for example) to infectious organisms from the environment. The earliest applications of this were in drinking water contamination. Appendix C1 is a 1991 paper that I did, which is currently my most highly cited paper. In this we outlined the risk from viruses and a particular type of protozoan that arise when they are present in finished drinking water that people ingest. We have extended this work to exposure to contaminated food, and most recently to risk from exposure to bioterrorist agents. Appendix C2 is a paper prepared just after the 2001 anthrax attacks in this latter area. I, and two colleagues at other institutions, collaborated on a book in this area published in 1999, and in 2005 received major funding ($2 million per year over five years) from US EPA and the Department of Homeland Security to establish a Center for Advancing Microbial Risk Assessment (CAMRA) (Appendix D1).

A second broad and long-standing area of interest is the analysis and design of processes for disinfection—how chemical or physical engineered processes can reduce the levels of disease causing organisms. In the 1990s, we looked at how to analyze the rates of chemical disinfection processes that made sense from an engineering point of view (Appendix C3). We have applied disinfection process analysis to many organisms, and our recent work has been to show how to couple this with models of how fluid moves in systems to use advanced computational techniques that could enable better design of such systems (Appendix C4).

External Funding

I have been funded continually while at Drexel. The major recent research funding is enumerated in the table. For three of these projects, awards letters are in the appendixes (Appendix D1 through D4).

Major Recent Research Funding

Role	Title	Agency	Duration	Funding Level	Collaborators
Principal Investigator	Evaluation of the Analytical Capabilities, Today and Near Future, for the Monitoring of Drinking Water for Accidental or Intentional Contamination	Philadelphia Water Department	2002–3	$100,000	No
Principal Investigator	Building Biodecontamination: A Process Engineering Approach	National Science Foundation	2003–5	$99,500	Yes
Principal Investigator	Workshop on Advancing the Quality of Water (AQWA)	National Science Foundation	2003–4	$99,000	Yes
Principal Investigator	Delaware Valley Water Source Tracking Effort (DeVaWaSTE)	Philadelphia Water Department	2004–present	$60,000 per year	No
Principal Investigator	Assessment of Physical Scale Models for Development of Room Decontamination Design Criteria	National Bioterrorism Civilian Medical Response Center (CIMERC),	2004–5	$55,000	Yes
Principal Investigator	Wastewater Disinfection Strategies for the Metropolitan Water Reclamation District of Greater Chicago	CTE Engineering	2004–5	$75,000	Yes
Principal Investigator	Expert Review of EPA Recreational Water Criteria – Scientific Basis	Metropolitan Water Reclamation District of Greater Chicago	2005–7	$25,000	Yes
Co-Principal Investigator	CLEANER Project Office[b]	National Science Foundation	2005–7	$200,000 (Drexel share)	Yes
Co-Principal Investigator and Co-Director	Center for Advancing Microbial Risk Assessment (CAMRA)[a]	US EPA and Department of Homeland Security	2005–10	$2,200,000 (Drexel share)	Yes
Principal Investigator	The Drexel University GAANN Fellowship Program: Educating Renaissance Engineers[c]	US Department of Education	2006–9	$168,000 (year 1)	Yes

[a]Appendixes D1 and D2.
[b]Appendix D3.
[c]Appendix D4.

This program of research has involved a diverse spectrum of local (Philadelphia Water Department, Metropolitan Water Reclamation District of Greater Chicago), federal, and private sector entities. It reflects both individual as well as collaborative research on a small and large scale. Both significant thrusts of interest (microbial risk assessment, disinfection) as well as other areas are reflected in this portfolio.

As three examples of the research efforts:

From the NSF-funded "Building Biodecontamination: A Process Engineering Approach" project, I and Professor Baki Farouk (Drexel) demonstrated that widely available commercial fluid dynamic computer models can be modified in order to describe how well disinfectants might act to kill infectious agents (such as anthrax spores) that contaminate an indoor environment such as a room or a suite of rooms.

In the NSF-funded "Workshop on Advancing the Quality of Water (AQWA)" project, we ran a three-day workshop on basic research needs in the field of drinking water treatment. This was organized around five research areas: biotechnology, environmental chemistry, novel materials, cyber infrastructure, and novel processes.

In the project funded by the Chicago Water Reclamation District ("Wastewater Disinfection Strategies for the Metropolitan Water Reclamation District of Greater Chicago"), I organized an expert work group to evaluate alternatives for disinfection at the three largest wastewater treatment plants in Chicago (totaling over 2 billion gallons/day flow).

Department/Institution Committee Service
Chair, Faculty Senate, 1995–1996

I served on the faculty senate from 1994–1997. In 1994/5, I was vice chair, and in 1995/6 I was chair of the senate. This was during the period when the President of Drexel (Richard Breslin) resigned and the search for a new president—which eventually resulted in the appointment of Constantine Papadakis—occurred. The senate officers were involved in multiple meetings with key members of the Board of Trustees during this period. Of course, the regular business of the senate (curriculum revisions, searches, and standing committees) was also under my purview. This period of service—only three years after I arrived at Drexel— gave me a very good orientation to the university, which has proven to be a major asset in the subsequent years. Appendix E1 contains my final remarks to the senate on the conclusion of my term.

Law School Development Committee, Member, 2004–2005

About five months after the administration initiated discussions leading to the development of the new Law School, I was invited to serve as a member of the Law School Development Committee. This committee met at approximately biweekly intervals leading up to the submission of the formal proposal to the State of Pennsylvania in the summer of 2005. This resulted in the preparation of a successful application to the State of Pennsylvania for permission to award the J.D. degree (Appendix E2).

Drexel Engineering Curriculum Revision Committee, Member, 2005–2007

During 2006, the College of Engineering embarked on a major revision of the freshman and sophomore "common core" curriculum (known as TDEC—"The Drexel Engineering Curriculum"). I was invited by the Associate Dean of Engineering for Undergraduate Education—Anthony Lowman—to serve on this. The committee completed a freshman curriculum revision that went into effect with the fall 2006 term, and then completed a transformed sophomore curriculum implemented in the fall 2007 term.

Administrative/Managerial Responsibilities

In 2005, I was appointed as Head of the Department of Civil, Architectural and Environmental Engineering, after having served for fifteen months as interim head. Appendix F1 contains a copy of the letter of appointment. In this position, I currently supervise five nonacademic staff, and manage a department with eighteen full-time faculty, almost 600 undergraduate majors and approximately

Figure 2

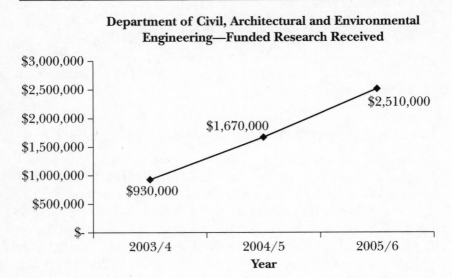

Department of Civil, Architectural and Environmental Engineering—Funded Research Received

100 graduate majors. The department offers ABET accredited undergraduate degrees in three disciplines and graduate degrees in both civil engineering and environmental engineering. I am responsible for a department budget of approximately $3 million.

During my time as department head, I have hired five junior faculty, and mentored three toward gaining tenure.

Growing the department graduate and research program is an important part of my duties. Working with my faculty to encourage proposal preparation and secure successful funding (as well as leading by example) has resulted in a dramatic increase in funding over the last several years as noted in Figure 2.

My responsibilities also include working with other department heads in the College of Engineering on issues common to the entire college. As an example of this, preparation for the ABET (Accreditation Board for Engineering and Technology) accreditation visit, which occurred in Fall 2007, was one such activity. My department has three ABET accredited undergraduate degrees, and so I worked with colleagues to prepare the three self study reports and manage details of the visit.

Mentoring Activities

As department head, I am responsible for mentoring the junior (untenured) faculty. I meet with them periodically as a group and am available to advise on their development on a one-on-one basis as needed. At the present time, we have five assistant professors. I have been pleased that during my watch, three assistant professors have been granted tenure. We have not had any departures of any junior faculty during this period and have hired five junior faculty.

I routinely advise five to seven graduate students (who are performing full-time research under my direction). In addition, I serve as the academic adviser to all undergraduate environmental engineering students (currently about thirty students). Some of the recent graduate advisees or undergraduates of whom I am particularly proud are:

2005 B.S. EnvE	Francis Haas (no relation)	Studying for Ph.D. at Princeton (Mechanical Engineering)
2005 B.S./M.S. EnvE	Sierra Dean	Working for Black and Veatch (Philadelphia) (major consulting firm)
2002 Ph.D. EnvE	Dennis Greene	National Technical Expert on disinfection, Metcalf and Eddy (major consulting firm)
2004 Ph.D. EnvE	Christopher Crockett	Manager of the Watersheds Program, Philadelphia Water Department
2001 Ph.D. EnvE	Paula Klink	Special Projects Officer, Queens University (Kingston, Ontario, Canada)

Contribution of Teaching, Research, and Service

I have found that these three activities are synergistic in my advancement as a scholar. There have been many cases in preparing for a course (either a new course or one that I had not taught in a while) that I have found myself in a thread for new knowledge in that area. In some of these occasions, I have actually noted a gap in information, which resulted in a new research branch for me, or in a short note for publication. My research in risk assessment started in the 1980s, and led me to develop (first while on sabbatical in 1986) a new course, which has now been made a matter of routine as ENVE 727. My external service (and consulting) has occasionally brought to my attention new problems or new areas in which my expertise could be used. My teaching in areas that I do not actively engage in with research has enabled me to retain some level of currency in the topics that I otherwise might not have. Therefore, I find the three activities to produce harmony in my development.

Contribution of Administrative, Managerial, and Mentoring Activities

My department is disciplinarily very diverse. My first task in becoming department head was to better understand what it was that all my various colleagues were engaged in. Doing this has required me to become acquainted with fields of which I had only rudimentary knowledge. I found this to be challenging, and it has enabled me to find the connections and intersections between fields that I can use to develop the department. I have found it more enjoyable than expected to mentor junior colleagues toward successful advancement. I have been able to work with senior colleagues to help meld a common set of visions and goals for the department.

Selected Professional Accomplishments

Membership on the Water Science and Technology Board (WSTB) of the National Academies

Since 2004, I have been a member of this board—which is an organizational unit of the National Research Council. My selection to membership was based in part on my extensive service on a variety of committees of the National Academies. WSTB is responsible for conducting a large number of studies for the federal government and other public and private sponsors on national issues concerning water quality and quantity— most particularly those that lie at the intersection between science and public policy. This has significantly enhanced my national visibility among the technical and environmental policy communities.

Development of the B.S. Environmental Engineering Degree

In 1997, after several years of development and planning—in which I took the lead—Drexel launched a new B.S. degree in environmental engineering. In 2001, this degree received its first accreditation by ABET. Since its inception, we have graduated over fifty students. With increasing interest in the environment by undergraduates, I expect that this program will increase in popularity.

Establishment of the Center for Advancing Microbial Risk Assessment (CAMRA)

In 2004, the U.S. Environmental Protection Agency (USEPA) and the Department of Homeland Security (DHS) issued a request for proposals for a major center on microbial risk in order to better inform policies and responses in the area of bioterrorism and emerging infectious diseases. Since this coincided with a major long-term research interest, I and colleagues at Michigan State University and the University of Arizona took the lead in responding to this Request for Proposal. We put together a team of seven universities and over a dozen faculty and in 2005 were awarded a five-year grant to establish CAMRA (with Michigan State as the lead institution). I serve as co-director (Appendix D1). In addition to providing long-term support for major multidisciplinary research programs of national significance, this has given us high visibility both with the USEPA and with DHS. This is the first center in the Homeland Security area in which Drexel has had presence.

Professional Goals

Development of Major Research Initiatives Engaging Many in the Department

I would like to catalyze a major research initiative involving a substantial number of faculty in my department, in collaboration with others at Drexel and elsewhere. At present we have been talking about several themes and are identifying targets of opportunity. Successful launching of this initiative could energize the department and bring it to the next level.

Achieving a More Responsible Academic Leadership Position

In my twenty-nine years of academic experience at three universities, and in the last several years as department head, I have started to realize that I could contribute to academic leadership of larger units. I believe that it would be good for Drexel to encourage a balance of promotion of leaders from within, along with recruitment from other institutions. I also believe that my multidisciplinary orientation has given me a greater comfort with understanding diverse disciplines, which would be a required skill in such positions.

List of Documents in Appendixes

B1—ENVE 300 Syllabus Fall 04/05

C1—Regli et al. Paper (JAWWA 1991)

C2—Haas 2002 Anthrax Paper

C3—Haas and Joffee Paper

C4—Dennis Greene Paper

D1—CAMRA Award Letter

D2—CAMRA Flyer

D3—NSF CLEANER Award Letter

D4—GAANN Budget

E1—Final Remarks at End of Term as Chair, Faculty Senate

E2—Application to State of Pennsylvania for Law School Approval

F1—Appointment Letter as Department Head

Foreign Languages and Literature

Sheri Spaine Long

Department of Foreign Languages and Literatures
University of Alabama at Birmingham
Fall 2008

Table of Contents

Integrative Prologue

> *The real voyage of discovery consists not in seeking new*
> *lands but in seeing with new eyes.*
> MARCEL PROUST

My current portfolio journey offers me rare reflective time and the "voyage of discovery" that helps me appraise my professional growth and development in teaching, research, and service. The outcome of the voyage will make it easier for me to chart a clear future professional course. My portfolio narrates **how I, the language and literature professor, became the global professor.** Repositioning my disciplinary role as a professor of Spanish to embed it in the larger sphere of international education provides avenues to connect my work in teaching, research, and service to greater issues on campus and beyond. Some of these are local, regional, national, and international topics such as charting literary globalization, expanding the teaching of critical languages, promoting study abroad, and addressing Spanish instructor shortages.

These connections help me **evolve as a teacher, researcher, and provider of academic services** by broadening my professional mission from a professor of Spanish to that of a champion for multiple languages and international scholarly pursuits. I can identify the two drivers of repurposing my focus—my professional service as a board member of the American Council on the Teaching of Foreign Languages and my role as the chairperson of the University of Alabama at Birmingham (UAB) Department of Foreign Languages and Literatures.

This year I have been engaged in academic activities in Beijing, Buenos Aires, Prague, and Salamanca. Bringing a global worldview to my teaching and research strengthens my ability to communicate with millennial students, my interaction with peer researchers, both domestically and abroad, and the comprehensiveness of my academic service. **Connecting the local to the global** has increasing currency in my professional life.

Teaching

Teaching Responsibilities

I teach **Spanish language, literature, and culture** at both the undergraduate and graduate levels. I teach just one to two classroom courses per year because I serve as Chair of the Department of Foreign Languages and Literatures. Typically I teach undergraduate Spanish classes and seminars at the graduate level. I also teach undergraduate Honors seminars. The courses that I teach at UAB are discipline specific and not required for the general core curriculum.

I teach Introductory Spanish and have provided course design, curriculum development and management for multisection classes. At the intermediate level, I teach basic language classes and have a particular interest in teaching writing process and content courses. At the advanced and graduate levels, I have been privileged to create and implement seminars (for example, From Local to Global: Madrid, Spain; Madrid-as-Text). Of my overall total instructional time, I have spent approximately 50 percent teaching introductory and intermediate language classes and 50 percent teaching more specialized seminar courses. I consider culture and cross-cultural themes to be an integral part of every class at all levels.

My complete **course list and select course syllabi** are found in Appendix A. Below are two representative courses. I teach Introductory Spanish I. The course on Madrid is characteristic of the theme-based seminars that I teach:

- Introductory Spanish I—SPA 101, enrolls twenty-eight students, not required (undergraduate)
- From Local to Global: Madrid, Spain (Golden to Terrorist Age)—HON 397, enrolls fifteen students, not required (undergraduate)

This Madrid course is currently being redesigned into a graduate-level seminar, *Madrid en ficción,* that includes city-as-text and literary and cultural theory.

Teaching Philosophy

The global professor knows that student anxiety runs high in foreign language classes due to the immersion environment and its built-in ambiguities. This has made me sensitive to the importance of a user-friendly, **low-stress classroom.** I also try to pass on to my students a **lifelong love of language, literature, and culture,** as well as a **cross-cultural perspective.** Embracing the philosophy of the *Standards for Foreign Language Learning in the 21st Century* (1999), my goal for both the learner and myself in the language classroom is to **communicate** in Spanish. Together we try to gain knowledge of Spanish-speaking **cultures,** to **connect** Spanish with other disciplines, to acquire information in Spanish, to **compare** through insights into the nature of language and culture, and to participate in Spanish-speaking **communities** locally and globally.

I view my role in developing content-based, standards-driven Spanish classes, workshops, publications, and textbooks as an important contribution to the focus on **best practices rooted in theoretical knowledge** to best serve the foreign language classroom. (See Appendix B.) The Standards have helped me to shift to a less teacher-centered classroom to one focused more on student learners who construct meaning.

The teaching of language and culture in **context** is part of my pedagogical mission. For my advanced undergraduate and graduate students, content-based instruction led me to develop the Madrid seminars that I have taught in both Spanish and English (domestically and on site). Drawing on interdisciplinary approaches and urban theory, students experience literature, film, and miscellaneous texts that feature Madrid, and they explore Madrid (or its construct) virtually or physically through mapping, synthesizing, and analyzing, while developing their own critical apparatus. In an introductory Spanish language class, I organize content thematically by focusing on Spanish-speaking cultures to develop critical thinking, both embedding structured input and grammatical explanation and facilitating vocabulary acquisition by connecting them with content.

My **instructional techniques**—group tasks, question/answer, lecture, role-play, and analysis through comparison and student presentation—always vary from course to course according to level (novice, intermediate, advanced). I was taught and learned to teach in the traditional foreign language classroom that centered on print matter. Currently I blend **traditional methods with new digital approaches** by using electronic activities for practice, film footage, and authentic audio to expose developing scholars of all levels to the many sights and sounds of Spanish-speaking world. Examples of these media can be seen in the ancillaries (CD-ROM, audio recordings, electronic workbook) to my coauthored textbooks (Appendix C). Because additional instructional approaches verify that student learning goes beyond the borders of the traditional classroom, **experiential learning** and **study abroad** should be part of the global professor's repertoire. I am committed to study-abroad programs for all students, because they offer both language and cultural immersion. I advise approximately seventy study-abroad students annually. In order to afford

UAB students a variety of opportunities, I work closely with the UAB Study-Abroad Director, foreign language faculty, and off-campus study-abroad providers to afford UAB students a variety of opportunities. (See Appendix D.)

Evidence of Student Learning

With the current emphasis on assessment, I realize that I will need to design activities or assignments or give pre- and posttests to **capture additional data.** I have just begun to do this. (See samples from the Madrid seminar in Appendix E.) I recently served as faculty mentor to an undergraduate researcher. Substantiation of student learning by Spanish major Brittlyn Hall is evidenced in her published poster on the Web site of the American Council on the Teaching of Foreign Languages (http://www.actfl.org/i4a/pages/index.cfm?pageid=4080). (See Appendix F.) I have been fortunate to have alumni corroborate in writing their learning experiences from my classes. (See select quotes in Appendix G.)

Teaching Improvement Efforts

Recently I designed and **piloted a paper project** with 150 under-graduate students enrolled in Introductory Spanish entitled "Spanish-Speaking Communities in Alabama Project." The project objective is to acquire knowledge about domestic Spanish-speaking communities through traditional research and a face-to-face inter-view with a person who identifies himself or herself as Hispanic or Latino. Designed to enhance student learning, the **project inte-grated three areas of UAB's Quality-Enhancement Plan** into the learning experience—Writing, Quantitative Literacy, and Ethics and Civic Responsibility. Students included were encouraged to reflect on what they learned from the project in their essays. (See Appendix H.) This project now runs each semester to develop multiple assessments of the learning experience.

Evaluation of Teaching

I have been privileged to be honored with **five teaching awards—** on my campus and in my state and region—that represent a combination of peer and student validation of my professional efforts (see Appendix I):

- Outstanding Woman UAB Faculty Member
  University of Alabama at Birmingham, 2005
- President's Excellence in Teaching Award
  University of Alabama at Birmingham, 2002
- Outstanding Foreign Language Teacher Award
  Post-Secondary Alabama Association of Foreign Language
  Teachers, 2000
- Outstanding Foreign Language Teacher Award
  Post-Secondary Southern Conference on Language Teaching,
  1999
- Ellen Gregg Ingalls/University of Alabama at Birmingham
  National Alumni Society Award for Excellence in Classroom
  Teaching, 1999

It is elevating to receive this type of recognition. However, I know that my teaching can always be improved, especially now that I am more assessment driven. I am more interested in measuring student learning than in achieving popularity with students.

That said, my student ratings are high. My students write positive comments about their learning experiences in my classes. Out of forty-two classes that I have taught at UAB since 1993, **96 percent of students who filled out evaluation surveys have rated me as "one of the best" or an "above average" instructor.** (See Appendix J for chart and comments.) I plan to do a further analysis of the hand-scored forms to assess whether my students are inspired to continue to learn Spanish. I choose this variable because it indicates my effectiveness in instilling the spirit of lifelong learning. Because my institution is implementing the IDEA survey assessment this academic year, it will become easier to collect more data about my own performance for improvement.

Research/Scholarship

Like my teaching, the underpinning of my scholarship is **inquiry into both Spanish language and literature in a cultural context.** From a traditional foreign language disciplinary perspective, some colleagues look at my scholarship and exclaim that there is a dual focus because part of my research centers on literature and the other portion addresses language pedagogy and study abroad. However, as a global professor, I believe that foreign language teaching as well as research can be integrative. Within the critical tradition, theories such as Iser's reading process and the world as social text for cultural studies inform my language and literary scholarship in a holistic manner. The integration is inspired by the *Standards for Foreign Language Learning in the 21st Century* (1999) and its interconnected "5 Cs" model (**C**ommunication, **C**ultures, **C**omparisons, **C**onnections, and **C**ommunities), and by Heidi Byrnes's scholarship on "multiple literacies" that defines an intellectual foundation of comprehensiveness and coherence as a way of bridging the discontinuities among the diverse scholarly interests typically found in foreign languages. I see myself as a **"bridge scholar" who embraces multiple literacies.** I believe that this validates what may appear to be the so-called dual nature of my research. All of my research is focused on developing cross-cultural literacies through literature, language pedagogy and study abroad. My research takes different forms and has different audiences, and I have delivered a variety of papers around the world. (See Appendix K.) Currently my research has three focal points:

1. **Madrid in literature:** the development of a volume, tentatively titled *Metro-Textual Madrid (1978—present)*
2. Introductory and intermediate **instructional materials for Spanish:** publication and development of textbooks and related pedagogical publications
3. **Study abroad:** experience abroad and student attitudes toward continued language study

Literary Research: Madrid in Literature

My interest in Spain's capital city dates back to my graduate studies and develops throughout my career in conference papers and publications. The **power and importance of place** as a structuring device and focus in language and literature classrooms has become vital to me as a scholar. I have published scholarly articles and have delivered conference papers that focus on Madrid. (See Appendix L.)

My interest in the **city-as-text** and its relationship with Madrid in literature intensified in 2000, when I directed the National Collegiate Honors Council's Madrid Semester Abroad at the Universidad de Alcalá. In Alcalá de Henares, now a bedroom community of Madrid, I taught a seminar exclusively on the literature of Madrid. I also designed field explorations that brought to life the literature of Madrid for thirty-three honors students. (See Appendix M.)

In 2002, I received the Robert G. Mead, Jr. Memorial Travel and Study Grant from the American Association of Spanish and Portuguese to conduct **on-site research** on literary Madrid. (See Appendix N.) In July 2004, I **codirected an international academic conference** in the Spanish capital: "Madrid in Spanish, Latin American and World Literature/*Madrid en la literatura española, iberoamericana y universal.*" (See Appendix O.) Scholars at this conference delivered more than sixty critical papers that focused on Madrid; as a result of this conference, I began to plan for the book on Madrid that I am currently authoring. At present there is no other book that focuses exclusively on contemporary Madrid during this period and explores it through carefully selected works of literature and film. (See Appendix P.)

Pedagogical Research and Instructional Materials

One of my areas of research is pedagogy. My **six coauthored textbooks** (and ancillaries) and **select articles on teaching** keep me up to date on the relationship between theory and practice. I believe that **best practices** in teaching must be grounded in research knowledge and reflection on teaching and that these practices should be shared through publication. My coauthored texts and ancillaries integrate the Standards for Foreign Language Learning and are influenced by the content-based instruction movement. Both editions of my coauthored Introductory Spanish book, *Nexos*, are being used at more than **seventy** U.S. colleges and universities. (See Appendix B.) Because of my background in pedagogy, The College Board and the Educational Policy Improvement

Center recently appointed me to the **World Languages Best Practices Commission for Spanish Literature.**

Study-Abroad Scholarship and Research

I have had the privilege of accompanying study-abroad student groups and conducting site visits abroad on numerous occasions. The **development of language and cultural competencies** in the context of international education movement is of growing interest to me. I owe much of my own language and cultural competencies to foundational study-abroad experiences. (See Appendix Q.)

Besides experience abroad, I began to reflect further on study abroad and language learning when I was invited to contribute a radio script entitled "Why Study Abroad?" that was aired on *Talkin' About Talk* for the 2005 Year of Languages Celebration. It was broadcast on affiliates of National Public Radio and subsequently published in *The 5-Minute Linguist: Bite-Sized Essays on Language and Languages.* (See Appendix R.) Writing it had a significant impact on me. It made me begin to ask harder inquiry-based questions about the **relationship between language learning and study abroad.** This has led me to a new project. I have developed a survey to study the attitudes of undergraduate students enrolled in the study of languages abroad and their attitude toward continued language study on returning to their home campuses. Study-abroad provider Cultural Experiences Abroad and its Global Campus Network has agreed to partner with me on this project and survey study-abroad students. This partnership provides the ability to survey a large cohort of students and has the potential to produce a significant data pool for analysis.

Service

For the global professor, service is a demanding job. There are three central tenets of my service. First, I am the editor of *Foreign Language Annals.* Second, I am the Chair of the Department of Foreign Languages and Literatures. Third, I am active in institutional committees and service organizations; a select list of activities is found in Appendix S.

The Editorship

Editing the journal is a specialized, scholarly pursuit that requires countless service hours. I was selected as editor as the result of a national search. *Foreign Language Annals* is the flagship journal of the American Council on the Teaching of Foreign Languages. Dedicated to the advancement of foreign language teaching and learning, the journal seeks to serve the professional interests of classroom instructors, researchers, and administrators concerned with the teaching of foreign languages at all levels of instruction. *Foreign Language Annals* is a double-blind, peer-reviewed journal published four times per year. I consider approximately three hundred manuscripts yearly. (See Appendix T.)

As the journal editor, I have a tremendous responsibility to my discipline. The **editorial role of gatekeeper** is a serious ethical and curatorial endeavor. This responsibility offers me another way to step out of my role as Spanish professor and **develop my global view of the foreign language field.** My work on the journal connects perfectly with my quest to improve student learning. A perk of editing is that the knowledge gained through reviewing manuscripts supplements my research. *Foreign Language Annals* enables me to **lead among my peers** and allows me to **shape research focus and the quality** of publications in the field. (See Appendix U.)

Department Chair

The leadership and organizational skills that I have developed as journal editor are often transferable to my work as department chairperson. Housed in the School of Arts and Humanities, the Department of Foreign Languages and Literatures has fifteen full-time faculty and three part-time faculty members. The unit has two half-time staff members and five work-study students. Currently there are 150 undergraduate foreign language majors and approximately 300 foreign language minors. I have been the academic and managerial officer of the department since 2002.

In general, I serve as the **leader** and **implementer** of our mission; chief **advocate** for high standards for the faculty, staff, and students; and **liaison** between administration, faculty, staff, students, alumni, and community members. In a small, closely knit department, it is important that the chair leads by example, brainstorms with the faculty, plays to the strengths of members on the faculty team, beats the drum for foreign languages and literatures, and makes one accessible to others.

Eventually when it is time to step out of the chairperson's role, I would like to be remembered as a **results-oriented chairperson** who strengthened teaching and our collective research profile, internationalized the department and curriculum, and improved the capacity to deal with the "language boom" that followed the September 11 tragedy. Below are **select administrative performance highlights** (percentages data source: UAB Planning and Analysis 02–07).

- Increased credit hour production: **40.6%**
- Increased enrollment in foreign language courses: **59.6%**
- Increased head count of majors
  - First majors: **133.3%**
  - Second majors: **78.9%**
- Secured major gifts ($420,000) toward endowment for French professorship
- Prepared department for successful accreditation review, 2005
- Directed renovation of foreign language central offices, 2005
- Launched introductory Italian and Arabic
- Directed community advisory committee
- Carried out student and faculty recruitment and management, advising, curriculum development, scheduling, and oversight of daily operations
- Established strong ties with UAB Study Abroad; promoted international education
- Introduced Fulbright Foreign Language Teaching Assistantship Program to department, 2007
- Lead in development of department's Strategic Plan, 2007

Overall, I have received positive performance feedback from my faculty and my Dean. On the IDEA Feedback Survey for Department Chair Report, administered in fall 2005, the **faculty rated me as outstanding** in these areas: "Guides faculty evaluative process," "Fosters good teaching," "Communicates department's needs," "Encourages balanced faculty," "Guides organizational plans," "Fosters faculty development," "Communicates administrative expectations," "Guides curriculum development," and "Rewards faculty appropriately." (See Appendix V.) However, as a chairperson I know that there is always more work to be done and that I will **need to improve continuously** in order to best serve the broad interests of the department.

Integrative Epilogue

Over 500 years ago, many of the voyages of the great European explorers led to so-called discoveries. These voyagers were focused on a mission. Like the explorers, a global professor needs to be faithful with her mission and align it with the greater mission, vision, and goals of the institution. The UAB Vision states that it is to be an internationally renowned research university—a first choice for education and health care.

The globalization of graduate education is easier to make possible because of its international agents and individualized nature. Regarding undergraduate education, I view the word *international* as key to connecting my academic activities within the UAB vision. The UAB Strategic Plan states: "We will achieve a highly effective undergraduate educational experience to give students the best possible preparation for productive and meaningful careers and lives that benefit society" (Goal 1). As a global professor, I find the objectives (of Goal 1) below particularly relevant to my role at UAB:

1. Offer exceptional curricula that are relevant, current, and comprehensive
2. Ensure high-quality instruction, advising, and student services
3. Expand opportunities for study abroad, learning communities, internships, service-learning, research, and honors experiences

Regardless of instructional level, I believe that **exceptional curricula must be internationalized.** It must include multiple perspectives. Quality instruction and research evolve out of **cross-disciplinary endeavors,** attention to theory and practice, and the development of multiple literacies. Within the foreign language and literature discipline, the notion of **global literacy** is yet to be fully defined. To that end, I am a committed advocate of student research, study abroad, and other forms of experiential learning that motivate students to discover **learning without (classroom) borders** and supplement traditional instruction. Most of our student protégés will become so-called global citizens who will serve society in a variety of ways. Therefore, global professors on the UAB campus and beyond must be prepared to see their teaching, research and service with new eyes.

Appendixes

A. Course List and Syllabi

B. Pedagogical Publications and Textbook Adoption List

C. Electronic Media

D. Cultural Experiences Abroad Advisory Board and UAB Study-Abroad Letters

E. Evidence of Learning

F. Student Learning Sample

G. Student Testimonials

H. Quality-Enhancement Plan Project

I. Teaching Awards

J. Student Ratings

K. Papers Delivered Internationally

L. Madrid Articles and Papers

M. Madrid Honors Semester

N. American Association of Teachers of Spanish and Portuguese: Research Grant

O. Madrid Congress

P.   Madrid Book Prospectus
Q.   Foundational Study Abroad: Council on International
      Educational Exchange
R.   Study-Abroad Essay
S.   Institutional Committees and Service Organizations
T.   *Foreign Language Annals:* Journal Profile
U.   *Foreign Language Annals:* Special Focus Issues
V.   IDEA Feedback Survey

Geology and Environmental Science

Ranjan S. Muttiah

Departments of Geology and Environmental Science

Texas Christian University

Fall 2008

Table of Contents

Service
    Department Committees
    Student Advising/Mentoring
    Contribution to TCU and Society
Integration of Professional Work
    Contribution of Teaching and Research to Professional Growth
    Professional Accomplishments
    Three Professional Goals
Appendixes

Purpose

My portfolio consists of teaching, research, and service accomplishments demonstrating my capabilities as an Assistant Professor and indicates that I'm worthy to move to the next stage of my academic career as Associate Professor. Attainment of Associate Professor will enable me to conduct new and exciting research in water resources and spatial analysis, and play a larger role in building a stronger TCU community as it grows and attracts diverse students. I have published eight papers, submitted eleven grants, taught ten courses, and built a regional reputation for the Center for Geographic Information Systems (GIS) and Remote Sensing. I believe TCU serves its students best through the fusion of research scholarship into teaching (and vice versa): the teacher-scholar model. I have advanced TCU's Vision in Action by offering GIS Certification, and incorporating service-learning in student projects.

Teaching

Teaching Responsibilities

My primary courses (Table 1) are: the Principles of Environmental Science (ENSC 10143), Geographic Information Systems (GEOL 50721/50723), and the sequence of one-credit hour remote sensing classes. I restructured the one-credit hour introductory GIS course to a three-credit-hour class with laboratory; I created a new course called "Hydrologic Modeling" (GEOL 50583).

    In **Appendix A**, other classes are listed along with enrollment numbers.

Table 1. Courses That I Frequently Teach

Term	Course	Enrollment	Elective/Required
Fall 2004	GEOL 50721	14	Elective
Fall 2005	GEOL 50723	9	Elective
Spring 2005	GEOL 50741	5	Elective
Spring 2005	GEOL 50751	3	Elective
Fall 2005	ENSC 10143	48	Required
Spring 2006	ENSC 10143	36	Required
Fall 2006	ENSC 10143	71	Required
Spring 2007	ENSC 10143	64	Required
Spring 2007	GEOL 50723	14	Elective
Fall 2007	GEOL 50723	8	Elective

Note: Those courses whose numbers begin with 5 are graduate/senior level classes.

Teaching Philosophy and Methodologies

I am striving to reach teaching excellence. With each passing year at TCU, I have learned new and improved teaching methods. Some of what I have learned has been through trial and error, and some I have learned from my esteemed colleagues in the department and from the Center for Teaching Excellence (CTE).

My teaching goal consists of challenging students to think through problems: to weigh the evidence and infer relationships between elements of knowledge taught in class. My teaching style could be classified as "lecture-demonstration" and "lecture-discussion." To determine retention of knowledge, I ask questions from students during lectures, have regularly (weekly/biweekly) quizzes, and conduct discussion to jointly arrive at answers. Recently I found that giving a motivational and emotional lecture (especially on topics such as human influence and species extinction for the freshman ENSC class), followed by discussion of the lecture material at the end of lecture, engages students well and inspires them to read and learn on their own. I had underestimated the importance of "cognitive attachment" in my previous lecturing.

At the freshman level (Principles of Environmental Science, ENSC 10143), I strive to make learning experiential: I illustrate difficult scientific concepts in terms of everyday experiences, I conduct small (kitchen science) experiments in class to demonstrate key points, and when appropriate, I lecture using modern visual and teaching aids such as classroom performance systems (with clickers that provide feedback from students).

For my GIS classes, I use a combination of lecture and hands-on skills learning. In a typical week, I lecture on a topic on Mondays, demonstrate and interactively walk through exercise problems on Wednesdays, and let the students tackle a problem on their own during the Friday lab periods. I have two tests: a written test and a test of their computer skills in which they solve problems on the computer within an assigned time period.

In my remote-sensing classes, I encourage students to discuss assignments in teams and then present their findings in front of class through a team leader. Team-based learning works particularly well when students are required to judge and render decisions.

Curricular Revisions

Since my first teaching assignment at TCU, I have changed my teaching style and method so that students can more easily retain the most important information from the class lectures. The undergraduate freshman class, for example, has a lecture and lab portion. I tell the students they will get an opportunity to take part in group activities in the lab, but that they must have a fundamental understanding of biological, chemical, and physical principles. I ask students to identify features on slides or ask them to list out features not present on the slides (for example, "Tell me what's missing on the slide"). I have also revised the course syllabus to reflect changes in my teaching style. The lesson plans are laid out by each day of lecture and lab exercise (see **Appendix B**).

Course Syllabi

In **Appendix B** are course syllabi for ENSC 10143 and GEOL 50723. For ENSC 10143, I use quizzes to monitor how well students are retaining lecture material, reading their assignments, attending classes, and coming prepared to attend classes. A unique aspect of my GIS classes is that students perform class projects on their own. They work on a project that's relevant to them (for example, ranch management students work on property management), or undertake projects with a local nonprofit organization (service-learning) such as the Fort Worth Nature Refuge. Project reports from the GIS class are available for ftp download on ftp://muttiahload@geo1.tcu.edu/ (password: 1muttiah1, under directory MuttiahPromo). The students present their projects in front of their peers and invited guests and then write a final report.

eCollege

I employ eCollege to post the course syllabus, lectures, educational Web sites, interactive practice exams, and grades, and to answer questions in the discussion forum. The students can check their grades anytime and take a more proactive role in improving their class performance.

Teaching Improvement Activities

After I attended a workshop on team-based learning, I used it in my remote-sensing classes. I grouped the class into small teams of three students, and then had each team identify geographic, vegetation, or geologic features from imagery depending on the lesson for the day. Each team was given enough time to complete the assignments, and then present their findings to the rest of the class. Often the presentations created new learning opportunities.

Student Evaluations and Teaching Improvement

Figure 1 shows the Student Perception of Teaching (SPOT) evaluation scores for ENSC 10143, showing that I have improved (based on three criteria) since I started teaching this course. There was setback in the spring of 2007, a primary reason being the difficulty of the second test (as seen in many of the student evaluation comments), and student morale didn't quite recover by the time of the last class. I have strived for teaching improvement:

- I discussed my teaching techniques with TCU Center for Teaching Excellence (CTE) personnel.

Figure 1. Student SPOT Evaluations Spring 2005 Through Fall 2007 for ENSC 10143

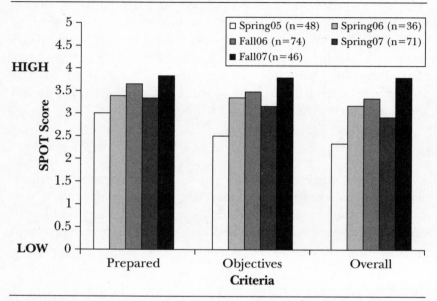

Note: The criteria consist of "Prepared," representing "teacher came well prepared for each lecture"; "Objectives," representing "objectives of the class were clear"; and "Overall," for "the teacher overall did a good job."

- I incorporated student comments and helpful criticisms in the course.
- I got feedback from the department head and other faculty who visited my lectures.
- I reformulated the course syllabus.

Figure 2 shows my SPOT scores for the remote sensing classes (GEOL 50731 is techniques of remote sensing, 50741 is computer processing of imagery, and 50751 is the interpretation of imagery) for the most recent semester of teaching (Fall 06) the class.

Team-based learning was a primary reason for the higher scores for the remote-sensing class. The small class size allows for additional experimentation of teaching methods and improvement in the remote sensing and GIS classes. Figure 3 shows my SPOT scores for the GIS class (GEOL 50723).

Figure 2. SPOT Scores for Remote-Sensing Classes

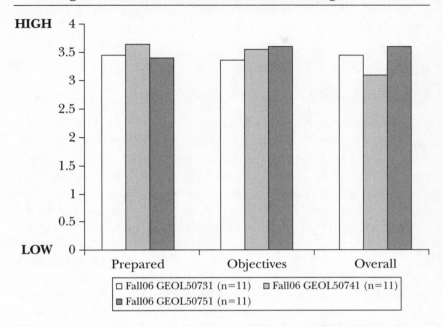

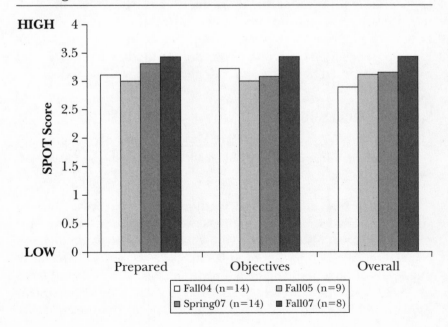

Figure 3. SPOT Scores for the GEOL 50723 GIS Class

Appendix C contains my Student Perception of Teaching (SPOT) and GIS certification evaluations. **Appendix D** contains letters from faculty who observed my teaching skills.

Research
Nature of Research

I have two areas of research: surface water resources, and bio-optics. In both fields, I work in a multidisciplinary setting. In surface water, I apply computer modeling to solve water problems such as impact of global climate change on water supply availability and the impact of small dams on vegetation communities growing on stream banks. I essentially bring new computational tools to solve complex water resources problems.

In bio-optics, I work with physicists to study how the internal leaf structure influences light scattering; the research will eventually answer the fundamental question of whether and how plant leaves use the polarization properties of light.

My publication record shows that I have performed research on my own, with TCU graduate and undergraduate students, and with collaborators from within my department and from other universities. My research does not lend itself to work in isolation whereby I can derive or prove a hypothesis on paper: field data must be collected or specialized experiments performed, models developed, and results interpreted by using computer and mathematical models.

Sample of Publications

Muttiah R. S., R. D. Harmel, and C. W. Richardson. 2005. Discharge and sedimentation periodicities in small sized watersheds. *Catena, 61,* 241–255.

I used a new mathematical method called wavelet analysis to analyze simultaneous relationship between sediment loading and river discharges. My paper was the first study that examined the correlation between sediment and discharge in terms of their frequency of occurrence. The data for my analysis were obtained from a nested watershed in Riesel, Texas. I collaborated with USDA-Agricultural Research Service researchers to perform this research.

Muttiah R. S., J. D. White, J. R. Duke, and P. M. Allen. 2005. Estimation of source water to cedar elm in a central Texas riparian ecosystem. *Hydrological Processes, 19*, 475–491.

I collaborated with Baylor University researchers to estimate the water source for cedar elm trees living downstream of a small dam near Waco, Texas. No one had back calculated, starting from the oxygen and hydrogen isotopes in the woody stems of plants, to trace the source of water to elm. A claim that was made before the above study was that mature trees were extracting water from the groundwater, and not the river itself. We conclusively showed (through my back-calculation technique) that cedar elms were obtaining water from the river—even the elms far from the rivers. What was happening was that the tree roots were creating hydraulic suction, and the water was moving up slope in conveyor fashion due to root suction.

Savenkov S. N., R. S. Muttiah, K. E. Yushtin, and S. A. Volchkov. 2007. Mueller-matrix model of an inhomogeneous, linear, birefringent medium: Single scattering case. *Journal of Quantitative Spectroscopy and Radiative Transfer, 106*(1–3), 475–486.

I have listed this paper, even though I am the second author, because of the long-term potential of my ongoing collaboration with my colleague from Taras Shevchenko University (Kiev, Ukraine). We're applying mathematical and experimental techniques to determine physical properties about media such as crystals and biological material such as leaves from light polarization. We have shown that light absorption by media is deterministically characterized by six physical parameters that quantifies anisotropy.

Appendix E contains a selection of my publication record.

Funding/Grants

- Spatial analysis for the Andes to Amazon Project: Moore Foundation Grant, Sub-contractor with Botanical Research Institute of Texas, $30,000. January 2005–December 2006.
- The products generated from this project included GIS maps on landslides, wetlands, and vegetation for the Peruvian

Amazon, training of students from BRIT in GIS, and the write-up of technical papers and a book chapter.

- Imaging spectroscopy for the Priest River Sediments, TCU Research Fund, $2,325. September 2005–May 2006.
- The product of this project was to analyze iron signature from soils to understand burial history of soils.
- TCU GIS Certification, TCU Vision in Action funding, $25,000. March 2005–May 2007.
- The goal of this project was to develop a GIS certification program for area professionals. This course has attracted interest from industry, nonprofits in the area, and the city government of Fort Worth.
- Mapping Plutons in the Baja Peninsular using ASTER, NASA Educational Grant to obtain ASTER imagery at no cost, valued at $2,500. March 2007–March 2010.
- The goal of this project is to map the plutons (intrusive rocks) that are commonly found in Baja, California. The project complements ongoing field activity by Dr. Helge Alsleben, who is a structural geologist at TCU.
- Mapping Wetlands of Madre de Dios, NASA Educational Grant to obtain ASTER imagery at no cost, valued at $2,500, March 2007–March 2010.
- The goal of this project is to compare classification procedures for wetlands in the Amazon of Peru from the LANDSAT and ASTER satellites.

   Appendix F contains letters from granting agencies.

Editorial Appointments/Offices Held

- Editor of book titled, *From Laboratory Spectroscopy to Remotely Sensed Spectral of Terrestrial Ecosystems.*
- Session chair, Geochemical Society, "Streams and Soils," May 22–25, 2007, Acapulco, Mexico.
- Session chair for American Geophysical Union, "Hydrology of Amazon," May 22–25, 2007.
- Faculty Senator, TCU 2007–present.

Sample of Conference Presentations

- Muttiah R. S., S. Khanal, J. Janovec, and H. Alsleben. *Stream complexity in an undisturbed watershed of the Amazon.* Fall 2005, American Geophysical Union meeting, San Francisco, California.
  I analyzed the structure of streams in the Andes and the fore-land basin of the Madre de Dios basin in Southeast Peru. The significance of this work was to show the limitation of stream complexity laws.
- Khanal S., R. S. Muttiah, and J. Janovec. *Landslides are common in the Amazon of SE Peru.* Fall 2005, American Geophysical Union meeting, San Francisco, California.
  I supervised this paper by my graduate student. Using spatial statistics we determined whether the landslide occurrence pattern was nonrandom. We eventually used spatial regression to determine the environmental variables responsible for landslides.
- Khanal S., and R. S. Muttiah. *Hydrologic Modeling of the Madre de Dios basin with MIKE-SHE using TRMM,* Joint Assembly of the American Geophysical Union, Acapulco, May 22–25, Acapulco, Mexico.
  We compared how the MIKE-SHE hydrologic model behaved when a single rainfall station was used versus geographically spread out multiple observations from the TRMM radar satellite. This work is important because the soil in the Amazon floods easily and the model results were sensitive to surface water ponding.

Supervision of Master's Degree Graduate Students

- Suresh P. Khanal, thesis title, "A GIS study of the landslides in the Amazon of SE Peru" (graduated in August 2006, and now employed as a GIS specialist with Eagle Mapping, Houston, Texas)
- Co–major adviser (other external adviser, John Janovec from BRIT), John Ethan Householder, "Vanilla in the swamps of the Madre de Dios Basin" (graduated in May 2007 and now working with BRIT team on forest inventory in Peruvian Amazon).

Currently I serve as a co–major adviser to the Environmental Science master's students Jorge Lingan and Andy Waltke.

Service

Department Committees

- Member of Committee on review of Environmental Science Department for the Dean of Science & Engineering
- Member of TCU Tsunami Relief Committee

Student Advising/Mentoring

I enjoy mentoring students because it leaves them with a long-lasting impression of TCU. For instance, I have mentored students who are interested in getting into a GIS-related field for their professional career. I encourage them to work with me on a small and manageable project of interest if they have one, or I assign them a project on which I am working (like mapping projects in the Amazon of Peru, impact of urbanization on the Trinity River). **Appendix G** contains example letters/e-mails from students.

Contribution to TCU and Society

- I am a Licensed Professional Engineer (PE) with the Texas Board of Professional Engineers. Noteworthy because I can officially give my professional judgment on surface water design and study plans.
- I initiated the Greater Fort Worth Microsoft Structured Query Language (SQL) 2005 monthly meeting for database specialists in collaboration with personnel from the city of Fort Worth. Noteworthy because these monthly meetings bring database professionals from industry (Freese & Nichols, DR Horton, Microsoft, Lockheed, city government employees) to TCU.
- I organized the Green Chair lecture by noted National Geographic Society conservationist Dr. J. Michael Fay at TCU.
- I participated in TCU Frog Camp 2005 to support TCU staff and advise incoming freshman (during camp students, staff and faculty go to a location outside TCU) and Frog Calls 2006

(in Frog Calls, TCU faculty visit our freshmen and sopho-
mores to find how they are faring in college).

Integration of Professional Work

Contribution of Teaching and Research to Professional Growth

Teaching is best when informed by research. Research complements teaching, and teaching complements research. The more I
perform research in the Amazon of Peru, the more I can provide
a unique and personal touch when I teach environmental science
to undergraduates. Or, if there's a real-world problem waiting to
be solved by GIS (such as application cost for animal manure on
cropland), the students learn to use GIS procedures. In a similar
vein, the better my teaching gets, the more I'm able to clearly
communicate my research findings to my peers: my presentations are organized better, more straightforward, and I'm able to
collaborate more effectively with my colleagues by working with
graduate and undergraduate students.

Professional Accomplishments

- I designed the new Geographic Information Systems (GIS) and
  Remote Sensing Center in the Department of Geology. The
  Center consists of twelve PCs running ESRI's ArcGIS program,
  ENVI remote-sensing software, MIKE-SHE hydrologic modeling
  package, and various other statistical programs. GIS software is a
  database programming system used to solve computerized mapping in a wide variety of scientific fields. I train students to apply
  sophisticated software in a number of scientific fields, ranging
  from hydrology to weather forecasting to geology.
- I started the TCU GIS certification program in the summer
  of 2006. In the certification program, I train area professionals in the use of GIS to solve spatial database problems. For
  example, the city of Fort Worth collects field data using Global
  Positioning System (GPS) and survey maps to lay pipelines.
  I train the city workers to convert and map such data in GIS
  systems. The center also serves as a center of excellence for
  TCU and Fort Worth, serving the spatial database needs of

the Sociology Department's Purple Bike Program and Fort Worth's Nature Refuge.

- I have strong working relationships with researchers (particularly, Dr. John Janovec) at the Botanical Research Institute of Texas (BRIT); this relationship has spawned a growing number of graduate (master's thesis) research in the Amazon region of Southeast Peru and brought about stronger bonds between TCU and BRIT.

Three Professional Goals

Premier GIS Center in North Central Texas

As director, my goal for the Center for GIS and Remote Sensing is to make it the premier learning center in the North Central Texas region. Prominent speakers have been brought to TCU by the center, the center has written its own user manual for GIS software, lecture videos have been made available online, lecture and skills exams have been shared with faculty at other GIS centers (for example, with Georgia Tech, School of Architecture), the center has a prominent collaboration with BRIT in the Amazon rain forest, and the center offers summer GIS certification that is being accepted and recognized by area professionals.

TCU Graduates in Leadership Positions

I want TCU students who've taken GIS and remote-sensing classes from me to be leaders in the industry. In order to do so:

- I worked with students on individual research projects so that they can explore the power of GIS.
- I gave students a competitive edge through teaching innovative technology.
- I facilitated summer internships and professional jobs for students.

New Research/Competitive Grants

A major goal of mine is to write up two papers on nonlinearity in long-term stream flows, and the presence of acceleration ("water waves") in the base flow of small-sized catchments. Ongoing research projects with BRIT and the Amazon Conservation

Association in Peru will create opportunities for writing large grants (for example, on the use of tall towers to measure rainfall canopy interception).

Appendixes

Appendix A: Classes Taught

Appendix B: Course Syllabi

Appendix C: Spot Evaluations

Appendix D: Faculty Evaluations

Appendix E: Sample Publications

Appendix F: Grant Letters

Appendix G: Service to Students

Jazz and Contemporary Music

Reginald Workman

Jazz and Contemporary Music Department
The New School
Fall 2008

Table of Contents

5. Integration of Professional Work Goals
   a. How Teaching, Research, and Service Contribute to My Professional Growth and Development
   b. Three Professional Accomplishments

Appendixes

Purpose

Because teaching is one of the most important professions in our country, it is important to me to be actively involved in establishing a high standard of pedagogy with regard to preparing aspiring artists to continue the work that we as their predecessors have established.

I am preparing this academic portfolio for several reasons—first, as a step toward preparing for my faculty appointment review. This teaching portfolio is being created to illustrate my teaching performance and effectiveness. Second, in the wake of seeking tenure appointment, this document will help me to present my ideal to the panel.

Finally, I think it will help to better mentor my colleagues regarding preparation for such a process.

Teaching

In 1987, I was recruited to the New School by administrators and faculty, who understood that my professional status (having worked with many world-renowned musicians who created the music commonly known as jazz) would be instrumental in attracting students worldwide to enroll in our program. I have included a short biography in Appendix A.

The concept of the school was to mix the academic requirements that students at any music school would receive along with the necessary element and information of professionals in the field.

Since I was attuned to the professional community of artists, I was recruited to help establish a program at the New School that would be built on high standards of performance and academics. My primary responsibilities were to recruit professionals who had pedagogical skills and were willing to commit themselves to mentor students for performance in the jazz community.

I teach the following courses:

Courses Taught Spring 2007

Class	Time	Course Number	Number of Students
Coltrane Rep. Ensemble	Mon.	1461	9
Improvisation Ensemble	Wed.	1444	7
Standard Music Ensemble	Wed.	1453	11
Improvisation Ensemble	Thurs.	5303	7

Courses Taught Fall 2007

Class	Time	Course Number	Number of Students
Coltrane Rep. Ensemble	Mon.	1531	11
Improvisation Ensemble	Wed.	1502	7
Futuristic Concepts Ensemble	Wed.	1529	9
Improvisation Ensemble	Thurs.	4129	9

My present teaching responsibilities with The New School's Jazz and Contemporary Music Department are to conduct four individual two-credit classes on the undergraduate level per week. Elective classes are the Standard Music Ensemble, the Coltrane Ensemble, and Futuristic Music Ensemble. The Improvisation Classes are core courses.

The Coltrane Ensemble is conducted every semester. The Futuristic Music Ensemble is scheduled to be taught every other semester, alternating with the Standards Music class.

In addition, I advise students (who are specifically string players) in the form of a string ensemble in which we examine the method of improvisation as it relates to string players; recognize if there are intonation problems and sighting ways of correcting them; and explore possibilities for improvising with string instruments in the style of contemporary jazz music.

Coltrane Ensemble

In order to understand concepts in this class, students should be among the more advanced population in the school. Therefore, they have to audition and be accepted to participate.

This class is approached as a repertory ensemble. Significant Coltrane compositions are chosen as vehicles toward understanding why and how Mr. Coltrane invented his new concepts of harmonization (the use of whole tone scales and the twelve-tone system, which give more flexibility to the improviser). Logical resolutions of extended chromatic passages, articulating densely notated compositions, and tasteful note placement in slower compositions represent challenges unique to Coltrane compositions.

The Improvisation Ensembles

Improvisation classes are a unique and important part of jazz curriculum, since becoming a convincing improviser is the goal of most performing artists:

- My classes always include a traditional exercise as a weekly challenge (rhythm progressions through the keys with alternate changes).
- According to the level of each musician in the ensemble, material is chosen that serves to illustrate specific changes regarding interpretation of the musical selection.
- There are two significant events in the course of each semester and a significant midsemester evaluation. The first event: Each

member illustrates and/or verbalizes his or her goal, concept, and instrumental ability during the first meeting. The midsemester evaluation: This is a monitored performance in which each ensemble illustrates their progress to an audience of professors from other classes.

Student Evaluations

Spring 2007 Summaries of Student Evaluations: Coltrane Ensemble, Standards Ensemble, and Improvisation Ensemble

Questions About the Instructor

Question 3: The Instructor presented the course in a clear way.

Class	Always	Often	Sometimes
Coltrane	5	3	2
Standards	2	1	4
Improv. (W)	6	0	0
Improv. (T)	3	2	0

Summary: Out of my four classes, 59 percent thought the course was "always" presented in a clear way; 22 percent said "often," and 29 percent reported "sometimes."

Question 11: I would recommend the instructor.

Class	Yes	Maybe
Coltrane	8	2
Standards	3	4
Improv. (W)	6	0
Improv. (T)	3	2

Summary: Out of my four classes, 66 percent said yes to recommending my class while 29.6 percent said they might recommend the course.

Questions About the Course

Question 1: All things considered, these courses were:

Class	Excellent	Good	Fair	Poor	Waste of Time
Coltrane	0	4	4	1	0
Standards	0	3	3	1	0
Improv. (W)	4	2	0	0	0
Improv. (T)	2	2	1	0	0

Summary: Combining the data from three classes, 59 percent reported my classes to be excellent or good; 33 percent fair; and some, as expected, were not happy. Of note here is that the Improvisation classes generally reported more satisfaction.

Appendix E contains more information on student evaluations.

Students' Comments

Question: What do you like about the course?

Class	Comments
Standards	"Playing (Practical application). Reggie's input and usage of very descriptive metaphors. Reggie has a lot to say."
Improvisation	"This is a great course and Reggie is a great teacher." "The info is straight from the horse's mouth— info from the man who physically was there." "Reggie is an inspiration and I like that we tried to interpret songs in different ways." "Great repertoire—Excellent advice from the teacher. Music was very challenging."

See Appendix F for additional student letters and other evidence of student progress.

Teaching Philosophy, Objectives, and Methodology

The most important aspect of teaching in a diverse situation like the New School is to bring a multitude of experiences into a common area where inspiring and meaningful presentations will take place. My goal as a professor is to guide each student to develop the necessary tools to accomplish this.

In my teaching, I like to draw on the built-in diversity of our student population. In this scenario, the students are the beneficiaries of each other's experience while developing techniques for successfully meeting the course requirements and developing technical proficiency.

As a team at the New School we have developed a method that ensures that each member of our staff monitors each student's development during the course of each semester. My objective in this process is to bring all the students to a common level whereby each one is able to practically apply and combine the technical and aesthetic elements of creative expression. Confirmation of their learning is demonstrated during assigned recording and performance projects at the end of each semester.

Description of Curricular Revisions

This fall, I incorporated a listening component and am encouraging my students to compose. I readily incorporate original student compositions in ensemble performances at Sweet Rhythms and recording projects. It is my belief that each student graduating should have recorded enough original material to compile a demo CD that will help the students as they begin their career.

Also, this fall I have prepared lesson plans that include a more in-depth examination of how the music was created. Through lecture and limited research, I want the students to realize art is not created in a vacuum but in context of the world from which it is derived. The New School Jazz and Contemporary Music faculty is a uniquely qualified group in that it consists of both musicians from the academy as well as the experientially based musicians who have performed themselves or in groups that were pivotal to modern music. New School students have the unique opportunity to draw on this wealth of knowledge as they develop, moving the music concepts and aesthetics forward.

I am proposing four additions to the curriculum for the 2008 school year:

a. Proposal–The String Summit

In the light of the dramatic increase in bassists and other stringed instruments, I want to establish the New School String Summit. The summit will concentrate on the development and improvement of improvisational techniques as well as prepare string players with a primarily jazz background to work in other genres of music. I am presently creating repertoire and considering guest artists to conduct master classes.

b. Add a Required Listening Component to My Courses

I want to incorporate/enhance a listening component in each course that I teach. This component will support the oral tradition as it relates to each respective course. Also, listening modules clearly illustrate to the students how artists of the past accomplished what they are now being asked to do. Particularly in the case of the Coltrane Ensemble, to fully understand the music of an iconic figure like John Coltrane, it is essential that students thoroughly examine Coltrane's musical path.

c. Add a Reading List to Each of My Classes

The program readily addresses the oral tradition; however, to get a full understanding of this great art form, I feel that students should also actively research the aesthetics as well as the lifestyle, society, politics, and culture from which this music has evolved.

d. Adviser/Online Radio Station

Having had experience on radio, I will act as an adviser as the online radio project gets off the ground.

Selected Course Syllabi and Other Course Material

I have provided my course syllabi in Appendix D.

Teaching Improvement Activities

Concerning my teaching improvement activities, I plan to take piano and arranging lessons. The piano lessons will be with an accomplished pianist and William Patterson University Professor, James Weidman.

Presently, I am working with a very well-established copyist, Randa Kirshbaum, on further developing my arranging skills. I am also working with one of her tutees, François Gruillot, who is tutoring on the Sibelius software program. This I think will be useful in seeing how my students are approaching composing using software programs.

I am also planning to take computer training at the Mac store to become more knowledgeable of the organizational software and other features of the Mac that can make me more efficient in handling my New School, business, and personal affairs.

Classroom Observation

The faculty members listed below have observed me in the classroom and submitted statements which I have added in Appendix C:

"His immediate insight into students' performance problems and ability to communicate that information with passion and humor is extremely compelling."—Jane Ira Bloom (Appendix C)

"And I understood why he established an international reputation as a great jazz educator. . . . I say this for two crucial reasons. First, he possesses an amazing amount of knowledge and deep insight of jazz music through his vast history of performances. Second and more importantly, Reggie possesses the special ability to convey his knowledge and love of jazz music to his students. That is even more rare."—Satoshi Inoue (Appendix C)

Research/Scholarship
Evidence of Research and Creative Scholarship

Research in the area of improvised African American music is unique. A large portion of the tradition is oral and relates to aesthetic values of the society. Daily there are new methodologies being created that lend to the futuristic quality of African American music commonly known as jazz. Since it is expected that our students will graduate with a thorough knowledge of theory and harmony in the traditional sense, I continually explore techniques of the older masters as well as contemporary scholars.

I submit the following as evidence of my creative scholarship:

1. Sound Spectrum Workshops: Created and implemented Sound Spectrum Workshop, a series of workshops aimed at providing greater understanding for novices (See Appendix G)
2. Sculptured Sounds Music Festival (see Appendix G)
3. Trio III: music, touring and marketing. The group consists of me, my fellow NS faculty member Andrew Cyrille, and Oliver Lake. The group has been touring, collectively composing new music for touring and recording (see Appendix G)
4. Educational workshops I am invited to conduct, particularly The Coltrane Workshop (Appendix G)

Proposed Research and Creative Scholarship

Because my definition of creative scholarship is outside the traditional realm, I submit the following creative projects as examples of my scholarly projects in progress:

1. Presently archiving, preserving, and transferring to digital historic air checks from WBAI radio programs from the 1970s to 1980s, which I hosted
2. Archiving music and personal music related documents
3. Composing music for various projects: Trio III (developing and composing for a CD project schedule)
4. Developing music for a string quartet project
5. Working with my cofounder to create a booklet of the Sculptured Sounds Music Festival programs and related notes for historical purposes
6. All the above will be used as classroom modules to further the students' knowledge of how to market their craft

Details of items mentioned above are available upon request.

For next year, I propose the following research and creative scholarship project, which would fit well into the goals of the New School strategic planning campaign.

Online Radio Station (See Appendix G)

Begin an online radio station to showcase the music of the New School Jazz and Contemporary Music Department. Most universities have campus radio stations, and in keeping with my idea that musicians should direct their own careers, I think that the New School should look to develop its own online radio presence. Other schools, Oberlin's WOBC and Columbia's WKCR, have become beacons in their respective communities. In keeping with the strategic planning goals of the university as a whole, the online station would incorporate students and faculty from various disciplines under the New School umbrella.

The online radio presence could also be instrumental in meeting several objectives of the strategic planning campaign:

1. Monetary support from sponsors would create new revenue streams
2. Stronger alumni affiliation, with alumni reconnecting with the university for interviews and live online performances
3. Audience development for the Jazz and Contemporary Music Department, as well as other departments involved in the performing arts. Online programs similar to television's Actor's Studio, or Onstage would provide publicity
4. With the Jazz and Contemporary Music Department taking the lead on this project, the online radio station would promote the presence within the university

External Funding/Grants Obtained

My cofounder and I created the Sculptured Sounds Festival to provide work opportunities for musicians, to showcase the many sides of futuristic music and to provide a hands-on, real-world experience for New School students to explore various musics as well as various aspects of the music business from promotion, to marketing, production, and performance.

Starting in August 2006, with limited resources to hire a professional fundraiser, we did not raise the monies needed for the festival and therefore had to rely on the door. However, believing in the project, the musicians worked with us on their fees, and we were able to obtain donations, cash, or in-kind from various sources.

For the Sculptured Sounds Music Festival grants and supporters, see Appendix G.

Selected Samples of Conference Presentations and Performances

- Invited to participate on the International Association of Jazz Educators panel (2007)
- Jazz Museum of Harlem (2007): Interview with Loren Schoenberg (Smithsonian Oral History Project)
- Jazz at Lincoln Center (2007): Participated in reading/open discussion of "The House That Trane Built" conducted by Coltrane biographer Ashley Kahn. Guests: Reggie Workman and Creed Taylor
- France—Son D'Hiver Fest: Roy Campbell, Jr. (Trumpet), Louis Belogenis (Sax), Andrew Bemkey (Piano), Reggie Workman (Bass), Warren Smith (Drums)
- TRIO III Tours (Fall 2006, Spring 2006, Fall 2007)

See Appendix I for additional performances, both historical and current.

Invited National/International Presentations

- Mexico—Quinto Encuentro Internacional de Jazz Y Musica Viva Monterrey (2007): An international music workshop including Faculty from United States/France/Germany/Mexico; commitment included introductory seminar; daily classes regarding respective instruments; daily musical workshops; final concert for students; final concert by faculty. Producer: Omar Tamez.
- Miles Davis Workshop (February 2006): The Miles Davis Alumni Clinics and Concert. Event was held in February 2006, featuring former Miles Davis musicians.
- High Point, NC, The John Coltrane Workshop: I've conducted the workshop three times since its inception in 1996.
- "Giant Steps" Seminar Panel Discussion and Award (Temple of the Arts Cultural Center, SI) (2007)

- The Sculptured Sounds Music Festival (2007) (see Appendix G)
  - Conducted workshop at Harlem School for the Arts (part of Sculptured Sounds Festival). Invited students from the College Prep Program to participate in rehearsal for the African-American Legacy Project, the fourth concert of the Sculptured Sounds Music Festival.
  - Sculptured Sounds Presents @ The Downtown Music Gallery (January 2007): Weekly showcase featuring kindred spirits in futuristic music.
  - African-American Legacy Concert February 2007, fourth concert of the Sculptured Sounds Music Festival: Free concert conducted by Charles Tolliver featuring the music of jazz legends, their offspring and progeny, designed to expose families and future generations to the wonderful legacy of African American composers and those who are carrying the legacy forward.
- Montclair Academy of Dance—Regularly co-conduct and teach drumming classes giving early music understanding to pre-K (3–5) and cultural understanding to youngsters and teens.

Service

Committees

1. Curriculum Committee Coordinator
2. Adjudicator—Sophomore juries (twenty years)
3. New School Outreach performances (informally since I have been at the New School)
4. Governance Committee (2004–2005)
5. Consultant to the Beacons in Jazz Committee (2003–2006)
6. Executive Committee—As a member of the full-time faculty, my responsibilities are not limited to classroom input. I am a member of the Executive Committee, which works in close proximity with the Curriculum Committee to ensure checks and balances regarding the Jazz Department policies.
7. New School Faculty Senate—(2007 to present)

See Appendix B for other administrative and New School committees.

Student Advising and Mentoring

Mentoring students through impromptu meetings and advisory sessions are also within my purview and are an essential teacher responsibility as the student develops toward work in the field and or graduate studies.

The undergraduate students I informally advised and mentored (through my classes and otherwise) total thirty-eight. I've listed several of my advisees below:

1. Ju-Ying Hsu—Now applying to graduate school at Queens College and NYU
2. Joon Hwa Jung—Is now attending the graduate program at Queens College
3. Stephcynie Curry—Working professionally in New York City
4. Jamire Williams—Performing professionally nationally and internationally
5. Rene Cruz—Attended the graduate program at Julliard
6. Yotam Silberstein—Emerging artist deserving greater recognition. Performing professionally
7. Hang Seoul—Worked with him through family challenges. Applied to Queens College graduate school

Integration of Professional Work/Goals

I define myself as a bassist, educator, and advocate for the arts. The order is dependent on the context and in my mind; all are equally important designations, and they are integrated in various ways.

As a bassist, I have been fortunate to have performed at the highest levels in the music world with such jazz icons as Elvin Jones, Lee Morgan, and John Coltrane and on to futuristic luminaries Oliver Lake, Cecil Taylor, and Marilyn Crispell. As an advocate of the arts, I have worked the past twenty-seven years, often teaming with many of my New School colleagues, actively championing the cause of arts education.

In more recent years, I have dedicated the greater percentage of my time to being an educator. For example, I created a workshop, the Sound Spectrum Workshop, an eight-week roundtable lecture/discussion designed to provide the nonmusician with a greater understanding of the concepts, forms, styles, and overall aesthetic of this great art form, jazz. The workshops, which were held at one of New York's top law firms, Debevoise and Plimpton, were well attended, with the firm allowing their summer interns time to attend the weekly sessions. Each lecture covered a different topic: comparing and contrasting the vocalists' approach to improvised music to that of the instrumentalists, a review of musicians accomplished in more than one discipline, a critical view of predecessors to today's rap and hip-hop, culminating with a autobiographical overview of the music, the social history of my musical journey, and a discussion of my upcoming music endeavors.

In addition, I created the Sculptured Sounds Music Festival (see Appendix G for an outline of the festival).

The Sculptured Sounds Music Festival was an exciting four-concert series of performances showcasing the many sides of futuristic music and concepts. Cocreated with Francina Connors (who also served as production coordinator) and under the umbrella of my production company, Sculptured Sounds, we "sculpted" an eclectic lineup of artists, some in unique configurations that heretofore I only imagined combining. Each concert had an entirely different theme. Festival concerts were held every Sunday in February 2007 at Saint Peter's Church.

We designed each week to consist of a demonstration/lecture, opening act, and headlining act(s). The opening and featured act(s) were performed in the sanctuary, while just outside, in "The Living Room," were multidisciplinary experiences of music-related demonstrations, lectures, and artwork by musicians.

The festival was organized in part to provide performing opportunities for many talented artists as well an opportunity to design a hands-on teaching vehicle for New School students.

Professional Accomplishments

Recent professional accomplishments of which I am especially proud:

1. Successful touring and response to production of CDs: I have toured more this year and feel that it has been very beneficial and necessary for me in many ways. It has allowed

me to maintain my visibility and professional standards. As a bassist, maintaining my technical proficiency is an absolute. Performing and touring has also made me focus on my composing. I strongly encourage developing composing skills in my classes.

2. Trio III compositions: These compositions are noteworthy in that they have received good reviews and have been well received by our touring audiences. I have also incorporated compositions from the recent Trio 3 Intakt CD "Time Being" into my futuristic class for the students to analyze and learn from.

3. Success of teaching seminars. I worked on several teaching seminars over the years.

4. The Sculptured Sounds Music Festival. As previously described, the festival was a huge commitment of my time, but I felt it to be a successful venture in many ways: it provided a practical experience for New School students in the areas of performance and production; it provided work opportunities for over eighty-two musicians, including several New School faculty members; and it illuminated my various concepts and involvement in diverse areas of music.

Accomplishments that I am most proud of in terms of my entire career include:

- The New School Distinguished Teaching Award (2007). It's an honor to be recognized for my service to the New School Jazz and Contemporary Music Program since its inception twenty years ago.
- Being selected as bassist for John Coltrane, Art Blakey, Thelonius Monk, and other pivotal jazz musicians.
- My Postcard Recordings (Summit Conference and Cerebral Caverns). I produced a kind of product that exemplified my thoughts about the music aesthetics and where my music has evolved.

Additional distinctions and special honors can be found in Appendix H.

Three Professional Goals That I Still Want to Accomplish

1. Touring—Increasing the marketing presence of and musical repertoire of Trio III (Note: Music composed by the trio is being studied in the Futuristic Concepts Class)
2. Archiving—my music and paper
3. Composing—The String Project, Trio III repertoire, and other affiliate ensembles.

Appendixes

A. Short Bio (Discography)
B. Administrative and New School Committees
C. Faculty Letters
D. Course Syllabi
E. Student Evaluations
F. Student Letters and other Evidence of Student Progress
G. Scholarly Research
H. Distinctions and Special Honors
I. Performances Historical and Current

Mathematical Sciences

Lisa A. Oberbroeckling

Department of Mathematical Sciences

Loyola College in Maryland

Fall 2008

Table of Contents

Purpose

The purpose of creating this portfolio is to organize all of my material to apply for tenure and promotion and to reflect on all aspects of my career. The main content of the portfolio should give the reader a sense of my accomplishments at Loyola College. The appendixes provide more detailed evidence of this.

Included in this document is an overview of my career at Loyola College in Maryland. This document is composed of four main sections, plus an appendix. The first section describes my teaching responsibilities and style, including evidence of my effectiveness. The second section describes my research program. The third section highlights a few service responsibilities, and the fourth section discusses the integration of teaching, research, service, accomplishments, and goals.

Teaching

Teaching Responsibilities

My teaching load is three undergraduate three-credit courses per semester with two preparations per term. Since the calculus courses are four credits and there is a one-credit MATLAB Laboratory (MA302) course offered in the fall, these extra credits of teaching are "banked" toward a course reduction. Table 1 lists the courses I've taught.

Teaching Philosophy, Objectives, and Methodologies

My philosophy and methodologies fall into three categories of courses.

The first is the Calculus type of course. This includes Precalculus, Calculus I, Calculus II, Calculus III, and even Introduction to Linear Algebra. Complex Analysis, for the most part, also falls under this category. These courses have a lot of material that is necessary to get through, and while it can be conceptual, many times the concepts are learned through a lot of exercises and homework. The Calculus courses have homework that is done online through WeBWorK, and I used WeBWorK in Linear Algebra. In addition, weekly quizzes are given in Calculus I-II.

Table 1. Courses Taught

Course	Name	Semester: Sections (N)	Role in Curriculum
MA109	Precalculus	Fa 2002: 01 (15), 02 (21)	To place in MA151 (Business Calculus) or MA251 (Calculus I)
MA251	Calculus I	Sp 2003: 01 (27), 02 (23) Fa 2003: 01 (23), 02 (29) Fa 2005: 04 (26), 05 (22)	Required of majors, minors, and most science majors
MA252	Calculus II	Sp 2005: 01 (22), 02 (21) Sp 2007: 02 (18) Sp 2008: 02 (20)	Required of majors, minors, and most science majors
CS295/ MA295	Discrete Structures	Fa 2002: 01 (15)	Required of computer science majors
MA301	Introduction to Linear Algebra	Sp 2004: 01 (24), 02 (29)	Required of majors; recommended for some science majors
MA302	MATLAB Laboratory	Fa 2004: 01 (10) Fa 2006: 01 (9) Fa 2007: 01 (24)	Required of all majors
MA351	Calculus III	Fa 2004: 01 (15), 02 (29) Fa 2006: 01 (15), 02 (26) Fa 2007: 01 (26), 02 (22)	Required of majors and some science majors
MA421	Analysis I	Fa 2003 (14) Fa 2004 (20) Fa 2007 (22)	Required of all majors
MA422	Analysis II	Sp 2004 (9) Sp 2008 (15)	Major elective
MA424	Complex Analysis	Sp 03 (13) Fa 03, Sp 04: Ind. Studies Sp 05 (11) Sp 07 (9)	Major elective

Complex Analysis has weekly homework that is mostly computational, with a few periodic proofs. Several exams are given during the semester with a cumulative final exam. The Calculus III and Linear Algebra courses have three or four projects due throughout the term. These are difficult book problems or problems that use the mathematical software MATLAB.

The second type of course is Analysis I and Analysis II. These courses are very proof intensive. The Analysis I course is vital for math majors to develop the ability to write proofs, in addition to learning the material, and Analysis II is an extension of that. Homework is collected biweekly. In order to further develop the writing component of the course, I've started a "rewrite" system that is a very minimal rough draft/final draft system to the homework. The student may choose one problem from each assignment to rewrite for up to full credit. They turn in both the original and rewritten problem the class period following the class the corrected homework was handed back. In class, exams are given, and either a comprehensive final exam (in Analysis I) or a final project (in Analysis II) is also given.

The third type is the MATLAB Laboratory course. This is a programming course that meets in a computer lab once a week. The students are exposed to MATLAB, a mathematical software package with high programming capability. Weekly programming assignments are given to expose them to various aspects of MATLAB, and the students are asked to use these for mathematical or statistical problems. Usually at the beginning of the class period, I talk about some of the syntax/ideas needed for the weekly assignment, then have the students work on the assignment the rest of the time. Attendance is counted in the grade, sometimes through a short worksheet or just by attending and participating. Some weeks I add a worksheet that is a short program, similar to something they will have to write for their next assignment. They are supposed to e-mail me the program by the end of class, and in a few cases they e-mail it to me by the end of the day. If the program doesn't work quite right or isn't exactly what I asked, I e-mail the student back with advice on how to fix it for the assignment. No exams are given in this course, but a final project is due at the end of the term.

Curricular Revisions

As this is my first postgraduate school position, there have been many courses that I hadn't taught before. But my graduate teaching fellowship at University of Oregon did give me a lot of experience teaching at the Precalculus and Calculus levels. What follows are changes or revisions made while at Loyola College.

- Changing Calculus I, II, and III from three credits to four credits. When I first came to Loyola, the Calculus courses were three credits and so met just three times a week. My second year at Loyola (2003–2004), a Calculus Committee was formed (of which I was chair) composed of the Mathematical Sciences faculty members who regularly taught Calculus. We successfully proposed changing the Calculus courses from three to four credits, meeting four times a week. With this change, the break in the material between Calculus I and II was also adjusted.
- The spring 2003 semester, I taught my first major upper-level course, Complex Analysis (MA424). I ended up designing the course to be too theoretical and chose a book that did not work at all for the students. The following year, I taught Complex Analysis both semesters as an independent study (one student each). I chose to use different books to see how they might work better. The book I chose for the spring 2004 independent study is the book I've since used for the spring 2005 and spring 2007 Complex Analysis courses. These courses were MUCH better received. In fact, the average of "Overall, I would rate the effectiveness of the instructor as" on the Course Evaluation form went from 3.21 on a 4.00 scale in spring 2003 to 3.82 in spring 2005 and 3.67 in spring 2007 (see Appendix B).
- Previous to Loyola College, I had never incorporated technology in any of the courses I taught. I allowed technology such as graphing calculators and even would mention them in class, but never created assignments that specifically used any technology. I have since incorporated the use of MATLAB in the Introduction to Linear Algebra (MA301) and Calculus III (MA351) courses. I give three to four projects throughout the

semester that use MATLAB. The projects use MATLAB to do some computations and/or graphing to answer more involved exercises than the typical homework assignment.

Teaching Improvement

One of the biggest changes I've faced in improving the Calculus courses is the use of WeBWorK. It is a free online homework system that was developed at the University of Rochester. This system allows me to select from a huge number of already written problems, or to create my own problems, for the students to complete. It is available through the Internet so all the student needs is the link to the page (which is made available on both Blackboard and the class Web site). When a student completes a problem, the computer immediately reports whether it is right or wrong.

Every student has the same set of exercises, but some of the numbers may be randomized or, in the case of a matching problem, they may be in different orders. For example, one student may have to compute the derivative of $cos(2x)$ while another student has to compute the derivative of $cos(3x)$. An example of a WeBWorK assignment for two guest students for Calculus II appears in Appendix A. Many students have found this system to be useful:

> "The webwork helped me a lot even though I did not like it at first."—Student evaluation comment, Spring 2007 MA252.02 (Calculus II)

Another teaching improvement I made was the idea of "redos" in Analysis I (MA421). As mentioned above, this course has a lot of proof writing in it, but there doesn't seem to be a good opportunity for a traditional rough draft/final draft writing system as in other courses. So I give the students the opportunity to redo a problem of their choice on each assignment. They turn in both the original and new version and can get up to full credit. Students commented positively about the redos:

> "Re-writes were a good idea of a different way to approach math homework."—Student evaluation comment, Fall 2004 MA421.01 (Analysis I)

Selected Course Syllabi and Other Material

In Appendix A are examples of the three types of courses discussed above. These are Calculus II (Spring 2007), Calculus III (Fall 2007), Analysis I (Fall 2007) and MATLAB Laboratory (Fall 2007). These syllabi are handed out the first day of class and are printouts of what appears on my class Web pages. Homework assignments, announcements, solutions, and handouts are also available on the class Web site. The interested reader may view a sample class Web site by going to http://www.evergreen.loyola.edu/~loberbroeckling/ma351f07.

Also included in Appendix A is a sample of a WeBWorK assignment for the Calculus II course and a sample review sheet for an exam for both a Calculus II and Analysis I exam. A review sheet is made available to the students a week before the exam, and solutions to the problems in the review sheet are posted on the class Web site. While it is a lot of work to type up the solutions to a review sheet for the first time, I've found it worthwhile, and students have commented to that effect on the course evaluations.

> "Keep making excellent review sheets for the tests."—Student evaluation comment, Fall 2006 MA351.01 (Calculus III)

Student Evaluation Data

My student evaluations have steadily improved while at Loyola College, which can be seen in Table 2. I've even received 4.00/4.00 in some courses on, "Overall I would rate the effectiveness of the instructor as . . ." (Fall 2006 Calculus III), "Was well prepared for each class" (Fall 2004 Analysis I), "Clearly laid out objectives" (Fall 2006 Calculus III), and "Communicated interest and enthusiasm" (Spring 2007 Calculus II). Table 2 summarizes the "effectiveness" question on the course evaluation. Appendix B includes more summaries of the course evaluations.

Classroom Observations

Our department at this time does not have a formal system of peer evaluation of teaching. This is a goal of several of the junior faculty to develop a better system to be used for evaluative purposes.

**Table 2. Course Evaluation: Question 13, by Year:
"Overall, I Would Rate The Effectiveness of the
Instructor of This Course As . . ."**

	4: Excellent		3: Good		2: Fair		1: Poor		Total		
Year	N	%	N	%	N	%	N	%	N	Ave	% ≥ 3
2002–03	38	38.8%	46	46.9%	12	12.2%	2	2.0%	98	3.22	85.7%
2003–04	59	50.9%	44	37.9%	11	9.5%	2	1.7%	116	3.38	88.8%
2004–05	71	64.0%	31	27.9%	7	6.3%	2	1.8%	111	**3.54**[a]	91.9%
2005–06	30	68.2%	12	27.3%	2	4.5%	0	0.0%	44	**3.64**	**95.5%**
2006–07	47	74.6%	16	25.4%	0	0.0%	0	0.0%	63	**3.75**	**100.0%**
Total	245	56.7%	149	34.5%	32	7.4%	6	1.4%	432	**3.47**	**91.2%**

[a]Averages that are 3.5 or greater and the % ≥ 3 that are 95% or greater are in
bold for emphasis.

Thus, in the Fall 2008 semester, I hope to have several classroom
observations made to include in this section.

Research and Scholarship

Description

My research is in Operator Theory, which is a specialization of an
area of mathematics called Functional Analysis. It is on the pure or
theoretical side of mathematics. This means that usually no direct
computations or computers are used; new results are proven in the
abstract setting using known results in texts and publications.

The description that follows is written for the nonmathemati-
cian; a more technical description can be found in Appendix C.

The first main project of my research involves what are called
generalized and Drazin inverses of linear operators. Linear operators T are functions or maps that have certain properties that
send or assign an input x to an output y. Frequently in mathematics or the sciences, an equation of the form

$$Tx = y$$

needs to be solved, where T is some operator, y is the known output,
and x is the unknown input. For example, T may be an operator

that computes the profit y of producing x number of units. The goal is to figure out what x needs to be to obtain the desired profit y.

To solve an equation of the form above, if T is what is called invertible, an exact, unique solution x can be found. However, if T is not invertible, then the equation may have no solutions or infinitely many solutions. In the case of no solutions, it would still be useful to find the best *approximation* to a solution. In the case of infinitely many solutions, the "best" solution would need to be found, with *best* usually meaning the solution of the smallest norm (magnitude or length). A generalized inverse can find these best solutions or approximations of solutions. Also, Drazin inverses can similarly be used to solve, or approximately solve, other types of equations. An issue with both generalized and Drazin inverses is that they may or may not exist.

My research project involves characterizing the existence of generalized inverses and Drazin inverses in special settings, one of which is called the Jörgens algebra. There are many important examples of these settings that are used to solve integral equations and physics applications. Using these results, other special situations are also considered. Also, a stronger type of generalized inverse known as the Moore-Penrose inverse (common in linear algebra) was studied. Generalized and Drazin inverses are widely studied in many settings, so this line of research can continue.

I've also started collaboration with a former colleague, Christos Xenophontos, whose area of expertise is more applied in what is called Numerical Analysis. While my collaborator does more computations and computer work, my contribution is in using the theoretical, analytical tools I've developed.

This project looked at a certain system of differential equations. In general, an exact solution cannot be found, so Numerical Analysis is used to find an approximation to the solution using easier functions like combinations of polynomials of certain degrees. There are two main goals in Numerical Analysis when approximating solutions; one is to analyze the accuracy of the solution, and the other is to determine the "computing cost" of this approximation. If the approximation is too difficult to compute or not very accurate, it is worthless.

Statements from Peers

The goal is in the next six months to be able to include statements from three peers.

Sample of Research Presentations

I've given a couple of research presentations at the Loyola College Mathematical Sciences Seminar. They are listed below.

February 5, 2003, "Generalized Inverses in the Jörgens Algebra"

December 11, 2006, "Drazin Inverses in Certain Banach Algebras"

Also, I've given presentations at national and international conferences which are listed in Appendix E. Two presentations are highlighted here.

The first presentation highlighted was an outgrowth of my work done during my junior sabbatical in spring 2006. This research was presented in the talk entitled "Generalized and Drazin Inverses in Jörgens Algebras of Bounded Linear Operators" at the International Congress of Mathematicians 2006 (ICM2006) in Madrid, Spain, on August 29, 2006. This is a conference that takes place every four years, during which prestigious awards in mathematics, including the Fields medal, are awarded. Over three thousand mathematicians attended this conference.

The second highlighted presentation is "An hp Finite Element Method for Singularly Perturbed Systems of Reaction-Diffusion Equations" at the Sixth International Congress on Industrial and Applied Mathematics (ICIAM2007) conference in Zurich, Switzerland, in July 2007. This is highlighted because again it is an international conference with a lot of potential visibility.

Service
Sample of Committees

Department committees:

Hiring Committee (2003–2004): Received over 200 applications and hired for two positions in Mathematical Sciences.

Calculus Committee (2003–present), *Chair* from 2003–2005: As chair, the first year we successfully requested to change Calculus I and II from three to four credits by researching other institutions and asked the administration to allow us to bank the extra credit toward a course reduction. We also decided what topics would be covered in each course. The following year we successfully requested to change Calculus III from three to four credits using the same banking system.

Institutional committees:

- Undergraduate Student Research and Scholarship Committee (2004–2007), *Cochair* 2005–2006, *Chair* 2006–2007: Plan the Undergraduate Student Research and Scholarship Colloquium, held March or April every year. During my time on the committee, the Colloquium began including poster presentations, updated its Web site, and added an online application system. The colloquium grew in size from thirteen presentations and twenty students to forty-six presentations and seventy students participating. As *chair* and *cochair,* I was in charge of the committee's budget.
- Phi Beta Kappa (PBK) (2002–present), *Secretary/Treasurer* 2005–present, member of Selection Committee 2006–present: The Selection Committee decided which students to invite to be inducted into PBK. As secretary/treasurer, I am in charge of the budget, including handling the dues, coordinating the induction ceremony and ordering for the event, and sending the dues and annual report to the PBK national office.

Integration of Professional Work and Goals

I feel that all three components, teaching, research, and service, must be interconnected in order to succeed as a faculty member. It is vital to stay current in the discipline through research in order to improve teaching. But in my discipline, the explicit connection between research and teaching at the purely undergraduate level is difficult to define. Only the most advanced students in the upper-level courses would comprehend a basic explanation of the research mathematicians are currently conducting. Indeed, if any of my department members or I were to give our conference talks about our research to each other, we'd be able to only understand maybe the first ten minutes of the forty-five-minute talk. This is a standard dilemma (to the point we don't consider it a dilemma) in mathematics. Thus we cannot very often show or discuss our research with the students in the classroom.

At the same time, I always try to mention something about my research or "mathematics beyond calculus" during a lecture. For example, in Calculus III, when we are discussing two- or three-dimensional vectors with real numbers, I mention that my research involves an abstract n-dimensional or even infinite-dimensional vector that may be composed of complex numbers. I don't go into details as I don't want to lose their interest, but I do want to portray that there is always something more beyond what they're currently learning (and I confess I enjoy the stunned looks on some of the students' faces).

Three Significant Accomplishments

- During my junior sabbatical and the time afterward, I conducted research in two very different projects described above, one of them in an entirely new area to me. As a result of these projects, I was able to submit a solo-authored paper, "Drazin Inverses in Jörgens Algebras of Bounded Linear Operators," and the project with my collaborator, Christos Xenophontos. We've had one paper published in *Applied Mathematics and Computation* and three others submitted.
- The improvement of teaching and the reputation I appear to have gained from it is another significant accomplishment. While I feel I'll always need to improve, I've had many compliments on my teaching in both personal interactions and the student evaluations. Recently in one section of Calculus III, I received 4.00/4.00 on the student evaluation question, "Overall I would rate the effectiveness of the instructor as . . ."
- A third significant accomplishment is the growing role that I've carved out in the department and college. While some would say my service at times was too heavy, taking away from my research, I've realized especially in the past year that many department colleagues come to me for advice or support.

Goals

- Feel more confident about my place in the college and in my research. My research got off to a very slow start after graduate school and is just now developing into a worthwhile program.
- Become more of a leader in my department and/or college. A senior colleague/mentor in another department once mentioned seeing me as a dean someday. I'd never thought of that until then, but have since thought in a positive way about my ability and desire to become chair or other administrator.
- Become even more of a mentor to students and young colleagues. As the senior untenured faculty member in my department, to some extent this has already taken place, but I would like to continue and improve this. I'd also like to be able to mentor more students to get them better prepared for graduate school.

Appendixes

A. Course Syllabi and Other Material
B. Student Evaluation Data
C. Research Description
D. Research Papers
E. List of Presentations
F. List of Service

Nutritional Sciences

Gina Jarman Hill

Department of Nutritional Sciences

Texas Christian University

Fall 2008

Table of Contents

Integration of Professional Work and Goals
  Professional Growth and Development
  Professional Accomplishments
  Professional Goals
Appendixes

Purpose

This portfolio serves to document the activities expected of a tenure track faculty member with the overall purpose to secure tenure rank. The materials are organized in such a manner to categorize within the elements of teaching, research/scholarship, service, and integration of professional work and goals.

The teaching section describes my teaching philosophy and serves to demonstrate teaching effectiveness, which is supported by student comments and evaluation data, description of course revisions resulting from student input, teaching improvement activities, and my own observations.

The research/scholarship section outlines the nature of my research and provides a sample of publications and conference presentations. This section also includes a description of involvement in professional societies and editorial appointments. The service section provides a sample of the committees on which I have served, my role on each, a record and description of student involvement and advising, and the record of service within the community surrounding the university.

The final section describes how the teaching, research/scholarship, and service contribute to one another and to my professional growth as a whole. Accomplishments and professional goals are highlighted. The accumulation of information for and creation of this document have revealed areas requiring improvement and emphasis over the next year.

Teaching

Teaching Responsibilities

The following chart summarizes the courses that I currently teach in the fall and spring semesters. The TCU Department of Nutritional Sciences does not have a graduate program. We specialize in the preparation of students for the nutrition field, where the majority of our graduates become registered dietitians.

Course Number	Course Title*	Student Enrollment	Required or Elective	Undergraduate
NTDT 30113	Infant and Child Nutrition	25–30	Elective	Undergraduate
NTDT 30331	Medical Terminology	26–28	Required	Undergraduate
NTDT 30333 Lecture and Lab	Medical Nutrition Therapy 1	14–30	Required	Undergraduate
NTDT 40333	Medical Nutrition Therapy 2	13–24	Required	Undergraduate
NTDT 40337 Lecture and Lab	Supervised Practice in Medical Nutrition Therapy, lecture and lab	10–16	Required	Undergraduate
NTDT 40363	Community Nutrition	25–34	Required	Undergraduate

*Note: See Appendix A for table of additional courses taught over past four years.

Teaching Philosophy, Objectives, and Methodologies

In the eighth grade, Mrs. Thelma Coffey was *not* my math teacher. I grew up in an incredibly small school where kindergarten through twelfth grades were housed in one very long building surrounded by corn and cotton fields. My math teacher had students in her room studying eighth-grade math, prealgebra, and algebra. I was in the middle group and was drowning quickly. My poor teacher was overwhelmed with junior high students studying different subjects in one room with too many hands raised and too little time. One day after school, Mrs. Coffey found me in a hopeless state and began tutoring me for a few sessions. Up to this point, I believed I was destined to be a math idiot. All it took was a few hours on her part, and to this day, I use techniques that she taught me through my blubbery tears and frustration to teach nutrition students how to calculate tube feeding regimens and total parenteral nutrition prescriptions.

Most people learn most effectively by doing. Book knowledge is important, yes, but it is not the end point. Students remember more and build confidence when they DO, when they use the information, and when they *practice* on their own what they have learned and then *use* it. As an assistant professor of nutrition, I introduce material and provide an atmosphere where students can learn and then practice using the information in a safe environment where they feel comfortable enough to ask questions without fear of embarrassment from me or their peers.

A good teacher facilitates learning. In my typical courses, I use a mixture of PowerPoint lectures, practice problems, case studies, nongraded quizzes, and guest speakers. I think that each of these is important because students tend to retain information best from different methods. I use PowerPoint in many of my classes because pictures are valuable for understanding. For example, if I want students to understand a concept about what happens in patients who experience insulin resistance, pictures can help solidify an idea much better than my drawings on a whiteboard. A picture of a person with goiter resulting from an iodine deficiency is much more memorable than words describing the appearance of goiter. Students work in groups in my classes to complete practice problems and case studies. In this way, they also hear others' ideas, which may help them solve similar problems in the future when they practice dietetics. I have found ungraded quizzes effective to help students review the previous class material and prepare them for what we are about to discuss. Guest speakers provide insight about day-to-day workings in specific fields that I have not worked in personally. For example, in Infant and Child Nutrition, a nurse from the Mother's Milk Bank of North Texas discusses how milk banking occurs and who benefits from mothers who have chosen to donate surplus breastmilk.

Curricular Revisions

In each course, I ask the students to give me feedback a couple of times during the semester about what things are helpful and what things are not working to help them learn. I have received great tips and suggestions that I have implemented to improve my classes and teaching methods. The following chart highlights examples of some of the changes that I have implemented as a result of student comments, my own observations, and teaching improvement workshops and courses.

Course	Opportunity for Improvement	Revision Implemented and Result
Medical Nutrition Therapy 1 (MNT 1)	Per students' comments and SPOT evaluations, MNT 1 was an overwhelmingly busy course. Students were required to learn medical terminology. However this requirement contributed little to their overall course grades, although it required significant amounts of study time throughout the semester.	Developed and received university approval to teach Medical Terminology as a separate one-hour credit course. Nutrition students are pleased with the course format. Additionally, other students outside of our department have enrolled in the course. It is required by many medical schools and physical/occupational therapy programs.
Medical Nutrition Therapy 2	Wanted to improve overall retention of information among students.	Incorporated un-graded quizzes for students to complete for the first 5–10 minutes of class. Students responded positively to the quizzes and were disappointed if they did not receive a quiz at the beginning of each class.
Community Nutrition	This course is typically scheduled for the last semester of a nutrition student's career. Students were unhappy with the time at which the course was scheduled due to inconvenience.	Completed requirements to become certified as an online instructor. Changed the class to be primarily online, meeting only for exams and informational meetings. Students expressed satisfaction with changes to course. Although SPOT evaluations are not available since this change was implemented, midsemester evaluations revealed that students were learning and pleased with the format.

Selected Course Syllabi and Other Course Materials

Infant and Child Nutrition

Students complete an infant nutrition case study, write a newspaper article comparing breastfeeding to infant formula feeding, develop an infant feeding brochure, and write a five-page persuasive paper about school food service regulations in this writing emphasis course. Guest speakers include a La Leche League leader, a registered nurse and lactation specialist from the Mothers' Milk Bank of North Texas, and a registered dietitian from the Birdville Independent School District.

Medical Nutrition Therapy 1

Students complete a nutrition assessment case study, a group educational presentation, and two journal abstract writing assignments, and develop an educational brochure for the lay public. Guest speakers include an enteral (tube feeding) company sales representative and a Certified Diabetes Educator (CDE). See Appendix B for the syllabi for this course.

Medical Nutrition Therapy 2

Students complete two intensive case studies. Guest speakers include dietitians from renal dialysis facilities. See the syllabus for this course in Appendix B.

Community Nutrition

Students create a bulletin board and complete online quizzes, online discussions, and a webliography, and write in their online journals in this primarily online course. Students must work in groups to develop a health fair. They secure a health fair site, develop educational materials, and obtain free advertising and free "give-away" products to attract participants. See the syllabus, bulletin board assignment, health fair assignment, and sample pictures of student health fairs in Appendixes B and C.

Documentation of Teaching Improvement Activities

* Completed eLearning Boot Camp, August 12, 2004. (See Appendix D for certificates of accomplishment for teaching improvement activities.)

- Learned to use eCollege. Have since developed eCollege Web sites for each course that I teach. Rely on this resource to disseminate grades, relay course materials, provide practice and graded quizzes, and post notes and lectures.
- Completed EDU 101B eCertification: Teaching Online Courses and earned recognition as an eCollege Certified Online Instructor, October 30, 2006. (See Appendix D for certificates of accomplishment for teaching improvement activities.)
- Chose to become a certified online instructor in order to teach Community Nutrition as an online course. Learned how to effectively communicate online course expectations, use threaded discussions, webliography assignments, and student journal entries. Taught Community Nutrition as online course in spring 2007.
- Attended Center for Teaching Excellence Workshop "Podcasting in the Classroom," May 3, 2007.
    - Several students in the Community Nutrition course suggested including recorded sound-bites within the online Community Nutrition course. Plan to implement recorded interviews with community dietitians for Community Nutrition course in spring 2008.
- Attended Center for Teaching Excellence Workshop "Classroom Performance System (CPS)," September 13, 2007.
    - Chose to attend this workshop to learn about incorporating CPS into courses to review and assess student learning.
- Attended "Using Online Learning to Compete Successfully in a Rapidly Changing Environment" at American Dietetic Association 2006 Food and Nutrition Conference and Expo, September 19, 2006.
    - Chose to attend this workshop knowing that I planned to change Community Nutrition to an online format. Learned to anticipate student expectations and frustrations that may occur regarding online courses. Discovered methods that I may use to avoid student frustrations.

(See Appendix D for certificates of accomplishment for teaching improvement activities.)

Student Course Evaluation Data

The following objectives were identified as holding primary importance by the Chair of the Department of Nutritional Sciences:

Objective	Year	Medical Nutrition Therapy 1 Score (Spring)	Medical Nutrition Therapy 2 Score (Fall)	Supervised Practice in Medical Nutrition Therapy Score (Fall)
I had sufficient opportunities to demonstrate my understanding of the course material.	2004	3.14 ($n = 14$)	3.67 ($n = 12$)	3.78 ($n = 9$)
	2005	3.37 ($n = 19$)	3.5 ($n = 12$)	3.8 ($n = 11$)
	2006	3.52 ($n = 22$)	3.26 ($n = 19$)	4.0 ($n = 14$)
	2007	3.19 ($n = 21$)	N/A	N/A
The instructor conducted the course in a way that helped me learn.	2004	3.07 ($n = 14$)	3.58 ($n = 13$)	3.71 ($n = 9$)
	2005	3.11 ($n = 19$)	3.42 ($n = 12$)	3.7 ($n = 11$)
	2006	3.18 ($n = 22$)	3.63 ($n = 19$)	3.92 ($n = 14$)
	2007	3.43 ($n = 21$)	N/A	N/A
The instructor was well prepared for each class.	2004	3.36 ($n = 14$)	3.83 ($n = 12$)	4.0 ($n = 9$)
	2005	3.26 ($n = 19$)	3.83 ($n = 12$)	3.7 ($n = 11$)
	2006	3.68 ($n = 22$)	3.79 ($n = 19$)	4.0 ($n = 14$)
	2007	3.67 ($n = 21$)	N/A	N/A
The instructor provided an intellectually stimulating learning environment.	2004	3.29 ($n = 14$)	3.75 ($n = 13$)	3.89 ($n = 9$)
	2005	3.26 ($n = 19$)	3.83 ($n = 12$)	3.7 ($n = 11$)
	2006	3.5 ($n = 22$)	3.63 ($n = 19$)	4.0 ($n = 14$)
	2007	3.57 ($n = 21$)	N/A	N/A
The instructor encouraged active student participation.	2004	3.57 ($n = 14$)	3.83 ($n = 12$)	4.0 ($n = 9$)
	2005	3.37 ($n = 19$)	3.75 ($n = 12$)	3.8 ($n = 11$)
	2006	3.59 ($n = 22$)	3.68 ($n = 19$)	4.0 ($n = 14$)
	2007	3.67 ($n = 21$)	N/A	N/A

Note: Score is based on 4-point scale, 4 being the highest rating. Number of respondents (n) completing evaluation are noted for each course.

Student Comments

- "It was a lot of work, but the information is really fun. I really like how the notes were done."—MNT 1, Spring 2004.
- "She drew us into each lecture with humor or just being pleasant. I really think she had a desire to make sure we understood what was going on."—NTDT 10403, Spring 2005.
- "I appreciate her style of teaching and her fair approach to testing. As a professor, I respect her level of knowledge and how she challenges us to learn the material."—MNT 2, Fall 2006.
- "I really enjoyed having e-college class; it allows you to monitor your progress as you go."—Community Nutrition, Spring 2006.
- "I feel like I learned the most in this class. And the way you taught, how you were interactive and always reviewed the class before, I really liked it; it helped me out a lot. I like that you expect our best effort. I don't think that you ever expected the impossible. And in return for our efforts you gave us your best effort. I enjoyed the class a lot; your style of teaching really helps me remember and learn."—MNT 1, Spring 2007.
- "This was my favorite class of the year. She was great. She made a fun environment of learning, and it was different than the same old taking-notes lecture. She made interaction available and let us voice our opinions. Everything in class was very interesting and I learned many things."—Infant & Child Nutrition, Spring 2007.

See Appendix E for further student cards and e-mails.

Colleague Observations

Dr. Bonnie Melhart, Associate Dean of College of Science and Engineering, observed Nutrition in the Life Cycle in Fall 2003. Excerpt from letter dated January 12, 2004:

It is clear that your students are engaged in what they are studying, as they asked questions and participated in the discussion. . . . I think it is commendable that you know all the students and called on them by name.

See Appendix F for the full letter.

Research and Scholarship

Description of the Nature of Faculty Research

The TCU Department of Nutritional Sciences prides itself on the fact that each of our undergraduate students completes an intensive research project prior to graduation. Although we are a small department with only five full-time faculty members, each student has a faculty member who guides her through the research project process.

I conduct research pertaining to the following four areas: medical nutrition therapy, lactation, dietary supplementation, and nutrition and behavior. Therefore students who are interested in these topics are directed to me. Examples of research projects conducted with students include:

- Eating patterns and diabetes knowledge among Meals on Wheels participants. Lacey Shield and Cristina Caviglia in conjunction with Meals on Wheels, Tarrant County.
- Marketing study to determine feasibility of for-profit home delivered meal program for Meals on Wheels. Krissy Chester for Meals on Wheels, Tarrant County.
- Influence of a nutrition education program among people living with HIV/AIDS. Kacie Beckett in conjunction with AOC (AIDS Outreach Center), Fort Worth.
- Dietary patterns among children living with behavioral difficulties. Kristina Keilson.
- Factors related to current eating habits among university students. Shea Saunders and Chelsea Cartwright.
- Neurotransmitter levels and nutritional intake among breast-feeding and formula feeding mothers. Jennifer Hunt and Laura Daughtery.
- Benefits and disadvantages of gastric bypass surgery. Shea Brumley and Katelyn Kelly.
- Factors influencing sports drink consumption among children attending sports camp. Shelby Pardue.
- Influence of media images on body image perceptions of college students. Rachael Heim and Leticia Wallace.
- Diabetes mellitus knowledge and concerns among African Americans. Amy Sin Wan and Nada Jawahery.

- Comparison of university students' actual and perceived food portion sizes to suggested food portion sizes and relationship to BMI. Rita Castillo and Nicole DeNes.
- Examining intentions to breastfeed among pregnant/lactating women using the expanded rational expectations intentions model. Mary Bishop.
- Folic acid knowledge and use among sexually active university females. Keely Hawkins.

Publications in Refereed Scholarly Journals

See Appendix G for full manuscripts.

- Jarman Hill, G., Arnett, D. B., Mauk, E. Breastfeeding intentions among low income pregnant/lactating women. *American Journal of Health Behavior.* 2008 March–April; 32(3), 125–136.
- Jarman Hill, G., VanBeber, A., Gorman, M. A. Breastfeeding promotion in Texas. *TAFCS (Texas Association of Family and Consumer Sciences) Research Journal.* 2007; 2(2), 21–22.
- Gorman, M. A., VanBeber, A., and Jarman Hill, G. Differences in serving sizes of commonly ordered foods at popular casual dining restaurants in Tarrant County, Texas. *TAFCS (Texas Association of Family and Consumer Sciences) Research Journal.* 2007; 2(2), 19–20.
- Jarman Hill, G., Hampton, S. Breastfeeding promotion among adolescent mothers. *TAFCS (Texas Association of Family and Consumer Sciences) Research Journal.* 2006; 2(1), 23–24.
- VanBeber, A., Jarman Hill, G. Increasing the awareness of folic acid: An important public health message. *TAFCS (Texas Association of Family and Consumer Sciences) Research Journal.* 2006; 2(1), 25–26.
- Jarman Hill, G., VanBeber, A., Gorman, M. A., Sargent, J. Knowledge of food portion size and typical food intake among university students. *TAFCS (Texas Association of Family and Consumer Sciences) Research Journal.* 2006; 2(1), 31–33.
- Hill, G. J., Shriver, B. J., Arnett, D. B. Examining intentions to use CoQ10 among breast cancer patients. *American Journal of Health Behavior.* 2006 May–June; 30(3), 313–21.

Grants Obtained

- Determining Intentions to Breastfeed among Women. Texas Christian University New Faculty Grant, $2207, Fall 2003.
  - This grant supported research that has been accepted for publication in the *American Journal of Health Behavior.*

- Influence of a Nutritional Education Program Among People Living with HIV and AIDS. Texas Christian University Science and Engineering Research Grant (SERC), $1300, Spring 2007.
  - This grant supported a research endeavor at the AIDS Outreach Center (AOC) of Fort Worth in which ongoing nutrition education was provided to those living in the community with HIV and AIDS. A manuscript is currently being written.

- Neurotransmitter levels and nutritional intake among breastfeeding and formula feeding mothers. Texas Christian University Science and Engineering Research Grant (SERC), $2000, Fall 2007.
  - This grant will support a research project that aims to compare nutritional intake and urinary neurotransmitter levels among breastfeeding and formula feeding mothers.

Editorial Appointments and Professional Offices

Editorial Appointments

- Texas Association Family Consumer Sciences (TAFCS) Annual Meeting Submissions Reviewer (2007)
- *TAFCS Journal* Reviewer (2007)
- Book reviewer for Wadsworth Thomson Learning. Nelms M, Sucher K, and Long S. *Understanding Nutrition Therapy and Pathophysiology.* Thompson Brooks/Cole, 2007.

Offices Held in Professional Societies

- American Dietetic Association Women's Health and Reproductive Nutrition Practice Group Nominating Chair Elect (2007–2008)
- Texas Dietetic Association Nominating and Awards Committee (2003–2004)

- Fort Worth Dietetic Association (FWDA) Board (2005–2006)
- FWDA Spring Seminar and National Nutrition Month Chair (2005)

See Appendix H for a list of additional offices held in professional societies.

Conference Presentations and Exhibits

Oral Presentations for Professional Continuing Education Credit

Continuing education credits were offered to professionals in attendance at each of these presentations, including registered nurses, social workers, health care administrators, and/or registered dietitians.

- Tarrant Area Gerontological Society Summer Forum, "Beyond Applesauce and Pudding: Nutritional Needs of Mature Adults," Fort Worth, TX, July 24, 2007.
- Alzheimer's Association 2006 Spring Symposium Key Concepts to Successful Dementia Care, "Designing a Diet for the Alzheimer's Patient," Fort Worth, TX, March 30, 2006.

Conference Presentations and Exhibits

The following conference exhibits were presented at the American Dietetic Association (ADA) Annual Conference. The ADA is the largest association of food and nutrition professionals with nearly 67,000 members.

- *Jarman Hill, G.,* Gorman, M.A., VanBeber, A. "All Natural" and "Organic Foods": Knowledge and Buying Practices of Specialty Foods Supermarket Customers. Presented at the 2007 Annual Meeting and Exposition of the American Dietetic Association, October 1, 2007, Philadelphia, Pennsylvania.
- Gorman, M.A., VanBeber, A.D., Dart, L., Hampton, S., *Jarman Hill, G.,* and Kistler, K. Diet and Dental Caries in Rural Guatemalan Children. Presented at the 2006 Annual Meeting and Exposition of the American Dietetic Association, September 19, 2006, Honolulu, Hawaii.

- *Jarman Hill, G.,* Gorman, M.A., Mauk, E., VanBeber, A. Examining intentions to breastfeed among pregnant/lactating women using the expanded rational expectations intentions model. Presented at the American Dietetic Association Annual Food and Nutrition Exposition, October 2005, St. Louis, MO.

See Appendix I for remaining conference exhibits/presentations and a full list of TCU Student Research Symposium exhibits.

Service
Sample of Committees

Department

- Coordinator of Medical Nutrition Therapy (MNT) rotations for Coordinated Program in Dietetics (2004–current)
- Director Didactic Program in Dietetics (2007–current)
- Student Nutrition and Dietetic Association Faculty Advisor (2004–current)
- Faculty Advisory Committee (2006–2007)
- Major Minor Fair Faculty Leader (2004–current)
- Committee Member, Faculty Search Committee, Management Coordinator Faculty (2007)
- Coordinator, Nutrition Care Process Seminar (2007)
- Co-Coordinator, Green Honors Chair Visit (2007)

University

- Faculty Senate Member (2006–2009)
- Academic Excellence Committee Member (2006–2007)
- Tenure Promotion and Grievance Committee Member (2007–2008)
- Undergraduate Council Member (2006–2009)
- Student Publications Committee Member (Spring 2005–2010)
- Graduation Faculty Marshall (Spring 2007)

Student Advising, Mentoring, and Service-Learning Activities

Fifteen students are on my regular advising list. We meet at least once each semester or more often if students have questions or are having difficulties with course work that may influence staying on their proposed degree plans. I also advise prospective students who visit TCU and are interested in our program, including those referred by the athletic department. I meet with such students approximately twice each month.

As the Didactic Program in Dietetics (DPD) Director for the Department, I advise graduating seniors regarding the Dietetic Internship (DI) application process. I meet with each of these students several times throughout the semester to help them complete the best application possible to help increase the chance of matching for a DI. This year I am advising eight graduating DPD students.

As the faculty adviser to the Student Nutrition and Dietetic Association (SNDA) I assist students in identification of programs that function as service-learning projects such as serving as nutrition experts at the local food bank or teaching inner-city children how to prepare healthy foods.

Community Participation

Everyone eats. Many people care about what they eat and how it influences their health. Employers want the employees to improve their nutrition in order to decrease absenteeism and decrease health care costs. Therefore, nutrition is a hot topic, and our department receives frequent requests for speakers and media interviews. Since arriving at TCU in Fall 2003, I have offered fifteen presentations to the public, completed ten newspaper interviews, six magazine interviews, and three television interviews. I also serve on the Tarrant County Meals on Wheels Nutrition Committee as a nutrition consultant.

See Appendix J for a complete list of community presentations and media interviews.

Integration of Professional Work and Goals
Professional Growth and Development

Each aspect of my job—teaching, research, and service—tends to improve each of the others. For example, I teach medical nutrition therapy to future nutrition professionals. By coordinating the clinical rotations in the TCU coordinated program in dietetics, students continue to apply this classroom knowledge that they obtain and grow in their confidence, until the time that they have earned the hours and experiences to take the registration examination for dietitians. While arranging these experiences for students and serving in my local dietetic association, I have had the opportunity to meet numerous nutrition professionals and find various locations to conduct research outside the walls of TCU. These relationships with nutrition professionals result in continual growth and freshness in the nutrition field.

Service both within and outside of the university has provided an avenue for professional growth. I have a much greater understanding of the importance of service for faculty and staff after serving on such committees as the Faculty Senate, Undergraduate Council, or the Student Publications Committee. Each committee serves a great purpose and is necessary for continued improvement in the education that we provide to our students at TCU. I serve outside TCU in professional organizations and as a frequent speaker in the community. These opportunities widen my network with professionals within and outside of my field.

Professional Accomplishments

Teaching

In my first four years at TCU, I have taught thirteen different courses/labs. I believe this is a noteworthy accomplishment because it shows that I am a willing and flexible member of the department. In my second year of teaching, I was awarded a Mortar Board preferred faculty award. I was very honored as a new faculty member to be recognized by a student as an especially effective teacher. *See Appendix K for the award certificate.

Research

Since 2004, I have served as the primary research mentor for twenty-two students, yielding twelve undergraduate research projects within the Department of Nutritional Sciences. These students participate in the TCU Student Research Symposium on research completion. Two of these students also presented their research at the Texas Dietetic Association conference.

Service

I have developed two new courses while at TCU. The first, Medical Terminology, was approved as a course for students within our department. However, other students have enrolled in this course after learning about the option since it is a prerequisite for other programs, including medical school and physical/occupational therapy programs. The second course I developed was Infant and Child Nutrition. It is a writing emphasis course offered as an option for students across campus, as well as those students in the newly developed multidisciplinary Child Development minor at TCU.

Professional Goals

- Publish a manuscript in the *Journal of Human Lactation* within the next three years. This journal is among the most respected research publications in the field of lactation.
- Serve as a spokesperson for the American Dietetic Association (ADA) within the next five years. ADA spokespeople are called on by media to interpret nutrition information for the general public.
- Develop a Continuing Professional Education home-study course for nutrition professionals within the next three years. Many registered dietitians rely on home-study courses to complete their requirements for continuing education. I believe that writing a peer-reviewed home study course would be a worthwhile accomplishment.
- Obtain letters to finalize professional portfolio. Request classroom observations and evaluations from two colleagues in the 2008–2009 year. Solicit statements regarding importance of my research from peers within the next six months.
- Continue to attend faculty development seminars/workshops to improve teaching techniques and overall student learning.

Appendixes

Appendix A: Listing of Additional Courses Taught

Appendix B: Selected Course Syllabi

Appendix C: Course Assignments and Sample Pictures

Appendix D: Certificates of Accomplishment for Teaching
      Improvement Activities

Appendix E: Student Cards and E-mails

Appendix F: Colleague Letter Regarding Teaching Evaluation

Appendix G: Full Published Research Manuscripts

Appendix H: Professional Society Offices Held

Appendix I: Professional and TCU Conference Exhibits/
      Presentations

Appendix J: Community Presentations and Media Interviews

Appendix K: Mortar Board Teaching Award Certificate

Pastoral Counseling

Kelly Murray

Department of Pastoral Counseling

Loyola College in Maryland

Fall 2008

Table of Contents

Purpose of Academic Professional Portfolio

The purpose of this academic professional portfolio is to encapsulate and speak to my teaching, scholarship, and service in one document for tenure/promotion. I will, narratively, discuss my philosophy of teaching and speak to my teaching responsibilities, syllabi, and course revisions. Included in this portfolio will be evaluations and statements from students and peers. I will also address the nature of my research and scholarship and how my research has evolved. Selected books and publications, along with conference presentations, will be highlighted. My administrative activities and my service will also be discussed. Lastly, this document, throughout, speaks to the integration of my professional career—my clinical work, my teaching, and my research.

Teaching Responsibilities

My teaching responsibilities in the Pastoral Counseling Department include teaching master's- and doctoral-level courses in psychology and counseling. The syllabi for the following courses are found in Appendix A.

Course Number	Course Name	Required/ Elective	Enrollment Number
PC678	Psychopathology	Required	20–30
PC778	Treatment of Psychopathology	Licensure requirement	20–30
PC661,662 PC663,664	Clinical Case Supervision	Required internship experience	6
PC675	Helping Relationship	Required	15
PC673	Crisis Intervention	Required	15–20
PC952	Theory and Practice of Supervision	Elective	10

Teaching Philosophy, Objectives, and Methodologies

My teaching philosophy and style have changed and developed over time. With years of experience, along with mentoring and discernment, I now have a more mature emphasis and commitment to the endeavor of teaching. My formation as a teacher has also been heightened by my time at Loyola and the basic Jesuit values of community and the ongoing challenge to improve. I have deeply incorporated the values of integration, service, and the whole-person perspective into my leadership style with my students both in and out of the classroom.

That style, in the past, was largely lecture, with an occasional open-ended question to get students involved. Their test scores were high, and my evaluations were good. Something, though, felt like it was missing. I wanted more from both myself and my students than to just memorize and store information. I wanted them to absorb it, ponder it, reflect on it, and then ultimately to incorporate and apply it. It was with this desire that I believe I truly began to develop as a teacher.

My style now is much different than it once was. With a deeper confidence in myself comes even more confidence in my students. I no longer think about what I MUST teach and about what I think they MUST know. I now think about HOW I am going to include the students and empower them in their learning process. Education is like the many paths that we journey through in life. As we forge a new path, it is nice to do so with someone who has hiked that particular trail before. It is from the experience of these seasoned hikers that we seek guidance, ask questions, know about the twists and turns of new terrain, and impart knowledge and information about the environment and culture in which we find ourselves.

Having walked the path my students are journeying, I am familiar with their pilgrimage. I have the knowledge to teach them about information they need to know. However, we forge the trail together, and I am interested in their perspective of the path and am curious about what meaning this knowledge has for them. My goal is to know how they encode the map of the journey and through what kind of lenses they see where they have been and where they are going. What do they take away from this journey? Could they walk this trail alone now? Are they confident in what they have learned, or do they need follow-on training in a particular area?

The answers to these questions can only be arrived at in collaboration with the student. I believe each student comes into the classroom experience with different readiness, experiences, motivations, and perspectives and will therefore have different needs from me as a teacher. While a lot of time is spent organizing, reading, and preparing, I do so with less anxiety and nervousness to be "perfect." There is a new acknowledgment within myself that there is a need to connect with my students and to make the classroom more collaborative.

Curricular Revisions

Over time, I have overhauled all of my courses and made significant revisions. However, one curricular revision has stood out to me as being both exciting in metamorphosis and in positive student feedback. One fall I taught Treatment of Psychopathology (PC778), which was a new class for me. I attempted to change the course to actively incorporate more theory into the treatment portion of the course. Initially I broke the students into groups of the main theories of treatment and assigned them readings and discussion groups, which they would then bring back to the class to share about ways they could treat particular disorders from their assigned theory. I got mixed results from the students about this approach. I liked the premise of interweaving more theory into a deeper understanding of treatment, and I also really wanted to delineate it from the students' first basic course in psychopathology.

The following semester I decided to teach the course through film while also incorporating symptoms, theory, and treatment. The students were assigned films to view outside class that corresponded with the disorder I was going to lecture on for that particular class and write a clinical paper for each movie that incorporated theory of understanding and treatment for a particular character from the film. I found through teaching the course with this format that the students were able to have a much more integrated and in-depth understanding of each disorder. The students reported on course evaluations that incorporating the medium of film was very powerful and that they felt much more in tune with the disorders through using multiple modalities to fully understand how these disorders are experienced and treated.

Course Syllabi

I believe that a course syllabus is like a map. It should be clear, easy to read, and point you in the right direction. As evidenced in my representative syllabi (in Appendix A), I lay out the expectations for the course, the course objectives, and goals. Required, recommended, and optional readings are listed. My methods of instruction, whether lecture, discussion, videos, overheads, small groups, and/or a combination of these, are delineated, as are student performance evaluation criteria and procedures. I highly value attendance and participation, and this is clearly stated, as are grading procedures. Weekly lecture topics and readings are clearly laid out. As a part of each syllabus are my home, work, and cell phone numbers, as well as my e-mail in case students have the need to contact me.

Teaching Improvement Activities

I am very mindful that the students in the Pastoral Counseling Department are all graduate students and adult learners. I came to Loyola after being on faculty at the United States Naval Academy, where the paramount teaching technique is largely lecture and the student population much younger. I learned, after a few semesters of both colleague mentoring and course feedback, that our students had different needs and a different style of learning. To ensure a shared learning environment, my style has developed where I lecture much less. The evolution in my style has been due to a deeper familiarity with the information I am teaching, more confidence in myself that comes with ongoing teaching, colleague feedback, and attending various seminars. I like my classes to proceed, when possible, in a seminar style. I have also learned, over the years, that students can learn as much from each other as they can from me.

Student Course Evaluations

During the academic year 2005–2006 we instituted a new student evaluation form within our department. There are forty questions on this evaluation, and students responded on a 5-point

Likert scale, with 1 being *ineffective* and 5 being *very effective*. The following table reflects the means from three selected questions from the new evaluation form for the semesters encompassing 2006–2007 and spring 2007 (Fall 2007 I was on maternity leave). The following three questions were selected: "My learning increased in this course," "Instructor's command of the subject matter," and "Overall evaluation of the course." See Appendix B for all student course evaluations.

Results	PC663,664: Fall, Spring 2006–2007 Spring 2007	PC678: Fall, Spring 2006–2007 Spring 2007	PC778: Spring 2006 and 2007
Learning increased	4.40,4.83,4.0	5.0,4.16,4.31	3.48,4.0
Command of subject matter	5.0,5.0,4.6	4.83,4.84,4.88	4.76,4.82
Overall evaluation	4.8,4.67,4.6	4.92,4.36,4.81	4.08,4.36

Colleague Statements

I am very fortunate to be a part of a supportive and enhancing department. When I joined the faculty, I was assigned a teaching mentor within my department, Sharon Cheston, who met with me frequently to discuss various teaching styles and techniques. She also asked me to videotape some of my classes, after which she and I would meet to review these videos. She gave me constructive feedback and suggestions, which were immensely helpful. Enclosed are also a few different colleague teaching evaluations. One observer, Joseph Ciarrocchi, noted, "She uses a deft sense of humor to enhance the pleasant learning atmosphere in the classroom as well as to highlight lecture material in a creative manner . . . particularly creative was the way she used case material as an instructional method to assist students in developing their diagnostic skills" (see Appendix C).

Nature of Research

Over the years I have researched and been interested in quite a few topics. My natural curiosity keeps piquing my interest to delve into unknown territories. However, I have come to realize that this tendency, while stimulating, does not offer me the opportunity to become an expert in a particular area and actually causes me to spend inordinate amounts of time learning new content areas. The past few years I have worked hard to narrow my focus of research, and I currently have two strands of ongoing research. The criteria used to narrow my research interests were to find areas of passion that integrated my clinical practice, my classroom teaching experiences, and my research. I have found, within the past few years, that I have two particular areas of interest that do indeed bring together these three areas. I have also discovered that integrating my practice, teaching, and scholarship has further synthesized and strengthened my performance across the board.

One strand of my research is focused on *practical clinical applications*. This clinical strand focuses on diagnostics and applicable interventions for various clients. Working in the area of personality disorders has, over the years, become a strong interest of mine, both in my clinical practice and in the classroom. I found that this particular topic is underrepresented in the literature and also in awareness in the general population. With years of clinical experience, I have come to the conclusion that deeply held personality characteristics are paramount to the relationships we have with ourselves and with others. These personality characteristics often go undiagnosed and untreated, which ultimately affects the way we interact with the rest of the world. As I became familiar with personality theories and interventions, I began to intervene at a deeper, characterological level and noticed that there was consequently a lessening of other major psychological disorders in my clients. Integrating this clinical work into the classroom has strengthened my teaching; therefore, it made perfect sense to also integrate work into my scholarship. I recently completed a book on personality disorders and relationships, and I have been asked by the publisher to further this line of writing with another book on personality disorders.

My second strand of ongoing research focuses on *spirituality*. Under this rubric, one's spirituality has been the main variable of interest. Within the past few years, spirituality has been found to be a separate construct from religiosity, and the interplay of spirituality with different variables is fascinating. My most recent and current empirical articles center on one's levels of spirituality and sexuality. Past research has looked at religiosity and sexuality, but there is little current research on spirituality and sexuality. Again, in my clinical practice, I see many adolescents with various psychological issues. I bring this interest into the classroom when I teach clinical courses and psychopathology and, in fact, I am the only full-time faculty member in our department who teaches both psychopathology and addresses child and adolescent issues.

Books and Publications

Research has been an active part of my academic career. My most recent scholarship achievement is the completion of my book, *Crazy Love: Dealing with Your Partner's Problem Personality*. This book was written for the general population and is the first book on the mass market to fully address all of the different personality disorders in the context of relationships. I also recently had an article accepted in the *Journal of Psychology and Theology* (rejection rate = 75 percent) that falls within the second strand of my research called, "Spirituality, Religiosity, Shame and Guilt as Predictors of Sexual Attitudes and Experiences." See Appendix D for a full accounting of my publications.

Conference Presentations

The opportunity to speak at conferences and seminars is truly a privilege. In June 2004 some of my colleagues and I gave a talk on, "Sexual Violence in Religious Institutions: The Case of the American Catholic Church," at Trinity College, Dublin, Ireland, at its conference on "Religions and the Politics of Peace and Conflict." To be a part of such an international conference strengthened me professionally, but also personally as I was called on to address and be a part of very real pressing global issues. This talk was followed by another similar one back home in America at the Mid Year Conference on Religion and Spirituality. A very recent seminar, one that I am quite proud of, was presented with my coauthor, Brad Johnson. We gave a seminar to approximately thirty clinicians on the topic of personality disorders. The feedback from the attendees was positive, and it helped us to plan for future seminars on the topic. See Appendix E for fliers from conferences and for attendee evaluations.

Service: Administrative Activities and Committees

I have numerous administrative activities as part of my duties in the Department of Pastoral Counseling.

- Faculty Senator is chosen by respective departments to represent those departments and the institution at large as part of the Faculty Senate. I have served as a Faculty Senator for the past $6\frac{1}{2}$ years.
- Director of Doctoral Clinical Education (hereafter director) has overall responsibility for guiding doctoral clinical education in the Graduate Programs in Pastoral Counseling and Pastoral Care, Loyola College, in Maryland. This includes implementing departmental policies and procedures for each Ph.D. student. I have served as the Director of Doctoral Clinical Education for the past five years.
- Chair, Faculty Search Committee 2002–2003; member, Faculty Search Committee 2004–2005, 2006–2007.
- Clinical Committee member 2001–Present.
- Director, Continuing Education Program 2003–Present
- Supervision, Mentoring, and Advising
  - Offer supervision to our M.S., M.S./Ph.D., Ph.D. students to help them acquire the theoretical body of knowledge and professional skills necessary for the counseling profession.
  - Provide individual mentoring to Ph.D. students as a way of offering unique teaching, consultation and evaluation vis-à-vis a student's professional and work.

- Offer student advising for academic planning and progress.
- Community service
  - Consultant to White House Medical Unit; implemented White House Crisis Intervention Team on Sept. 11, 2001.

Teaching, Research, and Service Contributions to Professional Growth and Development

I have found that my clinical private practice enhances my teaching. All of my course offerings are clinical in nature, which calls me to be up to date on the latest research, the most helpful and accurate intervention strategies and methodologies. Seeing patients keeps my diagnostic and treatment skills sharp and up to date. These experiences also translate well into case descriptions and studies in the classroom for my students. When I see a couple in my practice, for example, who have had relationship issues, and/ or psychological and personality issues, I will bring this case into the classroom for diagnostic and intervention discussion. My research strands spin off my clinical work and teaching, and consequently my work is integrated, and it feels as if I have completed the circle—one thing now flows easily into the others. This depth of integration allows me to grow in my work and research, thereby offering my students a grounded approach to learning.

Three Professional Accomplishments

I look back over the course of my academic career and I am delighted with where my road has led, and I am excited about what is ahead of me. I believe I have worked diligently to further my skills, and I am proud of my accomplishments. There are three accomplishments with which I am especially proud:

1. I am very proud to have grown and expanded as a teacher. I had a professor at Occidental College, Elmer Griffin, who was influential in my success and present career choice. He believed in me and held me to high standards. He was present, kind, and yet challenging. I firmly believe that I have grown into that example for my students, and I feel privileged to share their journey.

2. The completion of my first book has also been a big accomplishment. For years I wanted to write a book, yet time was limited, and I felt there were many other pressing issues to take care of first. When my colleague and I discussed the book and floated it by a few publishers to see what would happen, it was almost a shock when a publisher quickly grabbed it up and offered us a contract. The book is newly released.

3. Being chosen to teach at the Naval Academy is a big honor. There are only four active-duty Navy psychologists who teach at the Naval Academy, and it is a coveted and much-sought-after billet. Being selected to teach at the Academy is one of the highlights of my career. This opportunity was my first foray into teaching and academics. I am extremely thankful for that initial opportunity—it instilled in me a love of teaching and opened a whole new career path for me.

Professional Goals

I am blessed to be part of such a supportive department and institution. I have grown and developed largely because I have been given the encouragement and space to do so. I am delighted each year as I see my students progressing and finally graduating into competent and enthusiastic clinicians. With each passing semester and year, there are new opportunities and challenges. There are a few specific goals that I would like to accomplish before the tenure board convenes:

1. I would like to compile a few more statements from colleagues who can speak to my teaching style, skills, and way of being in the classroom.

2. I would like to collect three outside peer letters that address the importance of my research and scholarship to the field of psychology and counseling.

3. I would like to complete and submit an empirical paper, currently in progress, to a peer-reviewed journal by January 2008.

4. I would like to start and finish my new book on antisocial personality disorders and relationships by the end of summer 2008.

Appendixes

A. Syllabi
B. Student Course Evaluations
C. Statements from Colleagues
D. Evidence of Scholarship
E. Conference Brochures/Fliers

Pediatric Emergency Medicine

Annalise Sorrentino, MD

University of Alabama-Birmingham

Department of Pediatrics

Division of Emergency Medicine

Fall 2008

Table of Contents

Purpose

As a clinician in a highly research-oriented field, one challenge I have encountered is finding ways to illustrate my goals and accomplishments. We owe so much of what we have and are able to do today to medical research and the inquisitive minds that continue to seek out the answers. What sometimes get overlooked are the clinical contributions that occur on a daily basis. They do not necessarily come attached to a dollar sign or lead to a string of publications, but that does not make them any less important.

Scholarly activity comes in a variety of shapes and sizes, and it is all contributing to the good of the medical community. Whether it is by teaching students and residents, or giving your time and expertise to the community, it should be recognized and looked on as significant.

I am constructing this academic professional portfolio in order to highlight my contributions and accomplishments not only for the other people who might read it or review my performance, but for myself as I strive to have a successful career that is meaningful and noteworthy. I don't want to just look back on my career and be proud; I want to be able to examine it while it is happening, and ensure I am continuing in the intended direction.

Teaching

My teaching responsibilities include education at all levels. Working in the pediatric emergency department affords me the opportunity for bedside teaching on a regular basis. In this capacity, I instruct pediatric emergency medicine fellows, pediatric nurse practitioners, pediatric residents, internal medicine/pediatrics residents, emergency medicine residents, family practice residents, senior medical students, and nurse practitioner students. My role with each of them is distinctly different.

Pediatric Emergency Medicine Fellows

The pediatric emergency medicine fellowship at UAB is a three-year program with rotations in the emergency department, as well as anesthesia, critical care, toxicology, adult emergency medicine, and trauma. There is a research requirement to be eligible to take the board certifying exam. Copies of the fellow curriculum as well as evaluations by current and former fellows are included in Appendix 1. When working with the fellows, my teaching responsibilities include:

- Bedside assistance with critically ill patients
- Guidance with patient procedures
- Offering advice on clinical decision making
- Interesting case conference and evidence-based medicine conference annually
- Journal club with a fellow annually

Each of our fellows is distinctly different, which makes our fellowship program rich and full. This also allows differing levels of decision making and autonomy as they progress through their fellowship under the supervision of attendings like me.

Residents

The residents who rotate through the emergency department (ED) come from various backgrounds, including pediatrics, internal medicine/pediatrics, emergency medicine, and family practice. Resident expectations are outlined in Appendix 2. My roles with residents include:

- One-on-one collaboration with each patient
- Instruction on patient procedures
- Noon conferences
- Resident lectures
- Small group discussions/case presentations
- Mentoring

Many of my lectures come from cases I have seen in the ED, as adult learners seem to learn better from real-life experiences. I encourage them to do the same, researching interesting cases (and sometimes the not-so-interesting ones) as they see them. Often in a busy emergency department, it is difficult to take the time and instruct when you are just trying to move the patients, but I have found that even one or two small teaching points can make a big difference and one they will remember. Examples of conferences given to residents and evaluations of those conferences are included in Appendix 2.

I have also mentored resident research efforts, as evidenced by two previous presentations at a regional pediatric research conference:

- *Sorrentino, A.,* Hollingsworth, S., Railey, M.D. Atypical Presentations of Tuberculosis. *Journal of Investigative Medicine.* January 2005; 53(1): s279.
- Jackson, B. F., Monroe, K. W., Nichols, M. H., King, W. D., *Sorrentino, A.* Pediatric Eye Injuries in Alabama: An Epidemiological Review, 1989–2004. *Journal of Investigative Medicine.* January 2006; 54(1): s305.

These abstracts can be viewed in their entirety in appendix 2.

Students

I routinely work with two other types of students in the emergency department: senior medical students and nurse practitioner students. Both tend to be early in their training and love to learn even on the most basic level. They require complete supervision, and all decisions are cleared through a supervising physician, such as myself. They are at the stage of forming their foundation to build on, which is a crucial point in their careers. Medical student expectations are included in Appendix 3. I help them to construct a wide and stable base that they can foster, and I do so in the following ways:

- Bedside teaching
- Encouraging literature review
- Providing interesting articles/research on common pediatric emergency problems
- Providing lectures and case presentations

As the medical school has gone through a curriculum change, I have been able to participate in student education in the classroom. I am a small group preceptor for the Patient, Doctor, and Society (PDS) module, which is the first class they are required to take. A copy of this syllabus is found in Appendix 3. It focuses on issues such as ethics, professionalism, and communication, with the intention of helping them develop a better grasp of the topics before their first patient encounter.

Evaluations from students taught in the clinical setting as well as in the classroom can be found in Appendix 3. They include the following:

"Dr. Sorrentino was an engaging and caring preceptor. She offered much to us from her past experiences and current practice. She also expressed an openness to us to help us whenever we needed it, even after the PDS module is over. I appreciated her dedication to our group."

"Great rapport with students, easy to talk to, balances topic of discussion with relevant side stories which keep small groups interesting, encourages students to reflect on practical application of material, respectful of students."

"Outstanding at facilitating the discussion and integrating concepts learned in class with issues faced in the clinic. The biggest benefit was that she taught us that decisions were not simple; rather, they involved analyzing all stakeholders in different situations to make a proper clinical decision."

"I also serve as a mentor for medical students of all levels of training. My group consists of a total of nine students ranging from first- to fourth-year students. We meet two or three times a year, and I offer general advice and support on going through the process of medical school."

Medical Community

I am the medical director for our pediatric advanced life support classes, which are held four times a year for a variety of health care providers (physicians, nurses, respiratory therapists, para-medics, pharmacists, and dentists, to name a few). I have been able to use this experience to perform several different types of teaching. The course includes:

- Didactic lectures
- Small group discussions
  - Basic life support
  - Advanced airway management

- Shock
- Rhythm disturbances
- Hands-on learning
  - Bag-valve-mask technique
  - Demonstrating cardiopulmonary resuscitation
  - Endotracheally intubating mannequins
  - Placing intraosseous lines
- Skills lab
- Written and oral testing

The lectures are a combination of those provided by the American Heart Association as well as those created by the speaker. They cover such topics as Rapid Cardiopulmonary Assessment, Rapid Sequence Intubation, Sedation, and Status Epilepticus. A sampling of these lectures can be found in Appendix 4. Clinical cases covering each of these topics are reviewed in preparation for testing. The skills lab consists of endotracheally intubating ferrets with the assistance of the animal research department. Being medical director has allowed me the opportunity to be able to target certain audiences and adjust my teaching as necessary. Another challenge that comes with this job is keeping up with the changes in recommendations that occur about every four years. This requires me to not only gain expertise in the subject matter myself, but also to make sure that all the instructors whom I supervise are aware of the material and can teach it correctly. I am responsible for approximately sixty-five instructors.

Three times a year, I direct a pediatric advanced life support instructor's course. Students who have earned instructor status when they took the class itself are eligible to become instructors if they so wish. During this course, I give a lecture on the teaching basics when dealing with adult learners. The students are also required to take a test, which I have written. These documents may be found in Appendix 4.

Teaching Philosophy

Dedication to Lifelong Learning

In the ever-changing world of medicine, the concept of lifelong learning is crucial. What I learned in medical school may or may not be applicable to current medical strategies. So as I strive to teach trainees, I am also learning myself. Adult learners are a special breed, and I have the unique opportunity to experience them at all different levels. I have found it useful and successful to change my teaching style based on the student. Since *most of my teaching occurs on the individual basis,* my goal is to be able to identify the way each person learns the best and use that method. I find that although most adult learners do not like to be challenged, especially with something they may not know, they tend to learn and remember things better when faced with that type of situation.

I would like to be known as an innovative educator who is passionate and enthusiastic about what I am teaching. I feel that it is difficult to expect your students to be excited about something if you are not. I want to be known not just as a "good" teacher of clinical medicine, but as a medical educator who has developed methods, curricula, and improved understanding of educational processes that will make a difference in the development of the next generation of physicians. I want to be able to be the person who is respected yet approachable.

Maximizing the Learning Environment

Making the learning environment nonthreatening is important. We are creatures that become defensive when we feel we are "in danger" or under fire. I know that I don't learn well that way, so I just assume that other people are the same. We learn from our mistakes and from the mistakes of others. We need to be ready to take a risk and make ourselves vulnerable at times, and people are going to do that only if they feel safe. I deal with critically ill children every day, and as I attempt to train others to do the same, I try to impart the importance of urgency as well as keeping a cool head. In that situation, you must feel comfortable with your surroundings and with yourself.

Power of Positive Feedback

One thing that should not be forgotten is the power of positive feedback. Sometimes it just takes a seemingly very minor comment to make or break someone's day, and sometimes spirit. I try to be constructive with my criticism/suggestions, stressing that my way may not be the only way to do something, but I always try to couple that with something positive about the situation. Even if it just consists of saying "I thought you did a very good job explaining that to the parents" or "I liked the way you organized your power point slides," that will make a difference. We all tend to remember the things we do wrong, and many of us are quick to point those things out. It's important to remember the things we do right as well.

Research/Scholarship
Community Outreach

On a quarterly basis, I publish a newsletter called *The Polhill Report: Dedicated to Lifelong Learning.* This eight-page newsletter is distributed to pediatricians in Alabama, as well as former pediatric emergency medicine fellows throughout the country. The content is different issue to issue, but the general format is very similar. There is a review article of a topic that presents itself commonly to the pediatric practice or emergency department (for example, head injury, sinusitis, heat related illnesses). Next, there are three or four recent research articles that are summarized by me. These articles are chosen from journals that have been published in the previous three months. The objectives and methods of the studies are reviewed, and the results are highlighted. Copies of these newsletters and feedback I have received about them can be found in Appendix 4.

Professional Development

As a clinician educator in an academic world, it is sometimes a challenge to find the best approach to making your efforts known and appreciated. Scholarly activity has many valuable forms that should be recognized. I was fortunate to attend an Association of American Medical Colleges (AAMC) early-career women's professional development seminar. A conference agenda can be found in Appendix 5. I have been working with an associate professor colleague who attended the midlevel career seminar, and we have developed a lecture on strategic career planning that we have given on several occasions to varied groups, including women's groups and junior faculty. It has been very well received to this point. Although we alter the talk to fit the audience we are speaking to, a copy of one of the lectures as well as evaluations and feedback we have received can be found in Appendix 5.

We created a career development workshop that was held at the Southern Society of Pediatric Research meeting in February 2008 that highlights ways to use your strengths to function well in the workplace, how to accomplish graceful self-promotion, and the important role that mentoring plays. We helped workshop participants identify their personality strengths and annoyances, and helped them understand how to use that information to their advantage on the job. We received external funding to help support this portion of our workshop and offset the cost of supplies (Founder's Fund grant given through The Children's Hospital of Alabama). A copy of the workshop agenda is included in Appendix 5.

The emerging concept of academic portfolios is on the agenda of a growing number of institutions, and I have been fortunate to be able to work on the use of this unique tool in the clinical realm. I have developed my own academic portfolio, and am training to become a mentor for others wanting to complete the process.

Research/Presentations

Even though I am a primarily clinical faculty, I still perform and assist in some research studies. Each of the referenced studies below has resulted in oral or poster presentations at regional or national meetings. Some of the peer-reviewed abstracts are as follows:

- *Sorrentino, A.,* Monroe, K., King, W. D. Parental assessment of severity of illness and emergency department utilization. *Journal of Investigative Medicine.* February 2003; 51(1): 37.
- *Sorrentino, A.,* Monroe, K., King, W. D., Klasner, A., Nichols, M. Parental, nursing, and physician assessment of illness severity. *Journal of Investigative Medicine.* January 2004; 52(1): 315.

- *Sorrentino, A.,* Smith, G., King, W. D. A descriptive analysis of motor vehicle crashes at an urban children's hospital following an educational intervention on child restraint. *Journal of Investigative Medicine.* January 2007; 55(1): s295.

I have also contributed to the literature with original research:

- *Sorrentino, A.,* Monroe, K. W., King, W. Barriers to pediatric advanced life support training for pediatricians in the state of Alabama. *Pediatric Emergency Care.* 2003; 19(6): 408–411.

review articles:

- *Sorrentino, A.* Chemical restraint. *Current Opinion in Pediatrics.* April 2004; 16(2): 201–205.
- *Sorrentino, A.* Update on pediatric resuscitation drugs: High dose, low dose, or no dose at all. *Current Opinion in Pediatrics.* April 2005; 17: 223–226.

and book chapter contributions:

- *Sorrentino, A.,* Monroe, K. Glomerulonephritis and the Nephrotic Syndrome. *The Clinical Practice of Emergency Medicine.* 4th Ed. 2005: 1343–47.
- *Sorrentino, A.,* Baldwin, S. Heart Murmurs in Pediatric Emergency Medicine. *The Clinical Practice of Emergency Medicine.* 4th Ed. 2005: 1239–43.

Service

Through our day-to-day practice, many of us are presented with issues in need of improvement. They may be as simple as getting better smelling soap by the sinks, or as complicated as maximizing our Medicaid reimbursements. As these topics present themselves, committees are given the task of researching the problem and suggesting potential solutions. Sometimes the committees are already formed, but many times the development of a new committee is required.

Fellows

On an annual basis, we search out and interview applicants for our pediatric emergency medicine fellowship program. As our specialty has become more sought out and therefore more competitive, this is not an easy task. For those applying to this fellowship in the United States, an average of 70 percent receives a position. For our particular program, about thirty applications are received annually, and twenty to twenty-two are interviewed to ultimately fill three spots. My role as part of the fellowship recruitment committee includes reviewing the application materials for all whom we interview, personally interviewing as many as possible (usually 80–90 percent), and then participating in a division-wide meeting that ranks the candidates in order of our preference. The fellowship participates in the national match program, so that is where our control over the situation ends. Since I have been involved in the fellowship (eight years), there has not been a time when our program did not match the maximum number of fellows allotted.

Residents

There have been many changes recently in residency requirements that have affected the emergency medicine rotation. As part of the pediatric emergency medicine education committee, I have been able to help formulate an educational curriculum to attempt to maximize learning potential. In addition to their clinical responsibilities, residents are required to read articles and answer questions about those articles, attend lectures given by pediatric emergency medicine attendings and fellows, and participate in special topic activities that are specific to their level. For example, interns are required to spend time in the child abuse clinic, second-year residents in sedation, and third-year residents with emergency medical services. I help oversee these activities and handle issues that arise regarding this.

Another area which I am involved in is revising the resident noon conference schedule and content. Three days a week, the pediatric residents and medical students attend an hour-long lecture during their lunch that involves topics on a rotating basis. The goal is to present pediatric topics that relate to certain subspecialties and

identify potential board exam subjects. I personally have participated in this lecture series, and a copy of my lecture and evaluations
by residents can be found in Appendix 2.

Departmental/Systems

The department of pediatrics has a Clinical Outcomes Committee
that consists of representatives from each medical and surgical
division, as well as nursing, pharmacy, and administration. Their
job is to review clinical problems that arise, and identify the factors that contributed to the outcome. From that committee,
a subcommittee formed known as the Unplanned Transfers to a
Higher Level of Care Committee, on which I initially served as
member, and now am chair.

One high-risk area that we have investigated and researched
is the direct admit policy. There are many different points
involved in this process, thereby increasing the room for error in
patient placement and potentially delay in necessary treatment.
Our committee performed a failure mode analysis on this procedure, including a risk priority number calculator. The step that
proved to carry the most risk of misplacement was "inconsistent
incoming patient assessments." One step that has been completed to help remedy this problem is a direct admit patient form
that was developed by our committee and is now an official hospital form. A copy of this form and of the failure mode analysis
flow sheet can be found in Appendix 6.

State/Community

As medical director of our Pediatric Advanced Life Support
(PALS) classes, I have also become involved in its parent organization, the American Heart Association. For five years, I have
served on the Alabama Emergency Cardiovascular Care (ECC)
committee, whose goal is to monitor, evaluate, and ultimately
improve the quality of instruction that is being given throughout
our state. I am assigned certain training programs in the state to
review when it is time for their training status renewal, in the role
of PALS regional faculty. In the past year, I have been selected as
PALS national faculty. Each state has a representative who is in
contact with the national committee. I serve as the PALS expert

for our state and address any questions or grievances that may arise. A copy of my PALS national faculty card, as well as a description of expectations of those who hold this position, can be found in Appendix 4.

Another group that I have been fortunate to be able to serve is the Alabama chapter of the American College of Emergency Physicians. I have been a member for three years and have served as a board member for the past two years.

Advising

As my career has progressed, I have gotten the opportunity to mentor and advise various levels of students and colleagues. I am an adviser to pediatric residents (one or two) and pediatric emergency medicine fellows (one). My role with the residents is to help guide them in making career decisions, national boards preparation, and general residency survival skills and support. I do much of the same with the fellows, but also aid them in research questions, administrative issues, and job searches. I meet with the residents and students on a regular basis and discuss current issues facing them, making sure they are following the proper path for completion. Having been in the same shoes as the residents and fellows, I feel well prepared to help them in their journey. I still view the advisers I had with admiration and felt they had a strong impact on me and my career.

For the past two years, I have also been one of the faculty advisers for the Nuts About Pediatrics (NAP) group. NAP is the medical student pediatric interest group and consists of students of all levels. We meet three or four times a year and have different agendas for each meeting. The initial meeting is typically a panel of general pediatricians and pediatric subspecialists (on which I sit) who answer questions from students about our jobs and the paths we took to get there. Other meetings focus on specific topics of the students' choosing and include guest speakers.

Another group I am proud to be a faculty adviser for is the Coat of Arms resident committee. This is a committee made up of pediatric residents that is dedicated to community outreach and advocacy. They have sponsored such events as a 5 kilometer run, with all proceeds going to the UAB childhood obesity clinic, and food and supply drives for area families and agencies. Annually, there is a safety fair that provides neighborhood children with bicycle helmets and fittings, water safety tips, a review of house fire safety, and car/booster seat fittings. These fairs are very well attended and appreciated by the involved communities.

Across-the-Board Performance Reviews

Annually, I am required to report my progress, goals, and objectives to my division and department directors. The feedback I have received on my performance is excerpted below, with complete references available in Appendix 6.

> "Dr. Sorrentino continues to be an excellent junior faculty. She has assumed significant administrative responsibilities in the division/department. . . . She continues to refine and improve our divisional newsletter, which she personally created. Named in honor and as a memorial to Dr. Rud Polhill, the quarterly newsletter has been extremely well received by community pediatricians and promises to be a reliable, efficient source of continuing education."

> "Beginning in 2003, I have tracked the number of patients seen per hour in the emergency department by our division's faculty and fellows. Dr. Sorrentino continues to perform in the upper level in terms of patients seen per hour in the ED. She is also the only faculty member to receive all 'superior' ratings in evaluations done by the charge nurses in the ED. She is the first to volunteer to help out when division members are ill or have a family emergency. She also outperforms in other 'citizenship' areas like meeting attendance and division moral boosting."

Integration of Professional Work and Goals
Personal Growth and Development

When someone who is contemplating a career in medicine is asked why, what is the answer that is usually given? "Because, I want to help people." It seems like a very noble and admirable answer, and hopefully it even has some truth in it. I know those words have come out of my mouth at one time or another, and in reality, sometimes it sounds very rehearsed—almost trite. But is helping people the reason I am a physician? Reviewing the teaching, research, and service that I have performed tells me that intentionally or not, it is.

Being able to use my prior experience to help guide students, residents, and fellows on their journey through medical school and training has not only made me appreciate it all the more, but it has forced me to remember it, the good and the bad, and be able to help others not make the same mistakes I made. Those mistakes are not only made when making a living but also when making a life. Many times, the words "If I had to do it all over again . . ." or "If I knew then what I know now . . ." come out of our mouths. I can use those experiences to aid someone "doing it all over again" for the first time.

My contributions to the field of medical research are not going to be earth-shattering or landmark. I am not going to find the cure to AIDS or the common cold, but I might be able to help prevent an injury or inappropriate use of medical care. My literature reviews may help someone rethink a difficult case. Most important, all those things help me to be a better clinical caregiver.

My service contributions help to keep me grounded. Seeing, talking with, and treating the underserved population at a free health clinic or health fair helps remind me that what I do can make a difference in people's lives. It gives a face and name to the people some only read about or see on television. I get to meet them, hear their stories, and potentially touch their lives. What they don't realize is how much they have touched mine. So, am I a doctor so I can help people? Yes, I am, and people include helping me.

Accomplishments

As I reflect on my career to date, there are a few accomplishments of which I am particularly proud. The first is *The Polhill Report*. As mentioned previously, this is a quarterly newsletter that I edit and publish, that honors the memory of a pediatric emergency medicine physician who died unexpectedly in 2002. Rud Polhill was a mentor of mine during my training, and he introduced me to the concept of lifelong learning. As with many other important revelations, I didn't realize the magnitude and importance of what he was imparting to me. As editor, I enjoy writing about general topics, literature reviews, and bringing attention to issues that affect us all in a day-to-day practice. My hope is that if I can help others stay a little more up-to-date on subjects that are important to pediatric emergency medicine and do it in a way that is manageable and enjoyable to read, I am contributing to the lifelong learning that we are all striving for.

Another accomplishment that has special meaning to me is recognition of my teaching style and abilities. I have received two awards of which I am particularly proud. They are both teaching awards, and they were both awarded to me on the first year of their existence. The first one is the "Quarterback Club Subspecialty Education Award" given to me in my third year of fellowship (2002) by the graduating pediatric residents for excellence in resident education. The second award came in 2005 from the first graduating class of the emergency medicine residency program at UAB titled "Best Pediatric Emergency Medicine Faculty."

A third accomplishment that I hold in very high regard is the Chairman's Award. This was awarded to me in May 2007 by our Chairman of Pediatrics, Dr. Sergio Stagno. He states it is given "by me, when I want, to whomever I want!" It is an award that recognizes outstanding service to the department. As the youngest recipient to date of this award that has been given only fourteen times since 1990, I am in awe of the other recipients, knowing that many of them have helped me become the person I am today. Even more incredible to me was the echoing of support of the award by senior faculty whom I have admired and gleaned expertise from for several years.

Professional Goals

Even though the details of my goals may change, my overall purpose remains constant: to deliver quality health care to the children of Alabama and to teach others to do the same. In order to do that, I need to keep asking questions, keep searching for answers, and keep passing the information on to others. I will continue to do so at the local level, but I hope to be able to become more involved in pediatric emergency medicine at the national level, specifically through the American College of Emergency Physicians.

Another goal I have is to help others promote themselves. I hope to do this through continuing to host workshops on career development and by introducing others to the art of developing their own academic or professional portfolio. I feel fortunate that I became aware of these opportunities early in my career, and I hope to help other junior-level faculty do the same.

On a more personal level, I have a goal to improve my writing skills. As I have gotten the opportunity to do some factual medical writing, I have also become involved in a narrative medicine writing group. Being able to get down on paper some of the intense feelings and emotions, as well as some of the day-to-day issues, has proven to be a very therapeutic exercise. Many times, the subject is a difficult patient or undesired outcome. As physicians, I feel we are ill equipped to handle some of the aforementioned conditions, as we are not trained to do so. Narrative medicine has proven to be a great outlet, and it has allowed me to meet others around the university who feel the same. My hope is to introduce this art to others.

Appendixes

Appendix 1: Pediatric Emergency Medicine Fellow Documents

Appendix 2: Pediatric Resident Documents

    Teaching
    Service

Appendix 3: Student Documents

Appendix 4: Community Documents

    Teaching
    Service
    Scholarship

Appendix 5: Professional Development

Appendix 6: Departmental Service

Political Science

Carrie Liu Currier
Department of Political Science
Texas Christian University
Fall 2008

Table of Contents

Purpose

The purpose of this portfolio is to establish my record of teaching (section I), research (section II), and service (section III) in the discipline of political science and to establish my progress toward tenure at Texas Christian University (TCU). In the portfolio, I have laid out my professional objectives with regard to each of the aforementioned areas and how they have been satisfied over time. My intent is to demonstrate a strong record that upholds the criteria required of the teacher-scholar model in the pursuit of tenure and promotion. Since this track requires an exemplary record in teaching, research, and service, the sections outline my accomplishments and end with a discussion of my future goals and my plans to fulfill them. It concludes with a discussion of how the three areas are integrated and contribute to my overall growth and development as a teacher-scholar.

I. Teaching

My course offerings in political science have all been internationally focused, with an emphasis in the areas of Asian politics, political economy, and feminist theory. My current teaching load is 2–2, the result of a one-course reduction for my administrative responsibilities after being appointed Director of the Asian Studies Program in fall 2006. Each semester I generally teach forty to one hundred students and offer at least three different classes per year. I also teach at least one independent study, direct at least one senior thesis project, and serve on a few honors or departmental distinction theses committees each year (**Appendix 1.1**). All of my courses satisfy the requirements for the B.A., B.S., or BAIR degrees we have in Political Science, and our department does not have a graduate program. Additionally, two of my upper-division courses on China and East Asia are electives for the Asian Studies minor, my Feminist IR theory course is an elective for the Women's Studies minor, and all of my 20000- and 30000-level courses fulfill the Cultural Awareness (CA) and Global Awareness (GA) core curriculum requirements for the university as well as qualifying as international course electives for the international interdisciplinary minor. These courses were all essentially new preps for me, and all four of my upper-division course offerings are of my own design. The *undergraduate* courses I offer each semester (F = Fall, S = Spring) and the number of students (N) include the following:

	F04	S05	F05	S06	F06	S07	F07
POSC 10093—Intro to Political Science	N = 41						
POSC 20303— International Relations	N = 44		N = 29	N = 31		N = 34	N = 33
POSC 20303— International Relations (Honors)		N = 22			N = 25		
POSC 30303— Feminist International Relations Theory		N = 24		N = 21			N = 23
POSC 30303— Globalization and Political Economy	N = 25				N = 23		
POSC 30303— International Relations of East Asia			N = 25			N = 25	
POSC 30503— Politics of China		N = 23			N = 12		
Semester Total Enrollment	**N = 110**	**N = 69**	**N = 54**	**N = 75**	**N = 37**	**N = 59**	**N = 56**

Teaching Philosophy

My own interest in political science developed largely as the result of a dynamic and overcaffeinated professor who taught his introductory world politics course virtually bouncing off the walls, a remarkable achievement for a MWF 8:00 A.M. class. Apart from introducing me to the concepts of international politics, the class taught me important lessons about active teaching and learning, critical thinking, and developing writing and research skills. My own teaching philosophy incorporates each of these ideas, as I strive for students to think outside of their own experiences and build a more global perspective that sheds light on the interconnectedness of politics, economics, and society. One of the most important aspects of my teaching is for the students to examine how our actions and ideas in one particular locale can have global implications, essentially asking them to "think globally and act locally." These are views shared in TCU's mission statement, which asks us "to educate individuals to think and act as ethical leaders and responsible citizens in a global community."

Teaching Objectives

My objective in each of my classes is to challenge the students intellectually and to ask that they challenge themselves. I strive to meet three basic objectives in every class I teach: to create an active learning environment, to introduce critical theories and alternative global perspectives to the study of international politics, and to develop the students' writing and research skills.

First, with regard to an active learning environment, I want my students to come to each class prepared and willing to engage their peers in active and critical discussion of our course topics. All of my courses are designed to include time for relevant current events discussions and incorporate class participation as part of their grade. I also encourage them to ask questions, since I consider participation more than just regurgitating class material and think it is more important to ask thoughtful questions that stimulate further discussion and get us thinking critically and analytically about the subject matter.

Second, with regard to critical thinking, I do not ask that the students embrace or conform to a particular perspective or approach, but they do need to know the relevance of these theories to the discipline, how and why they have evolved, and how postpositivist or marginalized perspectives fit into what is called the "Third Debate" in the study of international politics. Occasionally this puts students out of their comfort zone, but the goal is for them to develop their own ideas and viewpoints, be able to justify their position, and learn the strengths and flaws of their own arguments.

Finally, I want the students in my classes to develop solid writing and research skills. I tell my students that writing is a lifelong skill that they will continue to develop over time. Even the most gifted writers go through several drafts before they have a finished product ready for someone else to see. Moreover, producing a quality research paper is more than just about the writing; it is also about the strength of the data and sources you consult. Internet researching is both dangerous and unreliable in terms of the reliability and validity of the information available, and quality research requires use of the library.

Teaching Methodology

I enter each class as if we were covering my favorite readings or topics for the semester, and aim to help the students see the interesting elements that led to my own continued study of political science. I come to class prepared and energetic and expect the same of them.

In my courses I generally use PowerPoint to display lecture outlines, charts reflecting global data and trends, maps, photographs and other images, political cartoons, interactive Web links, and MPEG news clips (see **Appendix 1.2** for sample slides). My use of technology in the classroom has made my teaching more dynamic and visually stimulating, and the students have commented on its usefulness. In my two Asian politics courses, I implemented a variety of new kinds of media in the class to enhance the visual component of the course as part of my Instructional Development Grant, "Visions of Asian Globalization" (**Appendix 1.3**). Last year I surveyed the students in my Politics of China seminar explicitly on the use of these technologies and found their response to my methods quite positive (**Appendix 1.4**). I also maintain links on my personal Web site (http://faculty.tcu.edu/ccurrier) to assist them with their research, and an extensive Ecollege Web site with maps, links to domestic and foreign newspapers, articles, and other related Web links. The students spend several hours on these sites over the semester, as evidenced by the user activity data on Ecollege (**Appendix 1.5**). Students also frequently send me new links, maps, and video clips to include in my lectures, indicating their continued interest in seeing these media included.

The other important component to my courses is how I personally interact with the students to develop their critical thinking and writing skills. I encourage the students to take an active role in their learning and not be afraid to present their ideas, even if they are still rudimentary. In my different classes I: (a) have students present analyses of current events articles and their application to course concepts/theories; (b) write critiques of journal articles in the light of our class materials; and (c) discuss the future of international politics and how those scenarios might change. These are activities that produce no single "correct" answer, but students are encouraged to base their arguments on evidence. When we discuss these ideas further, they see that their peers often come to different conclusions or justifications for debates such as "Is globalization beneficial?" or "Is the United Nations an effective institution?" Thus, in the end, we find ourselves with a better understanding of the concepts explaining international politics.

Curricular Revisions and Development

All four of my upper-division courses were new additions to the curriculum, and I continue to revise all of my courses to reflect the latest research in the discipline and in response to student suggestions (see **Appendix 1.6** for different versions of my course syllabi). I also add new or different types of electronic media to my classes, such as incorporating an interactive merchant Web game that demonstrates the "tragedy of the commons" concept, a short video clip that demonstrates nuclear weapons holdings across states by using bb's, or photo journals with audio commentary on the conflict in Darfur from the *New York Times* multimedia collection. This component of my class is updated virtually each semester to reflect contemporary developments in the study of international politics.

Two of the courses I have spent the most time developing, and which reflect my own theoretical orientations and research, are Politics of China (POSC 30503) and Feminist International Relations Theory (POSC 30303). The Politics of China course focuses primarily on domestic politics—examining the political history, political institutions, how the leaders have pursued development policies, and the future of democracy in China. The readings change to reflect the most recent leadership changes, the latest human rights cases, and the growing attention given to the social and environmental challenges to China's Olympic preparation. Given the growing importance China has in the world politically, economically, and culturally, it is helpful if students understand how it has transformed itself and at what cost. The last time I taught this course, I revised it to be a seminar with more rigorous oral and written assignments. Students were responsible for thirty- to forty-five-minute oral presentations—complete with discussion questions, critiques, and presentation of the main themes of their topics. For their writing assignment, I changed the research paper into a literature review, giving them a chance to assess the scholarly works written on their topic of interest and determine what new research projects might emerge from this body of literature.

In Feminist International Relations Theory, I introduce the students to several different feminist approaches and their importance to the study of political science. Depending on my own research projects at the time, we use these theories to analyze security (the military and redefining economic security) or transnational migration issues (with topics on the sex industry and economic development). Feminist theories help the students see how politics is really about the study of power and how it creates privilege and inequality.

Enhancements to Teaching

To improve the visual component of my courses, I received an Instructional Development Grant for my proposal "Visions of Asian Globalization" (**Appendix 1.3**). The grant funded the incorporation of foreign films, photography I conducted in China, and the use of new photo-imaging software into my courses. As a result of the grant, I revised my slides to include more recent images capturing the effects of globalization on China, and to produce more creative PowerPoint slides (see **Appendix 1.2** for sample slides). I also developed an Asian film series, accompanied by discussion of the film's themes and significance to the study of Asia, which included seven films over two semesters.

Grants

* "Visions of Asian Globalization," Instructional Development Grant, Texas Christian University, 2006–2007, $895

I also have been selected to participate in workshops that have contributed to my overall professional growth and development (**Appendix 4.1**). The focus of these workshops included teaching with technology as well as developing a professional portfolio, and were useful for the formal instruction and materials obtained in the workshops as well as the informal interaction and ideas I received from my peers.

Awards

Among my greatest accomplishments are the awards I have received from students to commemorate their positive experiences with me as a teacher and a mentor. At TCU I have been nominated for and have received several awards from students I either had in class or have mentored in the Connections program and the Asian sorority I advise:

* Three Senior Class Legacy Awards (2005, 2006, 2007)
* Nominated for Outstanding Adviser by Kappa Lambda Delta, Intercultural Services Banquet (2007)
* Mortar Board Preferred Professor (2005 and 2006)
* Brachman Hall Favorite Professor (Spring 2005)

Course Evaluations

The evaluations I have received in my courses by students and my peers have all been quite favorable. The following excerpts represent some of their overall impressions:

Peer Reviews (Appendix 1.7)

> "I thought that both of the classes I attended were very engaging intellectually . . . the [first] class was fact laden but also analytically rigorous and sophisticated . . . the [second] class was very fast paced, but students seemed to stay with it because the hour was punctuated by frequent student comments and questions."—Mike Dodson, Professor of Political Science (peer observation)

> "Carrie is well organized, enthusiastic, energetic, concise, up to date, and analytical (rather than descriptive). Her probing questions were carefully chosen to elicit answers from them that pointed to the complexities and nuances of global politics."—Manochehr Dorraj, Professor of Political Science (peer observation)

Selected Student Evaluation Comments (Appendix 1.8)

> "You were superfabulous, really energetic and it made me want to learn! I never cared about current events before this class but now I do."—Honors International Politics

> "Dr. Currier is the most passionate, well-prepared teacher I have ever had . . . I love the PowerPoint-lecture-discussion format—it made each class interesting."—Politics of China

> "One of the hardest courses I've had at TCU, but she is also one of the best professors I have had."—Globalization and Political Economy

> "Currier is clearly knowledgeable and has a passion for what she teaches. The course may be hard at times but that's because she wants to challenge us and make us capable to evaluate things in real life."—Feminist IR Theory

With regard to how my teaching compares to my peers in the Political Science Department (D) as well as the College of Social Sciences and Humanities (C), I have consistently scored above the mean for both (**Appendix 1.9**).

Mean Teaching Evaluations as Reported on Student Perceptions of Teaching (SPOT)

	F04 N = 110	*S05* N = 69	*F05* N = 54	*S06* N = 75	*F06* N = 37	*S07* N = 59
Course objectives were clearly communicated	**3.44** D = 3.56 C = 3.50	**3.67** D = 3.48 C = 3.51	**3.60** D = 3.53 C = 3.48	**3.75** D = 3.56 C = 3.51	**3.82** D = 3.47 C = 3.48	**3.66** D = 3.49 C = 3.51
Instructor was well prepared	**3.80** D = 3.73 C = 3.61	**3.83** D = 3.59 C = 3.62	**3.94** D = 3.63 C = 3.59	**3.91** D = 3.67 C = 3.61	**3.97** D = 3.61 C = 3.58	**3.87** D = 3.55 C = 3.58
Course was intellectually stimulating	**3.46** D = 3.39 C = 3.37	**3.58** D = 3.37 C = 3.43	**3.74** D = 3.38 C = 3.36	**3.70** D = 3.41 C = 3.41	**3.82** D = 3.38 C = 3.37	**3.61** D = 3.29 C = 3.41
Instructor encouraged active participation	**3.79** D = 3.41 C = 3.52	**3.72** D = 3.37 C = 3.55	**3.85** D = 3.44 C = 3.51	**3.78** D = 3.40 C = 3.53	**3.97** D = 3.43 C = 3.48	**3.74** D = 3.41 C = 3.53
Instructor was accessible to me outside of class	**3.67** D = 3.50 C = 3.49	**3.61** D = 3.44 C = 3.48	**3.66** D = 3.45 C = 3.48	**3.72** D = 3.51 C = 3.49	**3.85** D = 3.45 C = 3.48	**3.74** D = 3.44 C = 3.49
Instructor treated me with courtesy and respect	**3.56** D = 3.70 C = 3.66	**3.77** D = 3.70 C = 3.67	**3.77** D = 3.73 C = 3.65	**3.80** D = 3.71 C = 3.68	**3.82** D = 3.71 C = 3.67	**3.67** D = 3.67 C = 3.67
Instructor did a good job in this course	**3.52** D = 3.55 C = 3.50	**3.82** D = 3.50 C = 3.53	**3.68** D = 3.53 C = 3.47	**3.75** D = 3.56 C = 3.52	**3.85** D = 3.53 C = 3.48	**3.59** D = 3.45 C = 3.51

Note: Rating Scale (1–4): 1 = Strongly Disagree, 4 = Strongly Agree; N = Number of Students; F = Fall, S = Spring, D = Departmental mean; C = College mean.

My mean score for overall instructor effectiveness (E), as measured by "instructor did a good job in the course," is high for each of my individual courses.

	F04 N = 110	S05 N = 69	F05 N = 54	S06 N = 75	F06 N = 37	S07 N = 59
POSC 10093—Intro to Political Science	E = 3.59 N = 41					
POSC 20303—International Relations	E = 3.40 N = 44		E = 3.73 N = 29	E = 3.79 N = 31		E = 3.58 N = 34
POSC 20303—International Relations (Honors)		E = 3.75 N = 22			E = 3.80 N = 25	
POSC 30303—Feminist International Relations Theory		E = 3.86 N = 24		E = 3.75 N = 21		
POSC 30303—Globalization and Political Economy	E = 3.59 N = 25			E = 3.67 N = 23		
POSC 30303—International Relations of East Asia			E = 3.62 N = 25			E = 3.60 N = 25
POSC 30503—Politics of China		E = 3.84 N = 23			E = 4.0 N = 12	

II. Research/Scholarship

My research has primarily focused on the politics of China, examining both the domestic and international implications of the economic reforms that have been pursued since 1978, emphasizing their effects explicitly on women. This aspect of my research examines how women have been unexpectedly helped by reforms that on the surface have treated them as secondary workers and citizens compared to their male counterparts. My goal has been to study the impact of macro level policies (structural economic reforms) on the micro level (individuals and households). This research is based on survey work I designed and administered in China, where the survey asks questions on women's attitudes toward work and reform, their roles in the formal (paid) economy, their finances, the composition of their household and the division of labor within it, the use of modern innovations in the household (for example, washing machines, refrigerators), and what types of societal implications they see for their working status. My findings refute the popular claims that women have experienced increased gender discrimination and have fared worse in the reform era and challenges our understanding of communist regimes' adaptation to capitalism and marketization.

Publications (see Appendix 2.1 for full articles)

- Currier, Carrie Liu, and Manochehr, Dorraj. 2008. "Lubricated with Oil: Iran-China Relations in a Changing World,"*Middle East Policy* (March).
- Currier, Carrie Liu. 2007. "Labor and Identity: Who Are the New Beijing Women?"*Asian Journal of Women's Studies, 13*(3), 71–108.
- Currier, Carrie Liu. 2007. "Bringing the Household Back In: The Restructuring of Women's Labor Choices in Beijing,"*American Journal of Chinese Studies,14*(1), 61–81.
- Currier, Carrie Liu. 2005. "Politicizing Market Reform: Chinese Women and the State,"*China Public Affairs Quarterly, 1*(4), 269–292 [online journal].

Grants (Appendix 2.2)

- "The Impact of Economic Reforms on Women,"*Fulbright Research Grant,* for conducting survey work in Beijing (2001–2002), awarded $17,200.

Current Research Agenda

In addition to the work I already have published, I continue to develop articles out of the field research I conducted in China. I currently have several articles under review at journals (**Appendix 2.3**), including one on the one-child policy in China and one on Chinese foreign policy. I have also been contracted to write a book chapter for an edited volume on China's state-society relations and a compendium review article on the global commodification of women.

Invited Presentations and Scholarly Activities

In addition to my research and publications, my status as a China scholar has been furthered by the lectures I have been invited to give on my research outside the university, the offices I have held in professional societies, and the review work I have done in the discipline. Each year I regularly participate in two to three academic conferences in political science and Asian studies to present various stages of my work and to serve as a discussant or chair for panels (see **Appendix 2.4** for a complete list of conference participation).

Selected Invited Presentations (see Appendix 2.5 for a complete list)

- "China's One Child Policy and the Chinese Family,"*National Consortium for Teaching about Asia* (NCTA), University of North Texas, August 2, 2007. This is an all-day workshop I conducted for teachers interested in Asia. I was invited to do this presentation based on research I presented at the Southwest Conference of Asian Studies on the status of women and the One Child Policy in China.
- "Politics of China" and "Women in Comparative Government," *Regional Advanced Placement Institute* (Comparative Politics), Fort Worth, TX, July 18, 2007, and July 19, 2006. China has recently been added as one of the case studies in the Comparative Politics Advanced Placement Exam.

Selected National/Regional Activities (see Appendix 2.6 for a complete list)

- Comparative Politics program chair for the Western Political Science Association Annual Meeting, San Diego, CA, 2007–2008. After serving as a co-chair for the Women and Politics section of this conference (2005–2006) and as a co-chair for a paper award committee (2006–2007), I was asked to serve as program chair for the Comparative Politics section of the conference.
- Board member of Southwest Conference of Asian Studies (2005–2007). I serve as one of five board members guiding the

vision of this regional conference of the Association for Asian
Studies.
* National Advanced Placement (AP) reader for Comparative
  Government, Daytona, FL, 2007. I was selected as one of
  the readers for the national AP examination where we will
  score the exams to determine if the students get college credit
  for their work.

Review Work

* Currier, Carrie Liu. 2007. "Review of *Women Miners in
  Developing Countries: Pit Women and Others,* edited by
  Kuntala Lahiri-Dutt and Martha McIntyre,"*Gender Work and
  Organization* (forthcoming).
* Currier, Carrie Liu. 2005. "Review of Atul Kohli's *State Directed
  Development: Political Power and Industrialization in the Global
  Periphery,"Comparative Political Studies, 38*(9), 1162–1166.
* Manuscript reviews for Routledge, Longman, Houghton
  Mifflin, and Wadsworth Publishing companies.

III. Service

My service to the university is driven by: (a) a desire to promote
diversity and the status of women on campus; (b) an interest
in mentoring students; and (c) a sense of responsibility to my
colleagues—all of which I find personally and professionally fulfilling. Of my different responsibilities, the most significant has
been my appointment as Director of Asian Studies. I have worked
hard to make our program more student friendly, to raise the visibility of the minor on campus, to attract new students, and to
increase Asian awareness on campus in general.

Since becoming Director in fall 2006, I have scaled back my
other campus commitments and am more selective in the activities I pursue, given my new administrative demands. I still serve
as the TCU Truman Scholar representative, am a member of the
Women's Studies Advisory committee, and am responsible for
coordinating the Political Science department's funding and
scholarly activity files. I also give guest lectures and invited presentations for my colleagues or campus organizations as time

permits (**Appendix 3.1**), and serve as a faculty sponsor to Kappa Lambda Delta, an Asian sorority that was founded at TCU in Fall 2005. Thus my overall service can be divided into three basic categories: Asian Studies, other University/Departmental service, and student advising.

Asian Studies

I have been an active member of our Asian Studies program since I came to TCU in 2004. My goals have been to build both a larger China focus to our curriculum and to increase the size of and interest in Asian Studies on campus. In the past year we have accomplished the following goals: (1) a net gain of two new faculty members, (2) added Chinese language to the curriculum, (3) developed a line-item budget in the college, (4) created a Web site for our minor, and (5) hosted more events on campus.

Since I became Director, our affiliated faculty have grown from six to eight members, and our course offerings have expanded to include courses in Japanese religions, South Asian literature, and Chinese language. The addition of Chinese to the curriculum is especially noteworthy since it resulted from a proposal that I researched and wrote, prior to becoming Director, on behalf of the faculty of Asian Studies. The proposal outlines the increasing demand for Chinese nationally, among our peer institutions, and from our own students (**Appendix 3.2**).

In our efforts to be a more user-friendly minor for the students, I have implemented a variety of changes that I feel will enhance the program. One of the initial problems I noticed was that course scheduling conflicts presented obstacles for our minors and that we needed to be more aware of how we were scaring away students. To find out the full extent of our programmatic shortcomings, I began conducting exit interviews with our seniors. The results of these meetings led to several important changes in the program that make our requirements clearer and easier to fulfill, while providing more Asian-interest opportunities for the students outside the classroom. Our recent success in acquiring a budget for Asian Studies will also help us fulfill our future goals for the program (see **Appendix 3.3** for Asian Studies Annual Reports outlining programmatic accomplishments).

Other Selected University/Department Activities (Appendix 3.4):

- Truman Scholar representative (2005–present)
- Women's Studies Advisory Committee (2005–present)
- Honors Council Committee (2007–2009)
- Chair of the Wise Woman Award Committee, an award I helped develop that recognizes excellence in teaching and mentoring in Women's Studies (2006–2007)
- Coordinator and creator of a department portfolio on scholarships, internships, conferences, and external funding for political science students (Fall 2005–present)

Student Advising

My role as a faculty sponsor to student groups has largely involved the Asian sorority Kappa Lambda Delta (KLD) and the Connections program. I have been with KLD since its founding in 2005 and helped the women develop their constitution, attend and publicize their events, edit their magazine, and serve as a mentor. Several of these activities overlap with my work in Asian studies and build greater Asian awareness on campus. The mission of this organization is to be inclusive, empower women, and raise Asian awareness—all visions that I share in terms of my own service goals.

In addition to working with KLD, I have also been a faculty sponsor for two different Connections courses. The Connections program pairs two students with their invited faculty member into a nine-week mini-course that creates a smaller and more personable network for incoming students.

The interaction I have with students is fulfilling since it gives me a chance to serve as a faculty resource and a mentor. I have served or directed several honors and departmental distinction thesis committees over the past few years. I also have directed several independent studies, at the students' request, to develop research projects they began in one of my courses. Moreover, I am the academic adviser for the Asian Studies minor and am one of several academic advisers for the B.A., B.S., and B.A.I.R. degrees in Political Science. Between the two, I have approximately thirty to forty students per semester I am responsible for advising.

IV. Professional Growth/Development

Each time I teach a course, I learn something new, either by incorporating different materials or as a result of the interaction I have with students. I frequently change the readings both to update the course content and reflect my current research projects. This allows me to keep up with the latest developments in the literature and more effectively balance my time between teaching and research. Moreover, the interaction I have with students in my courses has furthered my professional growth by offering unsolicited assistance in searching for new media for my PowerPoint lectures, and by providing feedback on my research.

Goals

My professional development goals include: (1) participation in more teaching/research workshops, (2) conducting more fieldwork in China, and (3) building the visibility of the Asian Studies program. Over the past few years, I have participated in a variety of professionalization workshops that have been useful for refining my teaching and research skills (**Appendix 4.1**). These workshops were notable for the formal instruction they provided on different learning styles or research methods but were arguably more useful for the ideas that evolved out of conversations with other workshop participants.

My future research plans include more field research in China, implementing a second version of my labor survey in either Xian or Changchun. The results of the survey will be compared to the 2002 Beijing data and are designed to produce a monograph on the comparative intraregional effects of economic reform on the status of women's labor. In addition, the two other projects I am pursuing on Chinese foreign policy and on the growth of the sex industry also require a modest amount of fieldwork.

Finally with regard to service, I would like to continue to build the visibility of the Asian Studies program by inviting Asian scholars to give lectures on campus and developing a summer study-abroad program to China. In addition to the speaker series, we would like to develop a study-abroad program for summer 2009.

Appendix

Appendix 1: Teaching

    1.1 Student Advising

    1.2 Sample PowerPoint Slides with Graphics

    1.3 Instructional Development Grant

    1.4 Summary of Survey on Media Enhancements

    1.5 Ecollege Class Web Site Usage

    1.6 Course Syllabi

    1.7 Peer Evaluation of Teaching Letters

    1.8 Selected Comments from Students

    1.9 Perceptions of Teaching and Student Testimonials

    1.10 Student Perceptions of Teaching (SPOT) Evaluations

Appendix 2: Research

    2.1 Publications

    2.2 Fulbright Grant Documents

    2.3 Research Projects in Progress

    2.4 Conference Presentations and Participation

    2.5 Invited Presentations

    2.6 National/Regional Activities

Appendix 3: Service

    3.1 Invited Presentations and Guest Lectures on Campus

    3.2 Asian Studies Proposal for the Chinese Language
        Program

    3.3 Asian Studies Annual Reports

    3.4 University and Departmental Activities

Appendix 4: Professional Growth/Development

    4.1 Professional Development Activities

    4.2 Annual Progress towards Tenure Letters

Political Science

Marlene K. Sokolon

Department of Political Science

Concordia University

Fall 2008

Introduction

I graduated with my Ph.D. in political theory from Northern Illinois University in the fall 2003. From 2003–05, I was a tenure-track faculty member at West Texas A&M University (WTAMU) in Canyon, Texas; my primary responsibility at this small rural institution was undergraduate teaching. In 2005, I joined Concordia University in Montreal, Quebec, as the specialist in ancient political theory. The primary focus of this position includes innovative research publications and graduate training, as well as undergraduate teaching. Concordia is a large urban campus with a very diverse and politically active student body; political science is a dynamic department of approximately thirty tenure/tenure-track faculty, eighteen hundred undergraduate majors, and sixty graduate students. The most rewarding aspect of my four-year career has been the opportunity to experience teaching and research at such different institutions. This opportunity has provided valuable insights and broader perspective from which to develop research, teaching and service commitments and goals.

Teaching Statement

Responsibilities

In the last three years at Concordia University, I have taught the following courses:

Course	Level	Enrollment	Status
Introduction to Western Political Philosophy[a]	Undergraduate	90–100	Required
Hellenistic, Roman and Medieval Political Philosophy[b]	Undergraduate	40–50	Elective
Advanced Ancient Political Thought	Undergraduate	20	Elective
Honours Seminar	Undergraduate	15	Required Honors
Agricultural Biotechnology Policy[a]	Graduate	10–15	Elective

[a]Taught three sections.
[b]Taught two sections.

For a complete list of courses and teaching responsibilities see **Appendix A**.

Statement of Teaching Philosophy

The following five principles inform my role as a teacher and learner. I do not view these principles as discrete, but as interconnected parts of a continuing experience of learning and professional growth:

- A teacher should facilitate the development of independent and critical thinking skills by challenging students to gain not only mastery of the course material, but also of their perceptions and assumptions related to that material.
- A university education should encourage a lifetime of intellectual growth and self-examination.
- Teachers should foster environments that encourage self-advocacy and problem-solving skills.
- Teachers must accommodate variations in scholastic levels and individual learning styles by offering diverse learning opportunities.
- A constructive learning experience requires that teachers communicate clear expectations and genuine enthusiasm for the learning process.
- The most effective teachers are those who evaluate and learn from their teaching experiences and thus become a model of the learning process for their students.

Statement of Teaching Methods and Strategies

I work to incorporate my six teaching principles through conscientious course design and development as reflected in (1) comprehensive syllabi, (2) teaching methods and presentation, (3) teaching evaluations, and (4) course revisions and reflections.

Course Syllabi

My course syllabi include detailed course descriptions, objectives, academic requirements, a grading rubric, and a detailed weekly breakdown of topics and readings (see **Appendix B**, Course

Materials). I view a syllabus as an integral part of my teaching strategy and principle of providing clear expectations. A comprehensive syllabus should clearly introduce the course and explain the students' path toward academic success.

Teaching Methods and Classroom Presentation

As illustrative of integrating my first teaching principle of facilitating critical thinking, in my introductory courses I rely primarily on a Socratic method of presenting material, in which I ask questions that begin with basic reading comprehension, move to interpretive queries, and end with reflections of philosophic ideas on contemporary political problems. This teaching method fosters individual ownership of the material, since the students are not told answers but encouraged to think and formulate the answers. In junior-level courses, I monitor the responses of students by requiring them to hand in note cards of their responses to questions. In senior-level and graduate courses, students make classroom presentations and respond to other students' (and my) questions concerning their interpretations of material.

Other course material also reflects this diversity of pedagogical levels and learning styles (for copies of these described activities and assignments, see **Appendix B**, Course Material). In introductory-level courses, for example, I provide "Focus Questions" and quizzes to help the students prioritize their reading of philosophic texts. Introductory courses also incorporate learning activities such as exit quizzes, top-ten lists, interviews of their colleagues, and "races" in which groups compete to complete games such as crossword puzzles of key concepts. In more advanced courses, I continue to use quizzes but introduce more structured debates on philosophic ideas, in which students argue from both sides of an issue and link the debate to contemporary political issues.

Evaluation of Teaching

In general, my student evaluations reflect my success in implementing my teaching philosophy. My approach to student evaluations is to see them as important feedback in my ongoing efforts to improve my course design and approach to teaching. Teaching evaluation includes (1) Concordia's Teaching Evaluation Questionnaire, Social Science Sector, (2) student signed testimonials,* (3) peer evaluations.

As illustrative of my positive evaluations for the past two years of teaching at Concordia, the following ratings represent 164 completed evaluations of undergraduate and graduate students from all classes (with average response rate of 78 percent). Mean student ratings on a scale from 1 (strongly disagree) to 4 (strongly agree) follow:

Question	Instructor Mean	Political Science Departmental Mean	Faculty of Arts and Science (Sector) Mean
Does the instructor stimulate interest in the material?	3.64	3.47	3.41
The professor created a classroom environment in which students feel free to express their ideas.	3.82	3.59	3.54
The professor is accessible to students outside of class.	3.60	3.44	3.44
Overall this professor is an effective teacher.	3.66	3.57	3.50

Signed Student Testimonials

Following are representative examples from several students who have sent me notes over the last two years (see **Appendix C**, Teaching Evaluations). These testimonials, which are unsolicited,

---

*Concordia University does not permit anonymous student comments to be considered as part of teaching evaluations. Although I do use these comments for self-evaluation purposes, they cannot be included in portfolios or published material.

highlight my commitment to effective teaching and, in particular, my teaching principles of creating a positive learning environment.

> I would like to thank you for your help and guidance. I appreciate your goodwill and admire your professionalism and expertise. Your advice was really helpful in the development of my research.

> I just wanted to touch base with you and let you know that I am benefiting greatly from this experience. . . . How relevant these texts ARE for our field of study! I think your teaching method is very effective as well.

> I ran into several students from class the other day, and all agreed that you are the best teacher at the university.

Mentor and Administrator Evaluations

Written evaluations from administrators and teaching mentors reflect my commitment to creating a positive classroom for discussion and expressing genuine enthusiasm for the course material (see **Appendix C**, Teaching Evaluations).

> "The POLI496 [Honour's Seminar] evaluation results are outstanding. . . . I do hope we can attract more students to this obviously excellent class in the future."—Peter Stoett, Department Chair, Concordia University

> "[Marlene] has a skill for provoking good class discussions of the issues that arise in the classic texts of political theory. . . . As a classroom teacher, Marlene is a star."—Larry Arnhart, Professor of Political Science, Northern Illinois University

> "Marlene lectures to the point but in a 'talking with' rather than a 'talking to' manner . . . [she] is an unusually gifted, conscientious, and caring teacher who is moved by a love of her subject to wish to share that with others."—Gary Glenn, Presidential Teaching Professor, Northern Illinois University

Course Revisions and Reflections

I see curricular revisions as reflecting my teaching principle that the most effective teachers are those who learn from their teaching experience. My approach to revision is by assessing and reassessing student and observational feedback and self evaluations.

One particularly challenging course is the large, required introductory courses. In my first two sections of Introduction to Western Political Thought, I monitored student attendance and ensured completion of reading assignments by assigning 20 percent of the course grade to random pop quizzes (see **Appendix B**, Course Material). I found the pop quizzes were creating anxiety among the diligent students who could not prepare for them and in general were unreflective of the class average in other assignments. In response to this difficulty, recently I introduced scheduled quizzes to ensure completion of reading assignments and random small in-class activities to increase grade consistency with major assignments (see **Appendix B**, Course Materials). I have also introduced the Supplemental Instruction program as an additional aid to helping students who are experiencing difficulty with this course.

In addition, other course development changes improve on other avenues of difficulty as highlighted in student evaluations, such as speed and quality of student assignment feedback. In 2005, I introduced a standard rubric for grading (see **Appendix B**, Course Materials) and at the end of the term a student emailed the remark:

> Thank you very much for your extensive comments on my term paper. I am thankful for your encouragement on improving my paper. They will be so useful for when I write my undergraduate thesis.

Finally, to continue improving class presentation, I attended a full-day workshop on "Teaching as Performance," which included activities to improve presentation and lecture style (see **Appendix D**, Teaching Improvement Activities).

Reflection

Teaching is an ongoing and rewarding process that continues beyond the last class session. I am committed to improving my teaching through assessments of evaluations and recognize in this early stage of my teaching career that reassessment of course revisions may require several semesters of evaluations prior to implementing new changes. I am excited by and look forward to the rewards of this process.

Research Statement

Political theory is an exploration of widely shared ideas or principles of the political community, such as the purpose of political authority, the meaning of justice, and the extent of personal obligations to the common good. As these principles are often treated as self-evidence, political theory seeks to clarify ideas that underlie empirical political analysis and motivate contemporary political life. The fundamental organizing principle of my research agenda is to explore classical political theory (which developed in ancient Athens from the fifth century) as a unique perspective from which to understand enduring political ideas and concepts. My approach to research emphasizes an interdisciplinary perspective that brings together the discourse of diverse fields of the humanities, social sciences, and fine arts. My current research agenda has two key pillars of research: (1) political emotions and (2) literary explorations of justice and authority.

Pillar 1: Political Emotions

There has been increasing attention devoted to understanding the role of emotions in sociopolitical and ethical decision making. I contribute to this debate by exploring Aristotle's approach to emotions, which emphasizes emotions as complex responses that both provide essential contributions to ethical decision making as well as potentially undermine positive individual and social actions. An important conclusion of my research is that it emphasizes an interdisciplinary research perspective that includes political science, psychology, philosophy, and neurosciences. The main publication output of this research pillar is my book *Political Emotions: Aristotle and the Symphony of Reason and Emotions* (DeKalb: Northern Illinois University Press, 2006).

The book has been well received and reviewed in several journals (for complete list see **Appendix E**, Scholarship Reviews).

"Of the many books and articles published in the last few years on ancient Greek philosophy and emotions, this author's approach stands out in attempting to connect Aristotle's analysis of emotion with contemporary research on the emotions."—J. L. Miller, SUNY College at New Paltz, *Choice: Current Reviews for Academic Libraries 44,* 11 (2007).

"This is an excellent and comprehensive study of Aristotle's understanding of emotion that should be read by all serious scholars of Aristotelian political philosophy as well as contemporary researchers of the role of emotions in political life."—Ann Ward, University of Regina, *Canadian Journal of Political Science* (2007), 543–544.

"The book serves as an excellent resource for surveying the politically relevant emotions discussed in the Rhetoric and for encouraging conversation between current empirical political science and political theory."—Barbara Koziak, St. John's University, *Perspectives on Politics* (2007) 620–621.

This research pillar has also led to several shorter contributions. I contributed the chapter "Feelings in the Political Philosophy of J.S. Mill," to *Politics and the Passions in the History of Political Thought,* edited by Leonard Ferry and Rebecca Kingston (UBC Press, December 2007). This chapter focuses on the influence of John Stuart Mill's view of emotions for understanding the ethical theory of utilitarianism (see **Appendix F**, Publications). The anonymous reviews strongly endorsed this work (for full reviews see **Appendix E**, Scholarship Reviews).

Sokolon offers an overview of the conception and place of feelings in Mill's political theory, as well as an analysis and critique of his perspective. I think the dangers that she points out are worth taking seriously.

Although there has been a lot of scholarship on the emotions over the last twenty years that has begun to have an influence in contemporary political theory and its history, much more work needs to be done. This collection will play a large role in motivating this kind of work and it will set the standard of how it should be carried out for years to come.

This pillar researching political emotions has also resulted in an encyclopedia article, "Emotional Intelligence," in *Encyclopedia of Science, Ethics and Technology* (Carl Mitcham, ed., Detroit: Macmillan Reference, 2005) (see **Appendix F**, Publications), nine conference papers (see **Appendix G**, Conference Papers), and three grant applications. I was successful in one of these grant applications, Killgore Foundation Grant, which helped fund research into the role of emotion in deliberative political rhetoric. In this pillar, I have submitted two other article-length manuscripts for peer review and am currently revising two more for peer review (see **Appendix H**, Manuscripts in Progress).

Pillar 2: Literary Explorations of Justice and Authority

My second research pillar focuses on analyzing the meaning and ways in which political concepts, such as justice and authority, are communicated in the classical literary texts of Homer, Aeschylus, Sophocles, and Euripides. The main goal of this pillar is a book-length manuscript project currently titled, *Politics in Verse: Justice and Authority in Ancient Greek Tragedy.*

This pillar contributes to scholarship exploring political ideas not in philosophic texts but in literature, such as drama, poetry, and in the contemporary era, novels, and film. The general argument underlying this research is that dramatic works of literature contain social and emotional knowledge of political ideas not typically found in the rational argumentation of philosophy. As such, this research builds on my previous pillar exploring the political significance of emotions and continues to emphasize interdisciplinary research by bringing together scholarship from classics, political science, theater studies, comparative literature, philosophy, and history.

Thus far, this research pillar has resulted in five conference papers (see **Appendix G**, Conference Papers). One of these conference papers, "The *Iliad:* A Song of Political Protest," has been revised and submitted for peer review (see **Appendix H**, Manuscripts in Progress). The four other conference papers are contributing chapters for the book manuscript on this pillar, which is the focus of my current research.

This research pillar is also the focus of my current research grant applications. These grant applications are intended to facilitate my research by funding research time stipends, conference travel, as well as graduate research assistants. In 2007, I received a $3,000 General Research Fund (GRF), which is a faculty development grant from Concordia's Faculty of Arts and Science. In 2007, I applied and received a rating of 4A on my $96,000 Canadian Social Science and Humanities Research Council (SSHRC) application. The 4A designates that the research was highly recommended (in my case I was rated 50/142, with funding available for 48 grant proposals) but the Council had insufficient government funding to support the proposal. For full proposals and assessor evaluations see **Appendix I**, Grant Proposals.

Service Statement

The fundamental organizing principle of my service commitments is to engage and foster the development of positive research, teaching, and service communities. My service commitment emphasizes three main components: (1) collegiality and departmental service, (2) university interdisciplinary community service, and (3) service to the academic discipline and wider nonacademic community.

Collegiality and Departmental Service

I have been active in my commitment to collegiality and academic responsibility by attending all departmental meetings and serving on three important departmental committees (see **Appendix J**, Service). I am a member of the Masters in Public Policy and Public Administration (MPPPA) Admissions Committee for the years 2006–08, during which time we have evaluated 201 applications for admission. I also served on the Department's Standards Committee, which is engaged in the process of codifying departmental contract, tenure, and promotions standards. I have also participated in the growth of the department by being active on hiring and search committees (see **Appendix J**, Service, for full details).

University Interdisciplinary Community Development

In order to achieve my goal of fostering the interdisciplinary community at Concordia, I have been active in guest lecturing and joining committees and groups with an interdisciplinary focus (for full university service commitments, see **Appendix J**, Service). In April 2007, I was a guest lecturer for an introductory course in biology on biotechnology. In my lecture, I covered the ethical and social concerns of this technology. Dr. Pawelek commented (see **Appendix K**, Letters of Appreciation):

> [Your lecture] went over very well with the students! It was a perfect complement to the more technical information I had been teaching concerning these technologies.

I have also joined two important interdisciplinary groups (see **Appendix J**, Service). In 2005, I cofounded, with five other Concordia faculty members, the Consortium for Classical Thought @ Concordia; the purpose of this group is to raise the profile of classical thought on campus through public presentations and interdisciplinary events. In fall 2006, I became a member of the Advisory Board for the Centre for Interdisciplinary Studies in Society and Culture; its mission is to encourage the development of research ties and groups across the university.

Service to the Discipline and Wider Nonacademic Community

As part of my ongoing commitment to the discipline of political science, I have served as invited participant, chair, or discussant on ten different conferences (see **Appendix J**, Service), published a book review, and peer-reviewed two articles and a book manuscript.

As part of my commitment of outreach to the broader nonacademic community, I have given three public lectures (see **Appendix J**, Service) and was a volunteer judge for 180 high school students who were participating in a UN simulation.

Integration of Professional Activities

Growth and Development

The most significant experience of my career thus far has been to reorient from a small teaching-focused university to a large research-oriented faculty position. Experiencing academic life from these diverse positions has provided valuable insights and a broader perspective from which to develop teaching, research, and service commitments. The fact, for example, that I was the only political theorist at WTAMU is a fairly common experience in smaller teaching institutions and, thus, faculty at such universities tend to be part of an interdisciplinary community. At larger universities such as Concordia, where I am one of five political theorists, there is not necessarily the same impetus to join interdisciplinary communities. It was my past experience with such a community, however, that encouraged me to seek out Concordia's productive and dynamic interdisciplinary community.

Special Accomplishments

Although it is difficult to select only three professional accomplishments as representative of my teaching, research, and service goals, the following highlight successes of which I am particularly proud.

Student Development

The most rewarding experience of teaching has been to observe the personal success of my students. I require oral presentations in my senior classes, which for many students is their first experience with public speaking. I had several scheduled appointments with one bright young woman who faced a great deal of anxiety over public speaking. We spent time talking about content and developing a strategy to deal with her stress and panic. She did succeed with her presentations and is now in graduate school. In a recent e-mail she acknowledge how important overcoming her anxiety was for her goals (see **Appendix K**, Letters of Appreciation:

> Taking your class has given me the courage to speak in public and share my opinions with my classmates (this is helping a lot in my

MA classes because participation is a must!). Thank you very much for being a great teacher and a tough grader because it pushed me to always give 100% of myself and time to my studies. My goal is to be a professor later in life, and I truly wish I could be a good and fair professor like you.

Research Development

The most rewarding aspect of my research agenda has been the evolution of my research agenda. During my research into political emotions, I observed how much circumstance and events were important in emotional responses. This observation inspired my new research pillar, which explores how literature can capture these events and circumstances and thus provide the context for further exploration of the importance of emotions in political behavior. The most rewarding aspect of research is this ongoing process of inspiration and unexpected enterprises.

Professional Development

The most important element of my professional development has been the opportunity to work in a community of interdisciplinary research and scholarship. The two main groups I am working with are:

- Classical Thought @ Concordia (founded in 2005), which is a consortium of scholars from different disciplines interested in literary and philosophic heritage of the ancient world.
- Member of the Advisory Board for the Centre for Interdisciplinary Studies in Society and Culture (founded in 2007), which encourages interdisciplinary research through working groups and lectures.

The Future

The following are my teaching and research goals in the coming years:

Teaching

- In the fall 2007, the department introduced a Ph.D. program. I am currently working at recruiting Ph.D. students and look forward to mentoring and developing a new core course for graduate students specializing in political theory.

- I look forward to assessing and reevaluating changes introduced into my classes, such as scheduled quizzes instead of pop quizzes, for improved student performance as well as course evaluations.

Research

- I look forward to obtaining a SSHRC grant, which will assist in the publication of my second book, *Politics in Verse: Justice and Authority in Ancient Greek Tragedy.*
- My research into literature as a source of political knowledge has inspired me to include literary texts, such as Euripides and Sophocles, in course content. I also intend to use the experience of teaching with these texts to contribute to scholarship in teaching and learning in political science by attending conferences and publishing in the field.

Appendixes

A. Teaching Responsibilities

B. Course Syllabi and Materials

C. Teaching Evaluations (Student and Peer)

D. Teaching Improvement Activities

E. Scholarship Reviews

F. Publications

G. Conference Papers

H. Scholarship, Manuscripts in Progress

I. Grant Proposals

J. Service

K. Letters of Appreciation

Product Design

Robert Kirkbride
Product Design Department
Parsons The New School for Design
Fall 2008

Executive Summary

As part of the evaluation process for tenure, the enclosed materials reflect on the five years during which I have taught at Parsons The New School for Design, beginning in spring 2002 as a part-time instructor and concentrating on the period following my employment as full-time faculty in January 2005. Several syllabi and articles are included in full and may be removed from the dossier for further examination; some of these are also available on request at the dean's office.

The following points highlight the most important elements of my dossier:

- My teaching philosophy, methods of implementation, and evaluations from students and colleagues for my role as instructor and thesis coordinator in the Product Design Department (**Appendixes B–E**).
- A summary of my scholarship, its character, international presence, and relevance (**Appendixes F–H**).
- An overview of my service and efforts to improve the quality of the learning environment at departmental, divisional, and university levels, including my role as cochair of the University Faculty Senate (**Appendix I**).
- How my investigations have been recognized (Gutenberg-e Prize, Visiting Scholar at the Canadian Centre for Architecture), creating further research opportunities in and beyond the classroom (**Appendix F**).

Contents of Portfolio

Teaching

- Responsibilities (Courses, Coordination, Advising, Interns)
- Philosophy and Methodologies
- Curricular Revisions
- Course Work
- Teaching Improvement
- Student Evaluations
- Statements About My Work in the Classroom
  and as Coordinator

Scholarship

- Nature of Research
- Statements from Others About My Research
- Select Publications: Scholarship of Discovery
- Lectures and Conference Presentations
- Professional Honors and Recognition
- Editorial Appointments: Scholarship of Integration
- Design and Creative Research: Scholarship of Application

Service

Integration of Professional Work and Goals

- How Teaching, Research, and Service Contribute
  to Professional Development
- Select Professional Accomplishments
- Professional Goals

Appendixes

Teaching

Teaching Responsibilities

As Associate Professor of Product Design, I have taught and advised an average of fifty juniors and seniors per year in our undergraduate program. My experience in Parsons Product Design began as a part-time instructor of the thesis-related studio Information Design, which was conceived to enhance critical thinking in the thesis process. Subsequently, my involvement in the program parallels the growth of the department-wide initiative to diversify and deepen the pedagogy of product design. Over the past three years, I have averaged two six-hour studios and one three-hour seminar-studio (fifteen contact hours) each semester, frequently managing special projects (**Appendix B**). At the time of my full-time appointment, in January 2005, I was the coordinator and instructor for the Product Design Thesis + Analysis Studio, and redesigned the course Poetics of Design as a seminar-studio; additionally, I have redesigned and cotaught the Junior Furniture Design Studio and invented the seminar-studio Sites of Inquiry (syllabi, **Appendix D**).

Since 2004, as thesis coordinator, I have been responsible for coordinating thirteen faculty and calibrating syllabi across three thesis-related courses; writing and revising the syllabus for the Thesis + Analysis Studio; inviting guest presenters and critics; planning reviews; ensuring delivery of materials for the thesis show; dovetailing the grading process among several instructors; as well as participating in the hiring of new faculty. As thesis adviser, I meet with all seniors during the year to discuss their thesis development: in 2006–07 this included 175 individual half-hour meetings outside regular studio time (see **Appendix C** for chart and Thesis Overview). I also advised eleven Product Design juniors each semester and an additional ten CDT (Communications-Design Technology) graduate and undergraduate students in the spring for the interdepartmental Target Project. Additionally, this year I accepted student interns in my design work, for which students dedicate 120 hours: Veronica Choi (a recent Product Design graduate) assisted in architectural and graphic design, meetings with clients, and the production of a series of sculptures for an exhibit in Montréal (**Appendix H**).

In addition to my advising, during the 2007–08 academic year, I taught the equivalent of three courses each semester, including Thesis + Analysis Studio, Poetics of Design, and a new international intensive design elective studio, entitled *Ornamental Intelligence*. The Poetics course included a few new wrinkles: (1) students were interdepartmental, (2) my syllabus was cotaught (**Appendix D**), and (3) students had an opportunity to present their work at a scholarly conference. *Ornamental Intelligence* was a pilot advanced furniture elective studio in collaboration with Domus Academy in Milan, Italy; it matched seniors and juniors from Parsons with graduate students from Domus, offering an intensive experience in a world design center.

Teaching Philosophy

Research (thinking) and Design (making) are inseparable twins, a belief that infuses my investigation of connections between human behavior (ethics) and the sensual world (aesthetics). Are aesthetics and ethics at opposite poles or two sides of the same coin? At the heart of this question is the practice of sustainability, which is *systemic* and *poetic:* beyond industry standards and policymaking, it is an attitude—a *way of being*—that respects and enhances the mutual influences of personal and communal identity. For this reason I feel at home at Parsons and its association with The New School and the vision of its founders, including John Dewey, one of a legacy of scholars who have examined the fertile intersection of the mechanical and liberal arts. This legacy includes Hugh of St. Victor (1096–1141) and Nicholas of Cusa (1401–64), influential figures in my research and teaching, and more recently, the historian Ivan Illich, one of my mentors. Their fascination with the visible processes and products of material craft to explain and train the invisible workings of the mind reflects an ancient intellectual tradition of splitting ideas into categorical parts and compositional units (analysis) for innovative reassembly (synthesis).

Increasingly, a lateral approach to research, teaching, and design is demanded within and beyond the academy, where designers are called on to identify and orchestrate problem solving for complex, nonlinear issues, often in interdisciplinary teams. The New School's recent work with the ethnographic design consultants IDEO to program our new building at 65 Fifth Avenue (see Appendix J) offers one cogent example. In my interactions with clients, designers, and academics, it is clear that design—specifically the *design process*—is gaining new layers of significance as an analytical and synthetic methodology to appreciate the global impact of local conditions and the local impact of global conditions. Awareness of and participation in the expanding role of the designer reflexively fuels my teaching and design work.

With respect to disciplinary boundaries, my work explores a zone between architecture and product design, based on my experience that architecture often fails when it neglects the site-specific context, and that product design often fails when it forgets the universal. This principal has guided my teaching and the applied scholarship of my design practice through a focus on sustainable development, emergency dwellings, tangible goods, and intangible services that influence well-being at local and global scales (**Appendixes E, H**).

Teaching Methodologies

No method, however ideal in theory, is perfect in application. The unique character and needs of each student require a combination and tailoring of techniques based on observation. My task is to help students recognize and cultivate their aptitudes, equipping them with an ability to think broadly by forming incisive questions. Specialist skills may be acquired as needed, but the habits of critical thinking (historically referred to as *prudence*) are slower to develop, requiring patience, encouragement, and rigor.

Project-based learning is a catalyst to this process, with assignments that habituate students to rhythms of analysis and synthesis through research and design. This mode of learning achieves many goals simultaneously:

- Stimulates lateral thinking to form unexpected links and identify necessary skills
- Encourages social intelligence in a world and profession where teamwork is in growing demand to address complex problems
- Challenges individual development of multiple intelligences in a group dynamic, fortifying personal confidence in what one is "good" at by teaching others, while reducing fear of one's own "weaknesses" by learning from peers and "the task at hand"

Most important, perhaps, is that project-based learning is an egalitarian process where students learn from one another, and the instructor facilitates rather than imparts ideas.

Curricular Revisions

As Thesis Coordinator, I oversee the curricular evolution of "A Good Life," a complex endeavor now entering its fifth year. When I began this role in Fall 2004, one of my first activities was to create an "overview" that maps the thesis curriculum for students, faculty, and administration (see **Appendix C**). Each year, this overview and the syllabus require my revision, building on experiences gathered from the previous year and filtered with the core group of six instructors. As part of our social commitment to grow and deepen relationships with the nonprofit community we continue to explore techniques of engagement, from the Symposium Design for Change to community-based projects (see **Appendix B** for letters from community representatives).

Course Work

Several aspects of my course work might be seen as unique. Through the year, I invite guest speakers and critics to the Product Design Thesis + Analysis Studio from disciplines across Parsons and the New York for-profit and not-for-profit communities. Also of note are the alternative review formats I have tailored to build and/or challenge student confidence at threshold moments in the year. One example is the "open review," used at the end of fall semester and midspring, to allow students repeated conversational presentations of their thesis, thereby maximizing input from critics who, in an unusual twist, outnumber the students. In addition to specific pedagogical emphases, such as integration of full-scale hand-drawing and manual fabrication with computer-aided techniques, my Poetics of Design course complements a collection of challenging articles with an interlinking series of design exercises. Encouraging results are reflected in the following anonymous responses from student course evaluations (see **Appendix D** for examples of course syllabi):

> I think they [the readings] all added to the next one, making
> the class enjoyable. It was great how conversation started
> from every reading and we related it to our lives now.
> (Poetics F'05)

Although readings were quite hard I believe all of them were quite helpful. (Poetics F'05)

—————————

[The readings were] directly related to the projects as reference and inspiration. The reading and class discussions make you think unusually. (Poetics F'05)

Teaching Improvement

Beyond carefully planned curricular adjustments, it is extremely important to be able to respond swiftly to the inevitable "unforeseen circumstances." As thesis coordinator, I have learned to prepare myself and other instructors to expect the unexpected, developing exercises early in the thesis year to help us diagnose potential problems *before* they become crises. Direct feedback from students—whether by student evaluations, during advising, or less formal conversation—is the central point of reference for improving my teaching. As one example, during my first year coordinating Thesis Year, I was also one of the primary studio instructors. From student feedback, it became apparent that the challenge of coordinating three separate thesis sections *and* the precise needs of teaching one section of thirteen students—all within a six-hour time frame—was untenable; I shifted my approach to enable the other primary instructors more latitude with their own sections and sought different ways to more evenly engage all of the students through individual advising. This past year I developed new methods to improve my advising by tracking the number of meetings with thesis students (see **Appendix C**).

Student Evaluations

Tabulated below are the student course evaluations I have received since I began teaching in spring 2002 (not all copies were available). Note that I do not receive evaluations for coordinating and teaching Thesis + Analysis Studios (thirty-two to thirty-eight students each semester), and that I cotaught the Design Concepts and Information Design courses. Since Parsons currently does not include a numerical quotient for its student course evaluations, I have applied the following point system to quantify responses: 4 = always, 3 = often, 2 = sometimes, 1 = rarely, and 0 = never. Based on criteria from the evaluation forms, I then averaged the totals with the number of student respondents, on a scale of 0 to 4 (4 being highest):

Evaluation Criteria	Design Concepts S'07: Average + Number of Students		Design Concepts F'05: Average + Number of Students		Poetics of Design F'05: Average + Number of Students		Poetics of Design S'05: Average + Number of Students		Poetics of Design F'04: Average + Number of Students		Information Design S'03: Average + Number of Students	
Communication of subject	3.66	9	3.6	10	3.7	10	3.75	8	3.89	9	3.67	9
Class organization	3.2	9	3.7	10	3.1	10	3.75	8	3.89	9	3.11	9
Student enthusiasm	3.77	9	3.6	10	3.6	10	3.63	8	3.89	9	3.56	9
Critical thinking + participation	3.88	9	3.9	10	4.0	10	3.38	8	3.89	9	3.78	9
Concern about progress	3.55	9	3.7	10	3.9	10	3.75	8	3.89	9	3.67	9
Enjoys teaching	3.88	9	4.0	10	3.8	10	3.88	8	3.89	9	3.78	9

In addition to those previously mentioned, the following comments from anonymous student evaluation forms speak directly to my objectives and practices in the classroom:

[He was] passionate and able to transfer that into students. (Poetics F'04)

[He was] good at raising questions about presumptuous material and good at raising questions we don't typically ask of ourselves. One of the best teachers I've ever encountered. I feel lucky to have had such great instruction . . . very enlightening . . . I wish I had it as a class all four years. (Poetics S'05)

[Poetics of Design] has made a significant impact on the way I think about design and create. (Poetics F'05)

Statements About My Work in the Classroom and as Coordinator

The following are comments from colleagues and administrators at Parsons and at other institutions who have observed me as a teacher and/or coordinator "in the classroom," whether at The New School or in the field for a project in Sweden:

Tony Whitfield, Chair, Parsons Product Design (excerpt from Annual Performance Review, **Appendix B**):

> In [Robert's] role of coordinator of the Senior Thesis + Analysis Studio, he has vigilantly overseen the development of a curriculum . . . It must be noted here that Robert's commitment to the work of the classes far exceeds that of most faculty. Robert has become a powerful mentor and academic advisor for not only the motivated student, but also the struggling student.

Carlos Teixeira, Assistant Professor, Parsons Design and Management:

> Robert's systematic attention to methodical and rigorous design processes, as well as his unconditional demand for relevance and significance from students' projects, have been his main contribution to reposition product design students as strategic doers, instead of technical experts.

Lars Wieselgren, Project Manager, House of Design, Hallefors, Sweden (**Appendix B**), commenting on the [Little House on Black River]:

> I also had the opportunity to watch him [Kirkbride] as an instructor, both in New York and Hellefors. He had a very natural way of communicating with the students and motivated them through the whole project. The students showed great respect for his knowledge and the advice that he gave and clearly appreciated working with him.

Scholarship

Nature of Research

My scholarship reflects and recharges pursuits in the classroom and my design practice and has been central to an enjoyable and sustainable mode of living as a designer-scholar. To this end, I have been interested in the mutual influences of learning and design, and the role of the physical environment on the formation of memory and identity. This approach began in earnest from my master's thesis in architecture ("A Curiosity Shop," 1990), and spans my experience in curating and designing exhibitions, architectural design, furniture, and products, as well as in teaching, scholarly publications, lectures, workshops and my first book.

A particular point of concern is to help students recognize that they are a part of history and that a critical awareness of history offers invaluable perspectives on contemporary issues, revealing opportunities for design and political engagement. An example of my views on the political dimensions of design and scholarship is expressed in the video *Thinking and Making*, from a design charrette I conducted at the Cooper-Hewitt Museum (www.cooperhewitt.org/EDU/av_edu.asp?v=6).

Statements from Others About My Research

The following are comments from colleagues and administrators, peer juries and reviewers, regarding my scholarly and design research.

American Historical Association, Gutenberg-e Prize committee (for full jury comments and project synopsis, see **Appendix F**):

> [Kirkbride's] dissertation is a tour de force of scholarship and writing. It is full of insights, imaginative in its approach, very analytical and yet very elegantly written.

Caroline Payson, Director of Education at the Cooper-Hewitt National Design Museum:

> I had the opportunity to see Robert's work firsthand in Sweden. Because of that project and hearing Robert discuss the project-based approach in his work and teaching, I hired Robert to be a workshop leader and teacher at our annual Summer Design Institute here at Cooper-Hewitt.

John Hill's review of *Chora Four: Intervals in the Philosophy of Architecture* in "What Are We Reading? A Weekly Dose of Architecture" (www.archidose.org/books/chora4.html):

Kirkbride's essay on the Renaissance Studioli of Federico da Montefeltro give[s] great insight into lesser-known parts of a highly influential and studied time.

Shannon Mattern, Director of Graduate Studies in Media Studies, The New School for Graduate Studies, in a summary of *EARLIDS: A 3-D Aural Response to Noise Pollution,* a collaborative installation conceived by composer Melissa Grey (see **Appendix H**):

A prototype of Earlids . . . appeared in . . . a Lower Manhattan Cultural Council-supported exhibition that I directed in spring 2006. My own and other gallery attendants' observations revealed that Earlids was the highlight of the show. Its beauty earned it a prominent corner window placement . . . its interactivity inspired engagement.

Select Publications

In the past three years I have produced one book and five articles (two invited, two blind-juried, one juried), one interview, and one book review (See **Appendix A** for complete list and **Appendix G** for sample articles):

Architecture and Memory: The Renaissance Studioli of Federico da Montefeltro, experimental e-book with Columbia University Press (2008), recipient of the Gutenberg-e Prize, awarded by the American Historical Association. (For comments: http://www.historians.org/prizes/gutenberg/2004wins.cfm)

Invited to review *Urban Memory: History and Amnesia in the Modern City,* ed. Mark Crinson, for FutureAnterior, Columbia University's *Journal of Historic Preservation,* Vol. III, No. 2 Winter 2006, pp. 66–74.

"On the Renaissance Studioli of Federico da Montefeltro and the Architecture of Memory," in *Chora 4: Intervals in the Philosophy of Architecture,* eds. Alberto Pérez-Gómez and Stephen Parcells, McGill-Queen's Press (2004), pp. 127–176.

"Number Is Form and Form Is Number," interview of Anne
G. Tyng, FAIA, *Nexus Network Journal*, Vol. 7 no. 1 (Spring
2005), http://www.nexusjournal.com/Kirk-Tyng.html.

Lectures and Conference Presentations

Lecturing and conference participation is an integral component
of my research: over the past four years I have averaged five public presentations each year, by conference presentations and
responses (twelve), formal lectures at universities (six), panels
moderated (four), and lectures translated (one). (See **Appendix A**
for full list)

- McGill University: Montréal, Canada

  Speak, Stone: Geometries of Rhetoric in a Renaissance Façade,
  for the conference "Reconciling Poetics and Ethics in
  Architecture," History and Theory of Architecture Program;
  September 15, 2007. (article in full, **Appendix G**)

- Cooper-Hewitt National Design Museum: Smithsonian Museum

  NYC *Thinking and Making,* for "A City of Neighborhoods
  Program" with 40 K–12 public school teachers from New
  Orleans, LA; June 26, 2007. (Excerpt in **Appendix G**)

- Palazzo Ducale: Urbino, Italy (presented in Italian)

  *La Prospettiva della Memoria negli Studioli dei Montefeltro: la
  mestiere materiale e mentale nel quattrocento inoltranto* [Trans.
  The Perspective of Memory in the Montefeltro Studioli:
  Material and Mental Craft in the Late Quattrocento] for
  the conference "The Art of Mathematics in Perspective,"
  Palazzo Ducale, Urbino; October 11, 2006.

Professional Honors and Recognition

As a **Visiting Scholar** at the **Canadian Centre for Architecture,** I
enjoyed three months of access to "one of the world's foremost
international research collections of publications and architectural design documentation," in the company of talented staff
and fellow scholars. The residence enabled me to sharpen my
investigation of memory in the Renaissance *studioli* from the

Montefeltro palaces at Urbino and Gubbio, Italy, by composing a series of short historical fictions that illustrate how these remarkable chambers were used in everyday circumstances of diplomacy, dialectical inquiry, civil judgment, education, and leisure. Alongside these fictions, I developed the idea of a collaborative Web-based project to translate the research into an interactive digital environment. In the concluding week of my residence, I submitted this material as a proposal for the Gutenberg-e Prize. (letter of appointment, **Appendix F**).

The Gutenberg-e Prize, "the bluest of ribbons awarded by the American Historical Association," has enabled me to convert my dissertation into an experimental electronic book with Columbia University Press (launch, 2008). Following eight years of work, I greatly appreciated the response of the jury comments (for full jury comments and overview of Gutenberg-e, see **Appendix F**). "Designed to explore the potential of the digital environment to provide innovative models for the publication of peer-reviewed scholarly works," the award has provided funding ($20,000) for travel to Italy, purchase of documentary equipment (photographic, video and audio equipment) and related project costs. For my teaching, this opportunity also stimulated a new course, Sites of Inquiry, in spring 2006. The objective of this course was to generate an alternative point of entry to the online research, particularly for nonspecialist readers of varying ages.

Beyond recognition for my own work, I take special pleasure in the **achievements of former students.** Recently, Parsons Product alumnus Hideaki Matsui received the distinguished "Best of Category" award in the Student Design Review from *I. D. Magazine* for his project "CleanUp." Hideaki's product—land-mine-shaped soap conceived to "wash away" explosive devices worldwide—was developed as his senior thesis, in partnership with the U.N. sponsored nonprofit group Adopt-a-Minefield (**Appendix E**). I am pleased to add that among the 250 applicants, Mihoko Ouchi, another recent alumna from Parsons Product, received an honorable mention for her thesis, "Emotional Skin," which seeks to improve our psychological experience of elevators. This is a further tribute to the significant work being produced by our students and faculty.

Editorial Appointments

Since 2003, I have been an editorial board member of the *Nexus Network Journal,* an Italian-based peer-reviewed journal of architecture and mathematics for researchers, professionals, and students engaged in the study of the application of mathematical principles to architectural design. Recently, I have been invited to guest-edit a special issue of the *NNJ* for summer 2009. My working title for this issue is *Geometries of Rhetoric,* reflecting a focus on overlaps and differences among verbal and numeric modes of expression and how they are formally and figuratively embodied through design and architecture. (See **Appendix F** for a note about editorship and **Appendix G** for subsequent contribution.)

Design and Creative Research

In 1991 I launched *studio "patafisico,"* an ongoing endeavor whose projects encompass architectural design, ecological land planning, and installations; *Studiolo* subsequently emerged (1999) as an exploration of furniture and home provisions produced by regional craftsmen. Resulting work has been exhibited and published widely; in *Vogue, The New York Times, surface, Mark Magazine, Metropolis,* and the film *XX/XY.*

Recent Design Projects

- 2005–07. **O'Connor-Milstein Residence:** Apartment renovation. Barrow St. (West Village Houses), NYC. Construction document phase completed (8/1/07). With assistance from Parsons intern Kazushige Yoshitake. (**Appendix H**)
- 2006. **Wet Unit-Gatehouse** for *Little Houses on the Black River,* Hallefors, Sweden. 10m^2 communal space containing kitchen, dining/work area, shower and waterless Danfo w.c. to accompany two artist-in-residence dwellings designed and built by students from Parsons and St. Etienne. Project sponsored by Formens Hus (The House of Design); construction sponsored by IKEA. Built with support of Parsons staff and students in ten days.
- 2002–07. **Kirkwyd:** Land planning for and design of nine environmentally responsible homes for a conservation subdivision

to be built on 31.5 forested acres along the Brandywine Creek in Chester County, PA (final approvals received 7/2005). (**Appendix H**)

Recent Exhibited Work

In 2006–07 my work was exhibited in three separate shows in North America, including two installations of *EARLIDS: a 3-D Aural Response to Noise Pollution*, a collaboration with composer Melissa Grey, and *Culobocca*, a collection of experimental forms of continuous surface that were fabricated with assistance from Parsons intern Veronica Choi. (See **Appendix H** for images.)

CULOBOCCA

- 2007, September 15–November 15. Group show: *70 Architects on Love*, Centre de Design, Université du Québec à Montréal.

EARLIDS: A 3-D Aural Response to Noise Pollution

- 2006, November 9–December 15. *The 1st Reno Interdisciplinary Festival of New Media*, Sheppard Fine Arts Gallery, University of Nevada Reno (www.unr.edu/art/RIFNM/exhibit.html).
- 2006, May 9–20. Group show: "Channels: Emerging Media Publics," at 15 Nassau Street, NYC. Sponsored by Lower Manhattan Cultural Council and the Department of Media Studies and Film at the New School University.

University Service

Over the past three years, my service roles at The New School have centered on departmental, divisional, and university-wide space and academic issues. **Appendix I** includes a letter from the Provost's Office and a complete list of committee work and university-wide activities, as well as the following items produced by the University Faculty Senate (UFS) during my term as cochair:

- Minutes from a full session chaired in December 2006, which I designed to bring faculty and administration together to discuss physical and academic facilities
- Summary of work by each of the three UFS committees, with plans for 2007–08 session

- All resolutions passed by the 06–07 Senate
- Cover sheet of the Evaluation and Promotion Section of the Faculty Handbook
- The full Space and Academic Planning Document produced by the APC committee

The University Faculty Senate has provided a remarkable opportunity to work with faculty and administrators across the university to improve the quality of the learning environment. In my first two-year term in the UFS (2005–07), I was elected cochair of the 06–07 Senate and the faculty representative for University Facilities Planning. Both years, I served on the Academic Policies Committee, which supports university-wide academic, space, and information technology planning initiatives (Chair, 05–06).

As cochair of the 2006–07 University Faculty Senate, I guided its agenda and individual senate meetings for the 06–07 academic year with my colleagues Terri Gordon and Dennis Derryck. Beyond the planning of nine regular meetings, three of which I chaired, this included over fifty meetings during the year to plan UFS-related activities with fellow senators and members of the Provost's Office and Administration. Together, Terri, Dennis, and I sought to enhance the role of faculty in university-wide policymaking through increased efficiency of UFS committees and proactive engagement with the Provost's Office and Administration. Since being elected by the UFS as the faculty representative for university facilities planning (spring '06), I have been closely involved in the planning of the new building, as a member of the Provost's Task Force on Academics, Architecture and Facilities Planning.

Integration of Professional Work and Goals
How Teaching, Research, and Service Contribute to My Professional Development

Through architectural design and scholarly research, I examine the influences of the built environment on learning. In my teaching at Parsons, I experience firsthand the negative constraints that a lack of dedicated studio space presents for the Product Design program and, more generally, the problematic relationship between academics and facilities across Parsons and The New School. I aim in my teaching and service to direct this experience to positive ends by increasing opportunities for student and faculty participation in the planning process. Intellectually, I channel my research into course work to emphasize the significance of design for well-being. Service-wise, through my role of cochair in the University Faculty Senate, and as its elected faculty representative for facilities planning, I focus on improving the learning environment by viewing the quality of learning as inseparable from the quality of facilities. My work in these different facets has been mutually reinforcing and rewarding, even offering unexpected opportunities for design: for evidence of this cross-pollination, see **Appendix J**, a summary of the types of spaces encountered (for better and worse) during the "Little Houses" Project.

Selected Professional Accomplishments

Although selecting "top accomplishments" is akin to picking "favorite children," my first book, *Architecture and Memory: The Renaissance Studioli of Federico da Montefeltro* (Fall 2007, Columbia University Press), which received the Gutenberg-e Prize from the American Historical Association, represents many high notes. It was satisfying to apply the results of the research directly in a new course, Sites of Inquiry, where students learned that our "cutting-edge" technologies are strikingly complementary to those conceived five hundred years ago.

Little Houses on the Black River was a Parsons junior furniture studio centered on a year-long collaborative project with the Formens Hus, a design museum in rural Sweden, and two other design schools (Konstfack and St. Etienne). This project engaged all aspects of my work—research, teaching, and design—while offering students a remarkable opportunity as a real-world project for a community at a cultural distance. The project received the award for the top student design project at the 2006 International Contemporary Furniture Fair (NYC) and wide international press (**Appendix E**), as well as garnering support from corporations such as IKEA.

Gaining final approvals for the **Kirkwyd Conservation Subdivision**, a three-year ecological land planning project that I designed and hand-carried among all required agencies at the federal, state, county, and township levels, has opened my eyes to the real challenges confronting sustainable design in the United States and other parts of the world. I have funneled reflections from this process into my course Poetics of Design and the goals and methods of the Senior Thesis + Analysis Studio, in which students are required to envision the extended influences, geographically and temporally, of their product-system. (See **Appendix H.**)

Professional Goals

* To sustain a balanced integration among my teaching, research, and design, developing such project-based learning explorations as Sites of Inquiry and Poetics of Design as graduate-level interdivisional courses.
* To advise graduate students and doctoral candidates, and develop graduate-level programs: I will work with chair Tony Whitfield to plan a fifth-year M.S. program in Product Design.
* To establish a recurring studio in Italy, building on networks I have established, to broaden student experiences while furthering my personal research and professional work. As a step in this direction, Tony Whitfield and I cotaught an intensive advanced studio with Parsons students in conjunction with Domus Academy in January 2008 in Milan, Italy.

Appendixes

Appendix A: Curriculum Vitae

Appendix B: Chair's Annual Review and Letters from Community Partners

Appendix C: Thesis Advising Chart, Thesis Overview

Appendix D: Course Syllabi

Appendix E: Student Projects: Thesis, Sweden Project, University of Montreal

Appendix F: Letters of Recognition and Invitation for Scholarship

Appendix G: Examples of Lectures and Published Articles

Appendix H: Design Projects and Related Articles and Exhibitions

Appendix I: University Service: Letter from Provost and Materials from University Faculty Senate During Term as Cochair (2006–07)

Appendix J: Project Space Analysis for Work on New Building at 65 Fifth Avenue

Psychology

Pamela A. Geller

Director, Student Counseling Center–Center City
Hahnemann Campus
Associate Professor of Psychology, Ob/Gyn,
  and Public Health
Drexel University
Fall 2008

Table of Contents

B. Service to Drexel University
1. Campus Outreach
2. Consultation
3. Selected Committees
C. Service to Professional Community
1. Editorial Activities
Integration of Professional Work/Goals
A. Recent Professional Development and Goals
B. Future Research Agenda
Appendixes

Preface

When I joined the faculty of MCP Hahnemann University in December 1998, I was excited about the challenges this new position posed for my career in terms of integrating applied teaching, research and practice in clinical and health psychology, as well as the opportunity to gain administrative experience. The Psychology Department was then housed in the College of Nursing and Health Professions, and I was hired to direct the Student Counseling Center (SCC) that had been in danger of closing prior to the association (and ultimately, merger) with Drexel University. I viewed this as a remarkable opportunity to develop a high-quality training site for doctoral students in clinical psychology that would promote empirically based treatment and allow for clinical research, while providing top-notch clinical services for students in the College of Nursing and Health Professions, College of Medicine and School of Public Health. While working to achieve this vision, I also focused my efforts on developing an independent and systematic program of research in health psychology, particularly in the area of women's reproductive health, and have received national and international recognition for these contributions to the field.

With the formal merger of MCP Hahnemann and Drexel Universities, the Psychology Department is now housed in the College of Arts and Sciences. This reconfiguration necessitated the integration of applied training applications focused at the graduate level, with responsibilities from a more traditional academic perspective, including responsibilities for undergraduate students. The broader perspective of the newly integrated Psychology Department has allowed me to more fully utilize my varied skills and activities in teaching, research, service, and administration. Not only is there overlap among these aspects of academic functioning, but activities in one area also serve to inform and enhance productivity, and promote quality, in the others.

Although there is great overlap among my teaching, research, and service responsibilities, I discuss each area in distinct sections. I begin with an overview of my goals and accomplishments related to the Student Counseling Center as these reflect the expectations of my primary focus on my hire.

Directorship of the Student Counseling Center

The Drexel University Student Counseling Center at the Center City Hahnemann Campus (SCC) provides psychological services, free of charge, to Drexel University students, including crisis intervention; individual, couple, and group psychotherapy; disability determination testing and other assessment; and workshops and campus outreach. The clinical staff are advanced doctoral students in the Department of Psychology and some predoctoral interns who all work under the auspices of my Pennsylvania License in Psychology (see *Teaching*).

Shortly after my hire, I negotiated a cooperative agreement between the Psychology Department and the Office of University Student Life and now serve as a liaison between these two entities within which the SCC is jointly housed. Among other responsibilities, I coordinate and oversee all programming and activities of the SCC; manage the budget and payroll; supervise the associate director, secretary, and work-study students; provide training and clinical supervision for all clinical staff (see *Teaching*); lead weekly staff/training meetings; provide consultation for university faculty and staff (see *Service*); as well as provide direct clinical services to Drexel University students.

A. Highlights of SCC Development

My primary goal has been to build a student counseling center with professional integrity and a solid foundation for the provision of exceptional clinical service and student training where a program of high-quality clinical research could be initiated and sustained. These goals have been realized and even surpassed. Since my hire, the SCC has seen tremendous expansion and growth in terms of staff positions, types of services provided, service utilization by students, training opportunities for psychology graduate students, SCC resources, and campus visibility. My work has positioned the SCC to be a venue for active clinical research, including two randomized controlled studies—one examining Pennebaker's *Written Emotional Disclosure* paradigm as an adjunct to outpatient psychotherapy and the other comparing Beck's traditional cognitive therapy and an enhanced form of cognitive behavioral therapy, called Acceptance and Commitment Therapy (ACT).

1. Service Utilization Growth

Since my hire (December 1998), service utilization has increased from 54 students served in 1998–99, to 330 students served in 2006–07, an overall increase of over 600% (see summary table). Each year, utilization continues to rise.

SCC Utilization by Fiscal Year

Fiscal Year	Utilization (Students Serviced)
1998–1999	54
1999–2000	106
2000–2001	135
2001–2002	238
2002–2003	243
2003–2004	259
2004–2005	244
2005–2006	268
2006–2007	330

Total increase from 98–99 to 06–07: 611%

Teaching

My training and experience in the area of clinical psychology has reinforced the philosophy that each individual harbors specific strengths and resources and that attention to individual differences can help facilitate growth and change. It is my belief that to be an effective educator, it is essential to "meet students where they are" and attempt to bring them to the next level of development. My background in cognitive and behavioral theories and learning also has influenced my belief that students who have the opportunity to apply what they are learning in practical formats will not only learn most effectively, but also will develop confidence in their abilities more quickly. Therefore, one of my primary aims is to assist students in recognizing their current level of knowledge and abilities. Students who are willing and able to make honest self-assessments, and acknowledge and appreciate their strengths as well as areas in need of improvement, often are more open to the learning process.

I pay close attention to students' particular skills, level of motivation, and desire to learn and advance. When I first enter into a mentoring or supervisory role with a student, I provide them with various training opportunities or tasks that I perceive suits their current level of experience and training. How they function with these initial tasks helps me determine how to proceed with their training (for example, whether they need more support or whether they can function more independently; whether they are prepared for more sophisticated opportunities). I work closely with my students, attempting to model a level of professional demeanor and productivity, and also involving them in many aspects of my own work (for example, reviewing articles for journals, assisting with manuscript preparation, providing guest lectures in my classroom).

When highly motivated students are treated with a high level of respect and are provided with opportunities that involve real-life professional opportunity, with appropriate guidance, they often excel. To facilitate the success of students whom I mentor and supervise, I treat them as junior colleagues and provide them with such opportunities (for example, collaborative scholarship). I also encourage students to work independently and autonomously but to ask for assistance when needed; I maintain an "open door policy" and am available for consultation and supervision on an as-needed basis for all graduate students in the Psychology Department.

A. Teaching Activities

As assigned by the Psychology Department chair, I teach at the graduate and undergraduate levels with instructional responsibilities that involve both classroom and nonclassroom formats.

1. Classroom Teaching

At the graduate level, I have taught the required Psychopathology of Adults course consistently since my hire and the Clinical Practicum Seminar course for five years (1999–2004). Since 2005, I have taught the undergraduate Counseling Psychology course, which is an interactive class that introduces basic listening and counseling skills through didactics, demonstrations, and small group exercises. Each time I have taught these courses, I have implemented changes to improve the structure, keep up with advances in the field, and incorporate student feedback. This past spring, I developed a new graduate elective, Advanced Topics in Health Psychology, which emphasizes the preparation of a review or empirical or theoretical paper on a timely topic to submit for publication (see all course syllabi in Appendix 1).

Courses Taught Regularly

Course Name	Number	Typical Enrollment	Level
Advanced Topics in Health Psychology	Psy 865	6	Graduate
Counseling Psychology	Psy 342	30	Undergraduate
Psychopathology of Adults	Psy 520	24	Graduate

2. Clinical Teaching

As a scientist-practitioner, and student mentor and adviser, my role as educator extends well beyond course instruction. I provide some degree of clinical supervision to every student completing a practicum rotation at the SCC. As this type of teaching requires state licensure, and all clinical staff work under the auspices of my license, I completed the state licensing examination and became a Licensed Psychologist in Pennsylvania (in addition to being licensed in New York State) upon coming to Drexel University. In order to maintain my license, I complete thirty hours of continuing education credit each cycle.

In addition to the weekly SCC staff training meeting, I provide weekly clinical supervision to practicum students (and psychology interns and postdoctoral fellows, when on staff) in both individual and group formats (approximately ten direct hours per week, with additional time for reviewing charts and written reports). During supervision meetings, descriptions of the trainee's weekly therapy experiences and audio- or videotaped sessions are reviewed. Instruction and guidance is provided on a variety of topics and issues (for example, clinical methods and skills, diagnostic information and skills, various theoretical approaches, psychotherapy process, practical interventions, treatment planning, and ethical concerns and practices).

I also teach informally through several weekly and monthly Clinical/Research Team meetings in the areas of Women's Reproductive Health, and Stress and Medical Outcomes, where I cover topics related to current literature in the field, research methodology, and data analysis relevant to ongoing projects. I also provide instruction and mentorship on IRB [institutional review board] submissions, and poster, presentation and manuscript preparation. I encourage students to take the lead on components of projects and to submit their projects for presentation at national conferences, and for publication and awards (at which they have been very successful; see the list in Appendix 2). Clinical education and supervision also are included. For example, I arranged for students on my Women's Reproductive Health research team to attend grand rounds in the OB/GYN and Fetal Medicine Departments within Hahnemann University Hospital.

3. Student Advising/Mentorship

To date, I have been the primary research mentor and graduate adviser for nineteen students in the Department of Psychology (see table). My role as primary research mentor and graduate adviser to master's and doctoral program students has involved assisting with course work selection, assessing program requirement progress, chairing thesis and dissertation projects, coauthoring research, providing guidance for national clinical internship application and interviews, and ultimately providing guidance for postdoctoral fellowship and job applications. Those who have graduated have gone on to complete prestigious predoctoral internships and postdoctoral or other fellowships (for example, Massachusetts General Hospital). I encourage students to present and publish their work as well as apply for scholarships and awards (see Appendix 2). For example, one of my students recently received the Emerging Leaders Fellowship Award through the NIH Center for Scientific Review. In addition, I very often invite students to participate as coauthors on my own projects. Mentorship of my students also has involved providing guidance on their own classroom teaching by observing their guest lectures in my classroom, as well as giving feedback on their course syllabi and examinations for courses taught independently.

Number of Psychology Students for Whom I Am Primary Mentor, by Program and Status

	Master's	Ph.D.
In Progress	2	6
Graduated	4	7

B. Teaching Evaluation

Students have been very positive in their responses to the courses I have taught and ratings on course evaluations have been high overall (see the table and Appendix 3 for copies of formal and informal course evaluations). Consistently, students have ranked their clinical supervisory experience on practicum evaluation forms as superior overall (see Appendix 4) and have expressed appreciation for helping them extend their skills and articulate reasons for their clinical decisions, and encouraging them to develop their own independent clinical style while offering empirically validated treatments. Students whom I mentor and/ or clinically supervise nominated me for several mentorship awards, including the Women in Society Faculty Award, which I was awarded in 2007. Their nomination letters provide further support that I have been successful in my goals for teaching and mentorship (see Appendix 5).

	Term					
Course	Winter 2005	Spring 2005	Winter 2006	Spring 2006	Winter 2007	Spring 2007
PSY 342						
Q.1[a]	X[b]	4.5[c]	X	4.3[c]	X	4.4
Q.2	X	4.9	X	4.8	X	4.6
Q.3	X	4.8	X	4.7	X	4.4
PSY 520						
Q.1	4.4	X	4.4	X	4.5	X
Q.2	4.6	X	4.9	X	4.5	X
Q.3	4.4	X	4.7	X	4.5	X
PSY 865						
Q.1	X	X	X	X	X	4.4
Q.2	X	X	X	X	X	5.0
Q.3	X	X	X	X	X	4.7

[a]Q.1 = "Overall, I learned a lot"; Q.2 = "Instructor treated students' ideas and opinions with respect"; Q.3 = "Overall I would . . . recommend this instructor"/". . . rate this instructor as outstanding" [*form is not consistent across terms*].
[b] = course not taught during this term.
[c]Rated on 5-point scale.

Research and Scholarship

My research program maintains a focus on health psychology and public health, largely in the area of women's issues and reproductive health. I am interested in the study of stressful life events and psychosocial factors that can influence mental and physical health outcomes. I also am interested in determinants of behavior change and in the development of interventions and medical education. Among other projects, I have designed intervention protocols and surveys for women, adolescents, and medical trainees and conducted research that involved large, longitudinal data sets. A complete list of publications and presentations, as well as a summary table indicating number of publications broken down by various categories (for example, of my sixty-five peer-reviewed research presentations, forty-four were completed since coming to Drexel), can be found in Appendix 6. A description of currently funded research is presented below, and a complete list of funded and unfunded grant applications can be found in Appendix 7.

A. Current Work

When offered my current faculty position, I was excited by the opportunity to take on new career challenges in terms of the Student Counseling Center directorship, but also by the opportunity to create an independent program of research in health psychology. Since coming to Drexel University, my own research has blossomed, and I have been involved with three main topics of investigation: women's health (including medical education), adolescent health, and prevention/intervention. Many of my research projects have involved collaborative scholarship with students that I mentor (see *Teaching*).

During my years at Drexel University, I have earned national and international recognition of my work through my scholarly presentations, and published empirical articles and research reviews (See Appendix 6). For example, I served as an associate editor for the *Health Psychology* volume (volume 9) of the *Handbook of Psychology*, a twelve-volume set published by Wiley. I wrote the chapter covering women's health psychology for the volume. I chaired and presented in symposia at both the First and Second World Congress on Women's Mental Health in 2002 and 2004 and plan to do so at the Third in 2008. I was invited by the president of the International Association for Women's Mental Health to prepare an educational research review on the topic of pregnancy as a stressor for a special issue on women's mental health for *CNS Spectrums: The International Journal of Neuropsychiatric Medicine*. This journal is distributed to psychiatrists, neurologists, primary care physicians, and OB/GYNs who are able to earn continuing medical education (CME) credits through the Mount Sinai School of Medicine by responding to questions that I prepared for this purpose. I have been invited to contribute to Weiner and Craighead's upcoming fourth edition of Corsini's *Encyclopedia of Psychology*, to be published by Wiley. In addition to requests to write book reviews (for example, I reviewed *Grieving Reproductive Loss* for the journal, *Death Studies*), I serve as a reviewer for national and international journals (see *Service*). I also have reviewed grant proposals, such as one for the National Institute for Health Research in Great Britain. Moreover, I have been interviewed recently for a special program on the psychology of miscarriage for the *BBC Radio* and for the *BBC News*, as well as by a writer for the American Psychological Association for the *APA Monitor*'s special issue on women's health.

1. Women's Mental Health Following Pregnancy Loss

Using a longitudinal, NIH-funded data set from Columbia University/New York State Psychiatric Institute, one of the largest to include a miscarriage cohort and frequency-matched comparison cohorts of pregnant women and community women without recent reproductive events, my work with that of my colleagues has documented that in addition to increased anxiety and depressive symptomatology, miscarrying women have a 5.2 times greater risk for an episode of major depression (published in *Journal of the American Medical Association*), a 2.5 times greater risk for an episode of minor depression (published in *Journal of Affective Disorders*), and an 8.0 times greater risk for a recurrent episode of obsessive compulsive disorder (published in *Journal of Clinical Psychiatry*) in the six months following loss, than do otherwise comparable community women. I also seek to extend this previous work.

Building on my prior empirical work examining anxiety and depression following miscarriage described above and my published research reviews of the psychiatric and psychological sequelae of miscarriage (published in *Archives of Women's Mental Health* and *Journal of Psychosomatic Research*; see Appendix 6 for full list), I am completing an empirical paper examining the pattern of anxiety and depression symptoms for women during a pregnancy subsequent to miscarriage. With one of my doctoral students, we are examining predictors of grief and distress following pregnancy loss, along with collaborators at University of Utah

School of Medicine. Additional review papers are also being prepared. One in-progress paper examines "treatment as usual" in various medical settings for women following pregnancy loss and indicates that women who have experienced pregnancy loss often feel dissatisfied with post-loss follow-up care. In my reviews, I summarize my analysis of the literature regarding different psychosocial components of this important medical issue so that others in the field can also recognize this need. This last review further highlights needed areas of training intervention for medical personnel surrounding pregnancy loss.

2. Health Care Providers and Pregnancy Loss

In general, the traditional Western model of medical practice does not tend to recognize reproductive loss, particularly early miscarriage, as a death to be mourned, even when the woman herself experiences it this way. Medical doctors, residents, and students often feel unprepared to work with women and their families following loss, as they have had little training on how to deal with their distraught patients or how to make a mental health referral. At Drexel University College of Medicine (DUCOM) and Temple University School of Medicine, my doctoral student research team and I created and administered a survey to assess medical students' and OB/GYN residents' knowledge, training, and practices related to pregnancy loss and mental health. Our survey also provides an assessment of the perceptions and obstacles regarding communication between physicians and women following loss. A report of main survey results is currently under review.

Among other findings, our survey, confirmed by other published literature, revealed that the primary mental health referral resource on which physicians rely involves written material. Although far from ideal as a sole referral, since the provision of written material appears to be the current reality, and since consumers often search the Web for information, it seemed that a review of available Internet sites would make a valuable contribution. As such, I prepared a review of recommended Web-based resources for health care providers specific to pregnancy loss that was published in the *Journal of Gynecologic, Obstetric and Neonatal Nursing*. The manuscript contains a summary table that is a resource for professionals themselves and can be provided directly to patients as an "information prescription."

The work discussed above helped me to recognize the deficits in training and the desire of future physicians to gain knowledge and skills around psychological issues of death and dying and to develop competence in communicating effectively with women and their families following pregnancy loss. That such training is desperately needed has been further confirmed by my review of the educational objectives of the Council on Resident Education in Obstetrics and Gynecology (CREOG) and the Association of Professors of Gynecology and Obstetrics (APGO) Medical Education Foundation in Obstetrics and Gynecology, and also by my thorough review of the research literature. This preliminary work set the stage for my funded grant submission to APGO/Women's Healthcare Education Office for an Interdisciplinary Women's Health Competency Award. For my "Pregnancy Loss Curriculum Development Project," I collaborate with the OB/GYN Program director and associate dean of Graduate Medical Education at DUCOM to identify interdisciplinary curriculum to target core competencies identified by APGO in their document, *Women's Health Care Competencies for Medical Students.*

We have developed a practical and interactive Web-based curriculum for medical students and residents to increase knowledge about perinatal loss, as well as improve effective and sensitive communication, awareness of mental health consequences, and knowledge regarding mental health treatment resources and other referral options. The curriculum is delivered through state-of-the-art media technology and among other components includes didactics, videotaped clinical case vignettes, discussions/commentary by experts in the field (authors, clinicians, researchers), and interviews with actual patients. Validation of the curriculum is being conducted.

3. Additional Health Psychology/Women's Health Research

With my doctoral students, I am involved in a number of ongoing projects related to screening for postpartum depression, PTSD [postraumatic stress disorder] symptoms following solid organ transplantation, and HIV and pregnancy, for example. One student recently received the first-place Award for Health Psychology Research at a regional Psi Chi conference. Other active women's health research focuses on domestic violence. As a member of Drexel's Domestic Violence Task Force, I participated as a co-investigator in the preparation of two funded campus consortium grant submissions to the Department of Justice and Office of Justice Programs, Violence Against Women Office. The second, funded through 2009, involves a partnership with the University of Pennsylvania, Drexel University, and the University of the Sciences in Philadelphia to implement data collection, develop prevention/educational programs, and strengthen support services on campuses related to crimes of domestic violence, dating violence, sexual assault, and stalking. Wallet-size pamphlets have been created and distributed, and an educational video is being scripted and filmed.

Service

A. Service to Department of Psychology

1. Student Committees

I serve/have served as chair or committee member on twenty-six master's thesis and fifty-four doctoral dissertation committees (see the table below and the list in Appendix 8). I also participate in the administration and grading of Comprehensive Examinations in the Psychology Department, serving as a faculty examiner for the oral examination for approximately three to five students per year.

Number of Thesis and Dissertation Committees

	Chaired	Member
Master's Thesis	13	13
Doctoral Dissertation	11	43

2. Coordinator of Practicum Training

Between 1999 and 2004, I coordinated the practica for all psychology students in the master's, Ph.D., and J.D./Ph.D. programs, which involved placement of fifty to seventy-five students per year at thirty to forty-five sites. This position involved a variety of ongoing tasks and administrative responsibilities, such as maintaining contact with active practicum sites throughout the year (including periodic site visits); seeking out new sites; maintaining a database of sites; serving as liaison between the Psychology Department faculty and the sites; organizing and facilitating an annual Practicum Fair and creating the Practicum Handbook; matching students with sites; collecting and reviewing midyear and end-of-year evaluation forms from students and supervisors; monitoring student progress; and completing Affiliation Agreements (see Appendix 9).

B. Service to Drexel University

1. Campus Outreach

Since 1998, I have created and coordinated outreach programs, such as workshops, that are available to the university community. Through the SCC, an extensive series of mental health and wellness workshops for students and employees that run throughout the year and are facilitated by psychology doctoral students is offered. Topics have included stress management, study skills, healthy versus unhealthy eating, understanding anxiety and depression, and issues related to substance abuse, for example (see Appendix 10). I also have coordinated annual campus programs for National Depression Screening Day and our own Mental Health Awareness Day. I have taken part in other campus programs, such as presenting at new student orientations for many of the departments in Drexel's College of Nursing and Health Professions, School of Public Health, and DUCOM.

2. Consultation

As director of the SCC, I am often called on to provide mental health treatment referral information for employees, graduating students, and even alumni of the University. I act as a consultant for faculty and other staff (for example, the General Council, Dean of Students) who have mental health concerns about students. In 2001, I completed a forty-hour Pennsylvania state certification course in Domestic Violence Counseling/Intervention. Since then, I have been involved with developing domestic violence–related programs, clinical and consultation services, and research on the Drexel University campus to increase education and services (see *Research and Scholarship*).

3. Selected Committees

Since 2000, I have been an active member of the Academic Enrichment Services/Act 101 Advisory Board, established by the Commonwealth of Pennsylvania to provide academic support and funding for low-income undergraduate students. For the Campus Community Consortium grant to reduce violence crimes against women for which I am a co-investigator (see *Research and Scholarship*), I represent the Center City Hahnemann Campus on the Victim/Survivor Services Committee. I am a member of the Women's Studies Committee of the College of Arts and Sciences and have coordinated programming in honor of National Women's History Month.

C. Service to Professional Community

1. Editorial Activities

Between 1996–2007, I served as a member of the Executive Editorial Board for the *International Scope Review* (http://www. internationalscope.com), where I participated in decisions related to staffing, expansion, and other integral workings of this online journal and also reviewed manuscripts for contribution. The journal publishes multidisciplinary research on transformations in economic policies, management and capital-labor relationships, interethnic relationships, and interpersonal relationships taking place in industrialized countries. As an ad hoc editorial consultant, I provide peer reviews for fifteen additional research journals in my field (for example, *Journal of Psychosomatic Research; Sex Roles: A Journal of Research; Social Science and Medicine; Women and Health: A Multidisciplinary Journal of Women's Health Issues*). I have completed beta testing for a variety of clinical assessment instruments for Psychological Assessment Resources, Inc. (PAR), as well as the collection of standardized data for normative samples. This work has provided a resource for gaining access to new testing materials for the SCC.

Integration of Professional Work/Goals

I enjoy the diversity of experiences that my current position entails. My job involves varied responsibilities as researcher, teacher, clinical supervisor, mentor, clinician, administrator, and more. Every day there is a different task/challenge to attend to and something new to learn. I feel fortunate that I can incorporate my varied interests into my work and creatively utilize my different skills, and that my efforts are valued by my colleagues, supervisors, and students. A theme that unites my academic endeavors and makes them especially rewarding for me is that mentorship is involved with each. As a teacher and clinical supervisor for new therapists, it is rewarding to watch students benefit from the feedback and training that I provide. It is very satisfying to help them develop their own individual strengths and clinical style. I also learn a great deal from my students and from helping them confront the challenges they face in their training and research. I also have developed collaborations with colleagues from other countries, which has allowed me not only to extend my research and training efforts internationally but also to travel abroad, learn more about my field from a wider and more diverse perspective, and develop close friendships with psychologists and psychiatrists from other parts of the world. It is rewarding to be contributing on many levels to how society functions—on the smallest, most direct level of helping individual students and patients, but also on broader levels, like developing and facilitating the mental health services for our campus with such success, potentially easing the distress of women and families experiencing pregnancy loss through my writing and curriculum development for medical professionals, and contributing to the larger research literature and public health knowledge base through my research publications.

A. Recent Professional Development and Goals

I served as the research codirector for the Center of Excellence of Women's Health in the Institute for Women's Health and Leadership (IWHL) in DUCOM from 2004–2006 and continue to sit on the Research Advisory Board for the IWHL. Based on my collaborative research and educational efforts with individuals within the Department of OB/GYN at DUCOM/Hahnemann University Hospital, in addition to my joint appointment in the School of Public Health, I was named a research associate professor of OB/GYN within DUCOM in 2006.

In the past few years, I have focused my efforts to obtain continuing education credits required to maintain my Pennsylvania License in Psychology toward courses that would assist with grant writing and research productivity in the field of women's health. I also have become an active member of additional professional organizations that support research endeavors in women's reproductive health and medical education, such as the Association of Women in Psychology, Association for Professors of Obstetrics and Gynecology (APGO), American College of Obstetricians and Gynecologists, and the National Association for the Study of Psychosocial Obstetrics and Gynecology.

B. Future Research Agenda

My plans for research include the completion of several manuscripts that will further strengthen my already significant foundation of preliminary work for future grant submissions in the area of women's reproductive health. I will submit a proposal to the National Institute of Mental Health (NIMH) to examine rates of anxiety and depressive symptoms and disorders for women who have experienced "natural" pregnancy loss versus pregnancy loss following infertility treatment, and for women who have experienced multiple losses versus those who have experienced a single loss. Qualitative aspects of this stressful life experience also will be compared. Gathering input directly from women who have experienced pregnancy loss seems essential for successful intervention development.

In addition to the planned grant submissions focusing on pregnancy loss (described above), another is a revision of a recent R01 submission to NIMH in response to PA-03–135 (Women's Mental Health in Pregnancy and the Postpartum Period) that I will submit in July 2008. This new work represents a multidisciplinary attempt to elucidate the effects of prolonged exposure to antenatal and postpartum maternal depressive and anxiety disorders on offspring.

As an extension of my pending application for GRID funding (Grants for Research Impact at Drexel: A Distribution of Commonwealth of Pennsylvania Formula Tobacco Funds), which focuses on pregnant women's anxiety and decision making and implications on maternal and fetal health related to the American Academy of Obstetrics and Gynecology's 2007 recommended change in practice to offer first- or second-trimester genetic screens and/or diagnostic tests (such as amniocentesis or chorionic villi sampling) to *all* pregnant women, rather than just those considered high risk because of age or genetic family history, I will look to submit proposals to external agencies to examine the implications for women and health care providers of this significant national policy change.

Reviewing my professional career to this point, and reflecting on my goals and achievements since coming to Drexel University, has been both inspiring and challenging. The best of my own academic, clinical and research experiences have inspired me to strive to spark as much excitement and motivation in my students to develop their skills, employ creativity, and systematically examine the clinical and research issues that inspire them, as I have had for my own professional endeavors. I am proud of my accomplishments to date, but also look forward to further challenging myself with new opportunities such as conducting a large-scale research project that an award such as an R01 grant from NIH would allow, taking on greater leadership roles within the Psychology Department and the Institute for Women's Health and Leadership, for example, and collaborating with researchers from varied disciplines and agencies. I look forward to conducting interdisciplinary research that will help better the health and well-being of women and their families, as well as the professional competency of health care providers in the arena of women's health, and to the integration of this work into my teaching, mentorship of students, and service to Drexel University and the wider community.

Appendixes

1. Course Syllabi
2. Scholarship with Students and Student Awards
3. University Student Evaluations and Informal Student Evaluations
4. Practicum Evaluations
5. Letters of Nomination for Mentorship Awards
6. List of Citations and Summary Table of Research Productivity
7. List of Grant Applications (Funded and Unfunded)
8. Student Committees
9. List of Practicum Sites and Sample Handbook
10. Mental Health and Wellness Workshops

References

Curry, T. H. (2006, February). Faculty performance reviews. *Effective Practices for Academic Leaders, 1*(2), 1–16.

Diamond, R. M. (2004). *Preparing for promotion, tenure, and annual review: A faculty guide* (2nd ed.). Bolton, MA: Anker.

Froh, R. C., Gray, P. J., & Lambert, L. M. (1993). Representing faculty work: The professional portfolio. In R. M. Diamond & B. E. Adam (Eds.), *Recognizing faculty work: Reward systems for the year 2000* (pp. 97–110). San Francisco: Jossey-Bass.

Lynton, E. (1993, January). *The scholarly function: Common characteristics and criteria.* Paper presented at the American Association for Higher Education's Forum on Faculty Roles and Rewards, San Antonio, TX.

Miller, J. E. (2005, September). *Teaching portfolios for faculty and graduate teaching assistants.* Paper presented at the International College Teaching Methods and Styles Conference, Reno, NV.

Millis, B. (1991). Putting the teaching portfolio in context. In K. J. Zahorski (Ed.), *To improve the academy: Vol. 10. Resources for faculty, instructional, and organizational development* (pp. 215–232). Stillwater, OK: New Forums Press.

Seldin, P. (2008, February). *The academic portfolio.* Roundtable discussion at the American Council on Education's Leadership Development Program for Department Chairs, San Diego, CA.

Zubizarreta, J. (2006). The professional portfolio: Expanding the value of portfolio development. In P. Seldin & Associates, *Evaluating faculty performance: A practical guide to assessing teaching, research, and service* (pp. 201–216). Bolton, MA: Anker.

Index

Note to index: An *f* following a page number denotes a figure on that page; a *t* following a page number denotes a table on that page.

R

S

T

W

Z